THE A–Z GUIDE

FOR

Onglaze Decoration

THE A–Z GUIDE

FOR

Onglaze Decoration

Tricia Bradford

Kangaroo Press

Acknowledgments

It would not have been possible to compile this book without the help of many people, some of them well known to me while others will remain forever unknown. Much of the information came from artists and students who, like myself, had read or heard some item of interest and filed it away in the labyrinths of their minds; their source of information was almost certainly not the original one and it is therefore not possible to acknowledge these people by name. We can only thank them.

I can and do thank the many commercial people who gave their time and support in supplying me with information about their products for the first edition of this book and now for this, the updated and much enlarged and improved version. Good friends like Roger Lang of Alexanders, whose father Doug assisted with the earlier version, Fay and Elliott Good, Josie Robinson of Gilberton Gallery, Deirdre Fewell and Kit Ferry who helped introduce me to the ceramic world, and people like David Walker of Walker Ceramics, Michael Newman of Ceramic Solutions, Geoffrey Annett, a supplier of Duncan wares; also Australian Stained Glass Supplies, Northcote Potteries and those many others who have contributed in so many ways to my newfound knowledge about glazes and glass. Information repeated from the first version of the book came from Tetlows and from Peter Pritchard of Degussa who, when I said I was ignorant about gold, sent me three kilograms of information! There are also the artists who generously let me use their work to illustrate particular techniques in these pages. I cannot mention all those who have helped by name, as I would like to, but I thank them sincerely and suggest we continue to support them so that they may continue to support us.

I am also grateful for the art of painting on porcelain itself. Without it this book would never have been written. It has given me wonderful friends in many, many countries, world-wide travel, a consuming interest, much experience in many facets of management of exhibitions and other logistical exercises and a delightful way to spend my evenings.

Lastly, I thank my daughter, DanaKai, who volunteered to proofread and correct my errors. To this she added a zany sense of humour which frequently brought a smile as I bent over the keyboard in the many after-midnight hours.

COVER: *Porcelain and enamel on a porcelain canvas surface*
(T. Bradford)

First published in 1997 by Kangaroo Press Pty Ltd
An imprint of Simon & Schuster Australia
20 Barcoo Street (PO Box 507)
Roseville NSW 2069 Australia
Printed in Hong Kong through Colorcraft Ltd

ISBN 0 86417 888 3

Contents

Introduction I

Introduction to The A–Z Guide for Porcelain Painters: *'A survival manual for aspiring artists'*

This book is a combination of facts, figures, definitions and descriptions and my reason for writing it is that I have a lot of basic knowledge about the art of painting on porcelain, however whenever I wanted to reinforce or verify that knowledge I could never remember where I had read or heard about it or else I could not find the particular article or book in my chaotic library. Obviously there was a need for organisation in my life and library and rather than make a catalogue, which I had tried at one stage but soon tired of, I decided to collect all this information and keep it in a book and keep the book in my box of tricks! Maybe some of you have similar problems!

Collecting information was surprisingly interesting. It involved going through and skim reading every book, article and magazine I had or could borrow. Obviously, it would be impossible to differentiate between what I knew beforehand and what I gleaned from others, and to determine where information originated; there is so much that is said and written, passed on and reiterated that it becomes a mélange of fact, fantasy, rumour and myth, some of which works for some people and not for others.

Which brings me to the variables! And the most important variable is the human factor. When following a recipe for cooking, if one does not adhere strictly to the instructions the flavour is a little different, and you may or may not like the result. In porcelain art if you do not follow the instructions the same thing happens, only here the matter is complicated by other variables such as amount of paint or paste, thickness applied, medium, drying time, kiln, time/temperature curve, position in kiln and so on. They are endless, these variables; even the china on which we paint gives different results and the products we use may have similar names yet come from different manufacturers and their chemical content is very likely entirely different. Two artists, sitting side by side, using exactly the same materials, painting the same subject, will produce two dissimilar results.

Therefore, when you read this book and any other reference material, please keep in mind the factors which affect your work and make allowances.

Many of the terms used refer specifically to porcelain and the art of painting on it. Obviously, it would not have been practical to fill the book with terminology and give irrelevant definitions or meanings which refer to other activities. We have quite enough weight to carry around with us as it is!

The other limitations in this book are that I have only given brief and basic instructions for many of the techniques used. If you require further information, you will undoubtedly find it in one of the many books written on the subject. However, using the instructions included here and a little experimentation, you should be able to produce the effects you are looking for; your work will be all the more individual if you develop your own methods of application.

'Learn all you can from the mistakes of others.
You will not live long enough to make them all yourself.'

Introduction II

The A–Z Guide to Onglaze Decoration **(1997)**

I wrote the introduction to the first edition of this book, under another title, ten years ago. On reading it through now I do not want to change what I said then. However, I would like to add that much of the technology and techniques which apply to painting on porcelain also relate to other glazed surfaces and there is no reason why the potter or ceramicist cannot benefit as much from this book as the artists who use porcelain as a canvas.

Those of us who create, no matter what the medium, seem to be constantly craving for more knowledge, for other media which can enhance our endeavours, for new ways to express our creative abilities. Many of the artists I know have expanded their horizons into other fields, working with glass, folk art, screen-printing, and silk painting, all of which can be related to porcelain in one way or another. We can paint on glass and slump it in our kilns; we use the same brushstrokes for folk art as do artists who paint in the traditional European style; we screen-print decals for china and glass, and silk painting frequently acts as a backdrop for porcelain slabs or tiles. So versatile artists need to have this knowledge at their fingertips as they explore new products and venture with experimentation into tempting and fascinating worlds of colour and form.

Hence the reason for the expansion of this book to include a much wider variety of topics, techniques and terminology in these related art forms.

Tricia Bradford

A

Abbozo Oil painting term adapted to painting on glazed surfaces. First underpainting, frequently painted in monochrome.

Abrade To grind shallow patterns into glass with a grinding wheel.

Absorption Ability of bisque, unfired clay or plaster to absorb moisture when glazing, decorating or casting slip.

Abstract Concerned with pure form and pattern. Adaptation from the visible world in which shape, line and colour are given more emphasis than is evident in the subject being painted. The subject may be rendered unrecognisable by stylisation, repetition and deformation. It is only occasionally possible to identify the original model. There are many ways of approaching an abstract drawing because it is dependent on how the individual artist 'sees' or senses an object—however, simplification or distortion of a whole or part of the object is one way. Other techniques are to extend, twist, invert, evert, isolate and exaggerate. The design may then be expanded or contracted to fit the space you wish to fill.

Abstract expressionism The expression of emotion as opposed to reality in art.

Accelerated perspective Creation of a depth of field in a short space.

Accelerated test To test products such as paints and pigments in laboratory conditions.

Accelerator Substance which increases the reaction of a substance or its maturity.

Accent Strength of line or colour to emphasise detail and to attract attention.

Acetic acid Used as a binder for glass paints to harden the paint so that further layers may be applied before firing. Vinegar is not as strong but will serve the same purpose.

Acetone Very strong volatile solvent which is highly inflammable. Used for cleaning.

Achromatic colours Black, white and grey are termed achromatic colours—as opposed to CHROMATIC COLOURS.

Acid etch powder Used to etch a glazed surface. Mask that part of the glazed surface which is not to be etched with a masking lacquer. Mix a small amount of acid etch powder with a medium of your choice to milky consistency and paint it over the area to be etched. Pad gently with a silk-covered pad and leave for a period of time. The longer the acid etch powder is left, the deeper the etching. Remove masking lacquer and fire at 760°C (1400°F). *(Caution with acid.)*

Acid etching Removing glaze from a fired clay body with the aid of hydrofluoric acid. The area where the glaze is removed will be roughened and matt in contrast to the smooth high gloss in unaffected areas.

To etch with hydrofluoric acid (Caution with acid): Sketch a design and transfer it by tracing with the aid of graphite paper onto the glazed area. Paint the area *not to be etched* with asphaltum, completely covering the surface to protect it from the acid. Take care to see that the asphaltum is thick enough, and that there are no holes or brown areas. Cover all the surface not to be etched, including the back or base of the piece. The asphaltum may have to be thinned from time to time to keep it flowing. Allow to dry a day or so and then place the object into an acid bath of 50% hydrofluoric acid for 1–2 minutes or until the etching is deep enough. Remove and wash under running water to neutralise the acid. Wash with kerosene and then with hot soapy water to remove all traces of asphaltum and fire to further clean the piece. This is a brief outline only—please read more detailed instructions than these before you attempt to etch with acid. *See* Bradford, T. *Porcelain Art in Australia Today*, Kangaroo Press, Sydney 1984.

Take care not to Rustiban or any other acid touch your stainless steel sink. It will be permanently marked and scarred by the acid.

To etch with etching cream: Proceed as above until asphaltum has completely dried and then apply etching cream thickly over the areas to be etched. Leave for 12 to 24 hours, testing the depth of the etch occasionally. Clean as above. Etchall Cream is one commercial preparation; there are other, similar preparations; all such preparations should be treated with *extreme caution* as burns will result from the cream, just as from the solution. If acid comes into contact with your skin wash immediately in soda, soap and water to neutralise it. If the burn is severe, seek medical attention.

Acid etching on glass Flashed glass or glass

which has a different coloured coating is often used for etching. Part or all of one colour is removed (a design may be resisted with asphaltum) when dipped in hydrofluoric acid. *(Caution with acid.)*

Acid, hydrofluoric *(Caution with acid):* Very dangerous acid, which should be treated with extreme care, used to etch glass and remove colour and glaze from fired china and other glazed surfaces. Always wear plastic or rubber gloves, and protective clothing, and work in the open air or by an open window. If the acid comes in contact with the skin, painful burns will result; the fumes can be harmful if inhaled. *See* RUSTIBAN, HYDROFLUORIC ACID, ETCHING.

Acid polishing Glass or any glazed surface is dipped into an acid bath, usually of hydrofluoric acid and/or sulphuric acid, which will lightly etch the surface. Extreme caution is required when working with any acid. *See* HYDROFLUORIC ACID.

Acid resists There are several products which resist the action of acid on a portion of the glazed surface or glass, including asphaltum, strong adhesive-backed plastic, a mixture of beeswax, tallow and paraffin wax, liquid latex masking fluids and brand-name varnishes.

Acid under base A texture paste applied with a sponge, brush or pen to the glazed surface and fired at 780–815°C (1435–1500°F) to give an etched look without the use of acid. Gold or lustre may be applied over the resulting matt area.

Acids Silica, boron, antimony, tin, chromium, titanium and zircon are the most commonly used acids in the porcelain, glass and ceramic world. The acids combine with bases and neutrals and interact during the firing process to form a glaze.

Acrylic stains Hobby Colorobbia acrylic stains are non-toxic, intermixable, opaque, matt and offer a fast and economical decorative technique. The stains are water-based, self sealing and may be applied directly onto a porous bisque surface (or paper, wood, cork, plaster, etc.) where they become touch dry in a matter of minutes and one coat may be laid over another.

Action painting Broad sweeps of the brush to cover a large surface. Strong, forceful application of paint. (Difficult for the porcelain or ceramic artist on a 'canvas' where space is limited and heavy applications of paint chip off after firing.)

Add-ons Additional pieces of clay applied to a clay body, such as handles, spouts, etc.

Adherance Quality of adhesion of one substance to another, e.g. glaze to a bisque fired body.

Advancing colours Warm colours, e.g. the reds and oranges, which appear to be closer to the viewer.

Aerial perspective Distance implied by painting in pale and cool colours, e.g. blues, greys and mauves, and by ill-defined or blurred objects.

Aerograph Spray gun for applying paint in a fine mist.

Aesthetic Appreciation of beauty.

Africarn Manufacturer of hobby ceramic products.

After-image When the retina of the eye views a colour for any length of time it will eventually transmit an image of the complementary colour—this is the after-image.

Agate burnisher Agate set in a handle for burnishing or etching gold or metallic paint. The agate is rubbed on the gilded or painted surface to polish and bring it to a perfect shine.

Agate etching Highlighting portion of a design painted in gold. Several coats of burnishing gold are applied to a blank with each separate application being fired, burnished and rinsed thoroughly before the next is applied. Pen a design using powder paint mixed with pen oil to the consistency of ink, or with an ordinary HB pencil if you need guidelines. Fire and then highlight areas of the design with an agate etcher. This looks rather like a thick pencil with an amber coloured stone tip. Rubbing the tip on the gold will change and highlight the colour of the metal.

Aging Allowing cast slip to stand for several days to allow materials to blend and mature.

Airbrush Equipment for applying paint in a fine mist. It consists of a small container of paint, a 'brush' or fine spray gun, and a cylinder of compressed air, which is available in small cans or from a compressor. While smaller compressors do not have pressure gauges, large compressors do and, depending on the type of paint, the depth of colour and rate of delivery, the pressure should range from 15 to 40 lbs per square inch (psi). Select a low rate and increase it until you are satisfied with the delivery of the paint. Paints may be used directly or mixed with alcohol which dries rapidly and allows several layers to be applied. Follow the directions supplied with commercial preparations. Other evaporative solutions such as lustre thinner or nail polish remover may be used and you may like to experiment until you find the one most suitable for you. All gritty particles must be removed from the solution, otherwise the minute grains will clog the nozzle of the airbrush. Strain the paint through layers of nylon stocking, and mix particularly gritty paints with a mortar and pestle. Paints mixed with alcohol may be reused by pouring off the solution and drying the wet paint on a tile; the dehydrated paint may be returned to a phial and used as normal for conventional painting.

Airbrushing Clean your blank well prior to using the airbrush, as all grease and finger marks will show. Hold the airbrush approximately 30 cm (12") from the article to be painted and depress the lever. Paint will spray in a fine mist from the nozzle. Move the airbrush in a sweeping motion so that the paint covers the entire surface to be painted. By turning the article or changing the angle of the airbrush, you have some control over the placement and direction of the paint. Allow time for the paint to dry between coats.

Air twist Corkscrew patterns produced by twisting glass rods in which are embedded columns of air or threads of white or coloured glass or a mixture of the three.

Albany slip Low fusion point clay mainly used for glazes or in glazes for stoneware and porcelain. Deepness of brown colour depends on thickness of application. Temperature range of Cone 6–9 (1005–920°C, 1845–1690°F).

Alberta Manufacturer of hobby ceramic products.

Alcohol (absolute or pure) Ethyl alcohol is pure, with all water content removed. Ordinary alcohol (we use methylated spirits) contains about 6% water. Pure alcohol may be mixed with other solvents such as turpentine or mineral spirits. Pure alcohol is not readily obtainable.

Alkali In the glaze arts, an alkali such as soda is used as a flux. Potash and lithia are also used. Soda will also intensify the colour. Baking soda can be used where you would normally use flux to adhere incising glass beads in order to lift the glaze, and to adhere sand, stones, etc.

All'antica Painting in an antique manner.

Alla prima Italian term for a one-fire painting or painting completed in one session.

Allergies A matter for the individual. Avoid using any product to which you are allergic. There is bound to be an alternative.

Alumina Increases glaze viscosity, firing range and resistance to crystallisation.

Alumina hydrate A fine white powder which is an ingredient used in kiln wash or shelf primer to prevent articles in the kiln from fusing together. May be kept in a jar covered with two layers of fine muslin or pantyhose which can be used as a sprinkler to dust the kiln shelves.

Aluminum oxide Crystalline compound used in abrasives for grinding.

Analogous colour scheme Colours adjacent on the colour wheel which blend well because of their basic shade. Usually no more than three or four are used at one time.

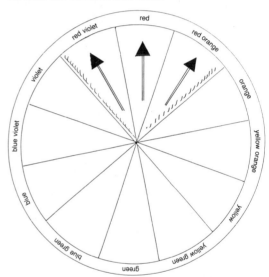

Analogous colour scheme

Anamorphosis A distorting technique which allows a painting to be clearly viewed from one angle only. All other perspectives are distorted.

Angled strokes For cross-hatching. Turn the brush to a 45° angle and pull in one direction, then in the opposite direction, to form a vague basketweave pattern.

Angular perspective Where only two faces of the subject are shown.

An-hua Chinese term meaning hidden or secret decoration.

Annealing The process whereby glass is cooled under controlled conditions to make it less brittle. An essential part of the firing of glass to reduce the risk of stress and subsequent (at any stage) breakage of the piece. Glass, particularly thick or fused pieces, and glass with a high coefficient of expansion, which has been heated to 800°C (1600°F) or more must be treated with care. It must initially lose heat rapidly, usually to around 580°C (940°F) (this depends on the thickness of the glass). It must soak for a period of time to anneal it, the time also depending on the thickness of the glass; examples would be 30 minutes for 3–5 mm and 90 minutes for 10 mm thickness. The glass must then cool slowly for the next 100°C (212°F) or so to allow the annealing to take place. This is called an anneal cool down, and usually takes several hours; finally the glass may cool a little faster to room temperature. Please read further on the subject of annealing as this is a simplified explanation.

Annealing range The range of temperature from just above the STRAIN POINT to the ANNEAL SOAK temperature. Depends on thickness and type of glass.

Anneal point The temperature at which glass has an acceptable level of internal strain. The annealing point is usually 5–10°C (30–40°F) above the strain point.

Anneal soak A cooling stage in which glass is maintained at a constant temperature to allow the glass molecules to stabilise.

Anther The foremost part of the stamen of a flower containing pollen and pollen sacs.

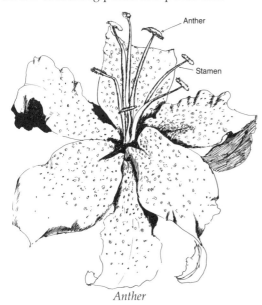

Anther

Anthropomorphism To attribute human characteristics to inanimate objects and animal or plant life.

Antimony oxide Lustrous white metallic element. When used in glazes with a high lead content, it will produce a yellow colour.

Antique etch Product which gives an appearance of erosion with age. Apply with an eye dropper or brush to cleaned greenware and fire to 1005°C (1840°F). *See* Carey's Products, page 95.

Antique glazes Trade name of glazes which have a frosted and aged appearance.

Antique look **1.** To obtain a crackled appearance with metallic lustres such as gold, platinum, etc. first apply a coat of a (usually dark) colour to the area and fire at a low temperature. Paint this fired area with Liquid Bright Gold or another metal of your choice and fire again at a normal temperature; the metal will crackle giving a crazed appearance. **2.** To apply one colour over another onto an uneven surface and then rub or brush off the colour on the raised areas, leaving the usually darker paint in the crevices.

Appliqué Fabric, lace, cord, string, grog, etc. applied to ware.

APT11 porcelain enhancer A product which varies the stability of the slip for draping, slip trailing or embossing. Sufficient may be added to thicken slip to moulding consistency.

Aqueous To contain water or be soluble in water, eg. powder paint mixed with water soluble mediums and applied with similar vehicles.

Arabesque Decoration composed of flowing lines and elaborate tracery.

Araldite Two-part glue usually used for jewellery findings and bases of urns etc. *To dissolve:* To unstick an object, place it in an oven which has been preheated to 180°C (350°F): 10 minutes for jewellery, longer for larger pieces; flick medallions out with pointed knife. *To repair scrolling:* If some paste jewellery or scrolling has popped off, colour some Araldite with the correct colour powder paint, allow to set until it holds its shape and repair your jewelling or scrolling as with enamel.

Arcanist A person with the knowledge of porcelain making. The dictionary definition of arcane is 'secret, mysterious', which leads me to think of artisans locked away, forbidden to have contact with the rest of the world so that they would not share their secrets.

Arnel Manufacturer of hobby ceramic products.

Art fundamentals The basis of aesthetically pleasing artwork. Knowing the principles to follow, and developing an intuitive and artistic approach using these principles, will increase your ability to paint well. The basic rules of art are:

Design: Usually composed of a theme or subject, a mass, lines of direction, negative and positive space or shapes, the size of these spaces, a centre of interest, the direction of lines and masses, areas of additional or supporting interest and values of shading either in colour or greys. Think in thirds. The subject should normally be supported by secondary mass or colour and distant or out-of-focus mass or colour. The space planned for the design area should incorporate all three depths of field with approximately one-third devoted to the centre of interest, one-third to negative space, with the remaining third being used for the supporting areas. The line of design is the direction which the eye follows as it winds its way through the pattern. It should twist or curve upon itself and not lead the viewer out of the painted area. The direction a line takes can indicate motion and strength, e.g. a vertical line indicates strength while a slanting line indicates action. A horizontal line is restful and a jagged line indicates restlessness. A curved line is usually peaceful and rhythmical.

Lines can be thick and thin, heavy or light, curved or straight, smooth or rough and short or long. Shapes and spaces are basically geometric, i.e. round, square, triangular; these can be formal or irregular.

Proportion: An important area which is often neglected. The design should suit the vehicle on which it is to be painted and once again space is to be considered. The subject matter should be drawn to scale, e.g. leaves and accompanying blossoms should be suited to each other and two or more blossoms of different species should be drawn according to their relationship in nature. Violets would not be the same size as daffodils in the same painting (unless it was a field scene with the violets in the foreground and the daffodils in the distance). *Relative size* is important. *Colour* is a visual sensation which arouses emotion. See COLOUR. *Texture* is both visual and tactile and should be appropriate for the design. *Balance* is usually attained by planning space and positioning subject matter. A large mass may be counterbalanced by two smaller masses, or a 'deep' area by two lighter 'deep' areas elsewhere. The painting should be able to be viewed from any angle and be pleasing to the eye. *Dominance* is the effect the centre of interest has over the rest of the design. *Contrast* is essential in all areas of design to add interest and give variety. No two lines should be identical or follow the same path, no two flowers should face the same way; variety of colour will help.

The ELEMENTS OF DESIGN are *colour, tone, texture, line, size* and *shape*. Each of these elements should exhibit the following *principles: dominance, harmony, contrast, balance, repetition* and *gradation*. Look for lack of balance; lines leading into corners, out of the 'frame', at right angles; dissociation of various areas, lack of proportion and lack of depth or third dimension.

Each time you paint a piece use the checklist below to see if you have all of the fundamental bases of design listed in the horizontal column for all the subjects listed in the vertical column.

Do not forget to check your 'Rule of Three' at the same time: Three colours for each area of painted space, leaf, petal, meadow, trunk of tree, wall, building or other shape. Three values of

Elements of Design Checklist

	Dominance	Harmony	Contrast	Balance	Repetition	Gradation
Colour						
Tone						
Texture						
Line						
Size						
Shape						

colour, and three areas of strength and weakness. Small, medium and large areas of each colour and small, medium and large areas of both colour and design. Original colour, shaded colour and reflected colour. Foreground, middleground and background. Highlight, shadow and reflected light. Areas in strong light washed out, areas in unlit foreground in focus and support areas slightly out of focus.

Art glazes Trade name for glazes which produce a blend of colours within themselves.

Art law Confusing legal scene where there are usually two or more sides and all of them are right, according to the individual sides. It is possible to obtain free interim advice from the Arts Law Centre, where members can seek help on a variety of matters at all times. But keep in mind that a good lawyer can actually prove that black is white. How, I do not know, but I do know that you will need a better one if you are on the other side.

Art nouveau Decorative style of painting from the late nineteenth century, often stylised. Influenced by folk art, plant forms, etc.

Asbestos Fireproof material composed of calcium and magnesium silicates once used in kilns as an insulator and to protect the surface. Now considered a health hazard. Gloves made from Kevlar are available for the glass worker to work with extreme heat.

Ash Residue from bones which provides some of the chemicals used in glazes: silica, alumina, potash, iron, magnesia, phosphorus and lime. A source of flux.

Ash (synthetic) Consistent mixture to replace variable and unreliable supply of natural wood ash.

Asphaltum Liquid tar or pitch which is used as a Resist when etching china or glass. May be thinned with mineral turpentine or thickened with talcum powder.

Asymmetry Not symmetrical. The human face and figure are asymmetrical, with the two sides being slightly but noticeably different.

Atelier Studio, often where there is a teacher and/or students.

Atmosphere With reference to the glazing process: the air in the kiln may have an excess of oxygen (oxidation) or be partially depleted of oxygen (reduction).

Atomiser Apparatus usually consisting of a glass jar, a screw top lid with two tubes, one to force air in and the other to force out a fine mist, and a rubber bulb which is used to project a fine mist or spray onto the work surface.

Aufsetweiss European enamel.

B

Background The supporting area for the focal point or centre of interest in a design. It is used to give an illusion of depth and natural elements as well as providing contrast for the subject. A background for a wipe-out painting is applied by laying different colours on in patches with broad sweeps of varying length in appropriate places. For example, paint pink for a rose theme where you might want your pink rose to be, or yellow for a building, green for foliage; paint less of the same colour a little away from that area for a supporting blossom, edifice, tree, and add more for reflection elsewhere in the design. Now add some blue and green in patches which vary in size around the pink area, going over it in a couple of places, drawing the colour out along the line of design, keeping close to it. Do not drag the heavier applications of colour out into the distant background areas as you will lose the design line and the work will spread, tempting you to fill it up with masses of design and colour which will detract from the centre of interest. For this distant background area use much lighter shades and tones of your chosen colour scheme. Place other colours for interest and, if you know where you want it, place some dark colour with a little of the pink or blue, etc. added to it to soften it. These strokes should be applied with Cross-hatching, i.e. a couple of broad flat strokes in one direction and another one or two strokes crossing the first two as an X or Z. A pattern of these strokes will give you varying degrees of colour with, hopefully, Windows of light which you will, once again hopefully, leave alone. The applied background is now blended by *filtering* or Feathering, *very* light brushstrokes which gently move the paint, blending and merging the colours without losing them. The heavier application of paint near the focal point is softened and merged with the lighter background. (*Exercise:* Paint an area heavily with a light colour, so that you can see the brushstrokes, then load your brush with a darker colour and feather the first application to blend the ridges and visible brushstrokes *without leaving dark paint* on them. It *is* possible!) To give the illusion of SHADOWS, grey your original colours with a tertiary blend and apply soft indistinct brushstrokes in the rough shape of a leaf or other subject. This can be done in the wet paint, over fired paint, wiped out of wet paint or shaped up with wet paint over fired paint, or any combination of these techniques.

Back painting Painting on a sheet of glass from the rear so that the design appears to be in the glass when viewed from the front.

'Back to front' Painting what would be physically at the back of the scene, e.g. mountains, first, then the middle ground and then the foreground, so that the closest part of the scene sits happily on the background. Not always easy for beginners to do because of their enthusiasm to rush into the focal point.

Baffle wall Barrier made up of kiln shelving or other refractory material to section areas in a kiln to diffuse heat or identify hot spots.

Baking soda/carb soda **1.** Use baking soda to neutralise acid when it is used to etch a piece, or if you should get it on your skin. **2.** May be used a fluxing agent.

Balance The design should be positioned on the blank surface so as to be pleasing to the eye, which should be able to follow the line of design around and within the object shape. A design which is top heavy will keep the viewer's eye on that part so that the remainder of the painting is ignored. Balance may be achieved by distribution of colour, continuation and direction of line, and tonal variation in the painting.

Ball clay Fine plastic clay used as a plasticiser in the making of porcelain.

Ball mill A jar filled with smooth stones or pebbles which is turned to fine-grind powdered glazes.

Balsam of copaiba An oil from South America which is used as a medium. Usually combined with other oils because of its fast drying action.

Banding Placing a band around the edge of a plate or drinking vessel, usually with the aid of a banding wheel or design tape.

Banding wheel Tool used to turn plates, vases etc. to allow a band or circular design to be applied. A record player turntable or lazy Susan may be substituted. Centre the plate on the wheel and spin to see if it is 'true'. Fix in position with Blu-Tack or plasticine. Dip a square shader in a mixture of turpentine and paint and with the plate spinning gently, hold the brush in position around the outer border. Continue towards the centre of the plate. Applications of paint in different colours and varying widths will make an interesting background for wipe-out florals. Another method is to lay paint fairly thickly on the plate, either when it is on the spinning banding wheel or before you place it on the wheel. Dribble turpentine onto the surface, spinning the plate rapidly to force the turpentine into rivulets through the paint.

Bandsaw Glass-cutting apparatus with stainless steel diamond blade.

Barium carbonate Component of some glazes. It is highly toxic and should not be used on functional pieces. Used in a high gloss transparent glaze, most of the barium should be dispersed in the silicate melt during firing; even so, don't use it on any functional piece.

Barilla A plant of the salt marshes in the Mediterranean region which was burned to make a soda ash, formerly used instead of potash as an alkali in the making of glass.

Baroque An art style of the seventeenth and eighteenth centuries which initially deliberately deformed or distorted figures or objects, frequently with ambiguous intent. The classic rules of art were broken to emphasise emotion and provoke a response in the viewer.

Basalt Dark coloured, fine grained rock used in making black and brown glazes. More fusible than FELDSPAR.

Basalt ware Decorative black ceramic stoneware which resembles the mineral. Developed by Josiah Wedgwood.

Bas relief Low relief sculpture which only slightly projects from the surface, with no part of the design undercut.

Base for raised gold White powder, similar in final appearance to enamel and not to be confused with raised paste. I find this an excellent texture paste which can be mixed with almost any liquid and which will withstand several fires. It may be coloured with the addition of a very small amount of powder paint and will tolerate foreign matter such as glass and sand. Applied over wet paint, it will absorb some of the colour. *See* Carey's Products, page 107.

Base glass The lowest, first or base layer of glass

to which other glasses are fused.

Base ring A ring of glass added to the base of a vessel after its body has been made.

Bases A term used for a flux which causes a glaze to become fusible. The chemicals which make up a glaze formula consist of acids, bases and neutrals. Alkalis and alkali earths are bases; those most commonly used are the oxides of barium, calcium, lead, lithium, magnesium, potassium, sodium, strontium and zinc.

Bassetaille Style of jewellery decoration where porcelain enamel is applied to metal which has been carved or etched in low relief. Each colour is allowed to dry before the application of the next and the piece is eventually fired after the final application of a clear enamel to bring the design flush with the surface.

Batch A mix of measured raw materials which, when melted and fused in the melting pot, will produce glass.

Batt wash Covering of a refractory material for kiln shelves and furniture to prevent glazes adhering to them

Batts Kiln shelves and pottery furniture. May be made of wood, plaster or clay.

Bead tree Kiln furniture composed of a stand and short nichrome wires to hold beads, etc.

Beeswax Available as virgin wax and white refined wax. Has numerous uses, e.g. in encaustic painting, as a resist and as a glaze for oils.

Bell china paints Prepared in cream form and designed to fire to Cone 018 (715°C, 1350°F); they may be applied to any glazed surface. Available in kits of 12 prepared colours.

Bell high-fire kiln wash Prepared liquid shelf primer which may be diluted for box tops.

Bell matting agent Used in equal parts with Bell china paints to produce a soft matt finish.

Bell mediums Range of mediums from slow to rapid drying for fine line work.

Bell 500 slip casting thinners (sodium silicate) Used to adjust consistency of slip to retain the stability of the formula.

Bell plasticiser (gum arabic in gel form) Makes clay more pliable.

Belleek Irish porcelain ware with iridescent pearly glaze, famous for its thinness and distinctive ring. American Belleek is soft paste porcelain with an ivory colour.

Bent glass Sheet glass which has been shaped by firing on, into or over a mould with the aid of applied weight which assists it to move before it would normally do so if slumped. Vehicle windscreens and curved architectural glass are manufactured in this manner.

Bentonite Plastic volcanic clay added to other clay to increase its plasticity. High shrinkage with stoneware temperatures and fuses to produce a typical brown colour.

Bevel The edge of a piece of glass ground and polished at an angle.

Binder An agglutinant or agent to hold together the pigment particles in a paint or glaze.

Biomorphic shapes Shapes and designs which are based on organic life.

Bird's eye view A view from above, used for panoramic scenes. All such drawings will be in oblique perspective with the horizon line very high or out of the scene.

Bisque 1. Clay which has been fired at a low temperature sufficient to harden the body for handling while allowing it to retain enough porosity to absorb a glaze. 2. Clay which has been fired to maturity and left unglazed. Unglazed chinaware or earthenware may be painted. 3. Bisque shapes are frequently used as moulds on which to slump glass.

Underglaze painting: A design is painted on a bisque blank with oxides or paint pigments and allowed to dry. The piece is then dipped in glaze and fired. For traditional bisque painting matt colours are used, as fluxed colours would be glossy on the matt surface, but not with their usual even brilliance. Matt colours are available; however, to matt normal colours mix 1/4 to 1/2 part of zinc oxide to one part of paint powder and make a stiff paste with grinding oil. Lavender oil is used as a painting medium. It is sometimes possible to remove lightly applied paint by soaking in vinegar overnight. Porcelain bisque should be smooth, fine grained and waterproof, although it is possible to fine-sand coarser bisque ware. Many artists are now pouring their own bisque ware so they no longer have to import painting blanks.

Because bisque is not glazed it will accept heavy applications of paint or paste.

To paint on bisque traditionally: Prepare a basic palette of light, medium and dark colours, plus white for highlights. Sketch the design with lead pencil. Using lavender oil as a medium, softly paint the subject first, then the background, feathering out into the negative space. Wipe out highlights *immediately*, as the porous surface and the rapidly drying paint will quickly make this difficult. Use the lavender oil to clean brushes between colours and to clear away unwanted paint. It is possible to paint a second coat prior to firing, using a very dry brush to add more detail, depth and colour when the first coat is dry. Add highlights with white paint and place in shadows and interesting brushstrokes. Fire at 700°C (1300°F). A higher fire will gloss the matt colours. Liquid Bright Gold is good for decoration—it fires matt. Enamel paste, penwork or scrolling all enhance bisque when well done. Bisque may be 'grounded' by applying a colour heavily and smoothly, either with oil and dry powder, or wet-grounded with mixed paint and a sponge.

A coating of gloss paste or enamel may be painted on bisque or the unglazed (back) surface of a tile and fired at around 800°C (1475°F) to 'glaze' a portion or all of the bisque surface. Depending on the paste and firing temperature the resulting surface may be either smooth or rough; it may then be painted with normal gloss paints. Globules of paste or enamel may be applied to fill a pattern and create the effect of a tiled or mosaic design, petals or a jewelled appearance.

Bisque eggs Painted as for bisque ware.

Bisque fire The first time a clay body is fired prior to its being glazed or being fired at a GLOST temperature.

Bisq-Stain Opaques Trade name of non-fired acrylic colours for bisque ware.

Black An achromatic colour derived from some of the following: cobalt, chromium, copper, iron and manganese. Care should be taken not to apply black too thickly, as it will chip off a glazed surface, particularly when used in pen or line work. Black is sometimes used to shade a colour and again should be used cautiously, to avoid 'dirtying' the colour. Works well when softened or greyed with blues or purples. Mixed with yellow, blacks will give a variety of interesting greens.

Black spot Mildew-like spot which appears after firing, caused by low firing at bisque stage. Fire hot; paint and fire again.

Blanc de Chine French terminology for white glazed Chinese porcelain.

Blanks Unpainted ceramic or porcelain pieces; glass cut to a pre-determined shape prior to treatment.

Blankschnitt A style of engraved decoration where the relief effect is enhanced by polishing the ground part of the intaglio.

Bleed When one colour migrates or spreads into another.

Blend 1. Mix two or more substances such as oil and paint pigments. 2. To move applied colour while still wet by filtering or with light brushstrokes.

Blender 1. Brush which merges colours together to remove harsh edges. 2. Appliance to mix glazes.

Blistering 1. Blister or bubble effect in a glaze caused by too high a fire on a soft glaze. Some English ware, Belleek and some American ware have soft glazes and should not be fired above 800°C (1470°F). 2. The bubble which occurs in sheet glass, which may be desirable from an artistic point of view but is considered a flaw for commercial purposes.

Bloating The formation of bubbles in the clay body during the firing process, usually caused by a build-up of gases, over-firing, interrupted firing or too much flux in the clay body. Try to fire more slowly and regularly at a reduced temperature or add more GROG to the clay to compensate for the high flux content.

Blocking in The application of paint in broad flat strokes within a previously sketched or designated area.

Block-out stencil Areas of a painting or a screen may be blocked or resisted with a water soluble glue. Not really suitable for intricate design but convenient when there is no commercial resist.

Block print Print made from carved solid material such as wood.

Blowing The process of shaping a molten mass of glass by blowing air into it through a blowpipe.

Blow-out Miniature volcanoes in a bisque or glazed surface. Usually caused by impurities in the clay or glaze.

Blowpipe A metal tube used to gather a blob of molten glass and through which air is blown into the glass to shape it.

Blown glass Glass shapes which are formed by blowing.

Blue A painting colour derived from cobalt. A lot of blues require the addition of a little flux to help them mature at the same temperature as other paints used at the same time.

Blunger Container with agitator for mixing slip.

Blunging To mix clay or slip with water.

Blushing To rub mixed paint into the design

Painting on onglaze surfaces with normal porcelain paints (T. Bradford)

ABOVE: *Painting on an onglaze surface with normal porcelain paints* (T. Bradford)

Mixed media *Diane Curtin uses silk as an integral part of her porcelain designs. The design is carried over into the silk background and all components are incorporated into a framed presentation* (Diane Curtin)

with your finger or a pad to tint it. As an example, dampen the tip of your finger with medium and pick up a little Blood Red. Gently rub the design with the colour and give it a blush of pink. Do not use too much colour.

Body The clay portion of a porcelain or ceramic piece.

Bone ash (calcined bone) 1. Essential ingredient in bone china producing translucent body. **2.** Secondary flux which gives a milky quality in glazes.

Bone dry (of greenware) Devoid of all water content.

Borax / sodium borax Strong fluxing ingredient for glazes which enhances colour; however, because of the risk of toxic effects it is considered dangerous, and care should be taken in its use.

Boric acid Flux which increases the gloss and elasticity of glaze. Particularly used when sodium oxide content of finished product is limited.

Boiling Blisters or craters forming on soft glazes after firing at too high a temperature.

Bone china Fine semi-translucent earthenware, containing kaolin and calcified bone, which resembles porcelain. The high proportion of BONE ASH (40%) lowers the melting point of the clay.

Bordering A term used in airbrushing referring to the paint becoming darker towards the edge of the object being painted. This effect may be obtained either by a heavier application of paint towards the edge or the use of a darker shade or colour.

Brass trims Variety of interesting decorative trims, usually intended for glass but suitable for porcelain and china ware as well. Available from Australian Stained Glass Supplies, Sydney.

Brilliant-cut A style of cut glass with very deep, complex and highly polished designs.

Broad glass Sheet glass made by cutting the ends off a long bubble of blown glass then cutting and flattening the resultant cylinder.

Brocade glazes Trade name of a glaze which is used for raised designs because of its torpid (inactive) qualities.

Broken colour Initially a term used by the French Impressionists to describe the application of various colours in separate short cross-hatched strokes to give the optical illusion of blended colour.

Brush cleaner Commercial preparation available for cleaning brushes—an alternative to turpentine.

Brushes Our most useful and often most necessary tools and probably those which cost the most and for which we have the least respect! Brushes come in many different varieties and are usually made from the bristles and hairs of animals—squirrel hair from various parts of the world, sable fur, fitch, skunk, badger, goat, camel etc. Some synthetic brushes are available as well, but these do not seem to have the flexibility of natural fur and are best kept for textured surfaces and harsh solutions.

Brush—acrylic: Made from nylon or acrylic fibres.

Brush—bristle: Made from special hog bristles.

Brush—hair: Made from flexible animal hair, the finest of which is red sable. A mixture of red sable and another cheaper hair such as ox hair or Russian sable is less expensive, as is badger or squirrel hair. Squirrel hair is sometimes called camel hair and is softer and more pliable than the more expensive hairs. Ox hair is more rigid.

Brush—quill: The hairs are fitted into a plastic holder called a quill, formerly from the feather of a bird.

Square shader: Straight-tipped flat brush varying in width from one millimetre to five centimetres. Used for washes of colour, shaded loads, cross-hatching, etc. The hairs may be short or medium in length.

Pointed shader: Full bodied pointed brush used in European or Dresden style painting. Used also for strong line work, folk art styles, shaded strokes and painting in a design.

Liner: Fine slender pointed brush used for delicate lines and fine detail.

Scroller: Long slender pointed brush used for lines and scrolls.

Long scroller: Longer than usual slender brush for extended line work.

Square quill: Full rounded brush with a blunt end.

Mop brush: Very large soft haired brush used for dusting.

Mini liner: Long very fine liner.

Long liner: Little shorter and thinner than a scroller.

Cat's tongue: Long flat liner.

Flo-line brush: Long haired brush with a full body which tapers down to a very fine point.

Stippler: Flat based brush either square or angled (deerfoot), which comes in various sizes from about 2 millimeters in diameter to about

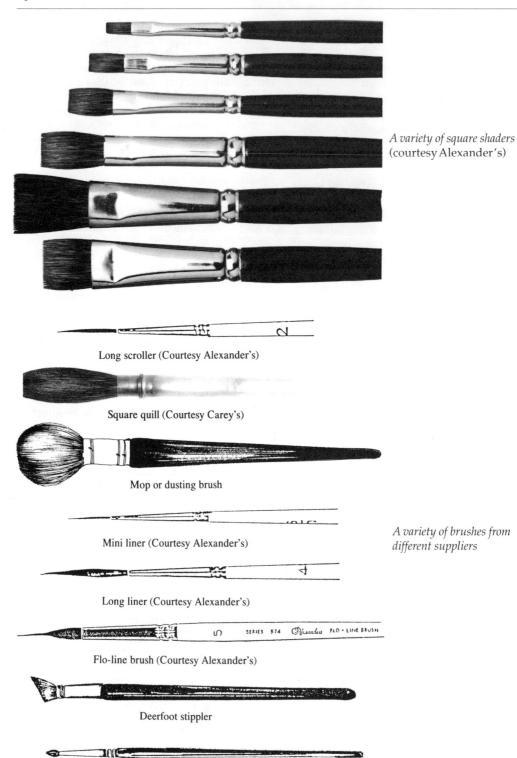

A variety of square shaders (courtesy Alexander's)

Long scroller (Courtesy Alexander's)

Square quill (Courtesy Carey's)

Mop or dusting brush

Mini liner (Courtesy Alexander's)

A variety of brushes from different suppliers

Long liner (Courtesy Alexander's)

Flo-line brush (Courtesy Alexander's)

Deerfoot stippler

Berry brush

one centimetre. Used dry to blend wet paint for foliage and stippled effect.

Deerfoot stippler: Flat based, angled brush for stippling.

Berry brush: Short full pointed brush, useful for European style painting.

Care of brushes: Brushes are expensive! With careful use they will last a long time. Here are a few general rules for care. Remember the hairs in a natural brush come from an animal and are similar in structure to your own hair. Always buy good quality brushes which suit your needs. Depending on your likes and dislikes, they may be long or short haired brushes, full or fine. A long haired full bodied brush is usually more flexible and carries more paint than the short haired variety. Do not bend a brush when the hairs are still stiff from lack of use (or care). Dip in turpentine or oil first and allow to soften. Do not bend a brush harshly at the ferrule—the hairs will break. Do not stab your brush either into the jar of turpentine or onto your plate. If you would like a stippled effect for fur or foliage keep an old brush for this purpose or use a stippler. Do not discard all old brushes—there are a number of uses to which they can be put such as applying resists and textures, cleaning, painting on a 'toothed' surface; the handles may be used as a tool, as a holder for a pen nib or as a quill ferrule. Do not stand your brushes on their painting tips as this will result in a permanently bent shape. Also do not stand them for great lengths of time the other way up, as this allows oil, turpentine and paint, dirt, etc. to run into the ferrule and cause the hairs to separate. If you are not going to paint for a time, place all your brushes flat in a covered container after first washing them well in turpentine, then methylated spirits and finally in an oil like lavender oil to keep them supple. Once they are oiled, pull them gently into shape and make sure that they cannot subsequently be jammed against anything which will cause them to bend (fine brushes may be kept in a drinking straw). To expel excess oil, place the hairs on a lint-free cloth and gently press with your finger. Do not pull on the hairs as they are only glued in. Washing brushes occasionally with soap and water or a shampoo is good but make sure they are completely dry and oiled again before painting. Brushes should be conditioned before each painting session.

Brushstrokes Conventional brushstrokes are like scales for a pianist. They must be practised before you can use them skilfully: 'paint is applied with one stroke and removed with the next'. If you can make your brushstrokes work for you, your painting will not end up overworked or muddy. For individual results, however, you cannot blindly follow a set pattern of strokes to form a leaf, flower or pattern, for example. If you do, your leaf, flower and pattern will be the same as everyone else's leaf, flower and pattern.

Flat load: The brush has an even coat of one colour right across its width.

Shaded load: The brush is loaded with paint in a circular motion, going into the mound of mixed paint (from right to left in an anti-clockwise direction for a right handed person; left handers left to right in a clockwise direction) and gradually taking up paint. The stroke will apply a heavier application of paint on the left side (right side for left handers), shaded to the right (left) with a lighter colour tone.

Side load: Only one side of the brush is loaded.

Mixed load: When two or more colours are loaded onto the brush usually with the shaded load or side load technique.

Straight strokes: Pull the loaded brush towards yourself or slightly to one side. Vary the length of the strokes. Used for backgrounds, washes, cross-hatching and tints.

Comma stroke: The loaded brush is held at a 45° angle and pulled towards the painter in the shape of a C, either short or long, back to front, or normally. Pressure is applied to the brush at the top of the stroke and lifted as the stroke is executed. An elongated comma stroke will give a long-tailed effect. Used to frame and cut in.

Dash: Fully loaded brush is used on its tip so that a narrow band of colour is applied. Useful for branches, veins, etc.

There are obviously many other positions for your brushes which you will discover by experiment or accident. Use as many as you can to become versatile.

BTU (British Thermal Unit) The quantity of heat required to raise the temperature of one pound of water one degree Fahrenheit.

Build-up Line or mound of thick paint caused by too much paint or oil on the brush, inexpert application or grainy paints.

Bullseye confetti Paper-thin shards of blown glass, both transparent and opal.

Bullseye fusible sheet glass Single rolled hand-cast glass with a slightly wavy top surface and a texture on the underside of the sheet in a wide variety of transparent, solid opal and streaky opal colours, and with fractures and streamers on white opal and clear glass. There are also transparent, solid opal and patterned iridescent glass, thick rolled glass and standard dichroic glass.

Bullseye non-sheet glass frits Crushed, screened, cleaned and tested compatible glass comes in transparent and opal frits.

Bullseye stringers Threads of glass pulled from re-melted sheet glass. May be tack fused or torch worked over a candle flame to make fine line designs for fusing onto sheets.

Burnish To rub Roman Gold or burnishing gold with a burnishing cloth, burnishing sand or fibreglass brush to give it a rich satin finish. The best results are obtained when this is done while the piece is still warm from the kiln.

Burnishing gold Most golds, other than Liquid Bright Gold have to be burnished. Made from pure metal from which the alloys have been removed. See individual names such as ROMAN GOLD, FLUXED GOLD, UNFLUXED GOLD.)

Butting To apply glazes adjacent to each other but not touching.

Byron Manufacturer of hobby ceramic products.

C

Cache-pot Small lidded container or larger bowl or pot used to conceal an unattractive plant pot or other container. (From French *cacher*: to hide.)

Cadmium Element used in some very bright (letter box/Santa) reds. Should only be fired once at a very low temperature, e.g. 700°C (1400°F), after all other painting has been completed.

Calcine Chemicals reduced to powder with heat.

Calcium borate Strong flux which intensifies colour and assists in resisting crazing.

Calcium carbonate A fine white powder which occurs naturally as chalk, limestone, marble, etc.

Used in kiln whiting or wash.

Calcium chloride Acts as a flocculent or suspension agent.

Calcium magnesium carbonate Natural mineral which is used as a secondary flux. *See* DOLOMITE.

Calcium oxide Quicklime, made by heating chalk, used in the manufacture of glass.

Calligraphy Formal script written with a pen or brush.

Calyx Outer protective envelope of flower.

Calyx—consisting of SEPALS

Camaieu French terminology for monochrome painting.

Cameo Small relief carving, usually in two layers, the lower one a different colour to form a contrasting base for the relief layer.

Cameo glass Glass with two or more fused layers of different colours, the outer layer etched or carved to create a multi-coloured design in relief.

Camera obscura Apparatus for projecting a design onto a surface where it may be traced. A modern day technique is to project a slide or image onto a wall and make an enlarged tracing which can be reduced to the desired size on a photocopier.

Camieu French terminology for silhouette painting.

Candles It is possible to paint on candles as you would on soap, also on waxed surfaces such as the inside of a milk carton, waxed paper and plasticised surfaces, although all these surfaces tend to show scratch marks. Using a fast drying medium, paint as though on glaze. The finished design may be sprayed with hairspray and then with a craft lacquer to preserve it. It is better to use an aerosol lacquer, as it is possible to move the paint using a brushed-on sealer.

Cane Fine glass rods in many colours used for ornament, millefiori and many other decorations.

Canvas porcelain Very thin porcelain (1–2 mm thick), also called porcelain canvas. It is slightly rough in texture with a matt surface and is usually only available in comparatively small tiles. The rough surface or 'tooth' is hard on brushes, and paints will not fire evenly as a rule, so the use of a matt art varnish spray when the work is completed is advisable. There is sometimes a difference in the two sides but it does not really matter which one is used for painting. Normal porcelain paints are used and the pieces are fired either flat or supported in an upright position. As the tiles are slightly transparent, an interesting effect is obtained when they are lit from behind.

Carb soda/baking soda 1. Baking soda is used to neutralise acid when it is used to etch a piece, or if you should get it on your skin. **2.** May be used a fluxing agent.

Carbon paper Used to make a copy of a design. If you must do this, and it is necessary for some subjects and for some beginners, try graphite paper.

Carborundum Trade name for SILICON CARBIDE, very hard abrasive. Fine grades are suitable for grinding glass.

Cartouche Framed ornamental panel with symbols or inscriptions. A cartouche is made up of scrolls (or other shapes) of varying sizes which make a 'frame' which may be round, oval, rectangular or free form. They may be ornate or simple and the interior of the shape may be left blank, filled with a lattice pattern or a complementary floral design to suit the vehicle. For exact symmetry, draw one corner or side of the cartouche and trace the rest of your design to complete the boundary.

Carving clay Leatherhard clay may be: **1.** Carved with a tool to incise a design, shape an edge or penetrate the wall and make holes. **2.** Etched with a solution: the design is drawn onto the dried clay, areas to be left unchanged are coated with a mask such as Gare Hi-Lo or Gare Wax Resist and the remaining areas etched with Gare Thick 'N Etch.

Cased glass Glass with two or more layers of different colours, often with the top one or two layers cut away to create a multi-coloured design.

Casting Forming a shape by pouring liquid clay into a plaster mould or glass into a refractory or sand mould. For best results, moulds should be clean and dry, and care should be taken to pour evenly and slowly to prevent air bubbles or pinholes forming. Avoid brittleness, cracking and casting spots caused by the addition of too much deflocculent. Too long a casting time is caused by too much water and damp moulds.

Casting slip Liquid clay held in suspension with a deflocculent such as sodium silicate.

Cast shadow Shadow thrown by object in the path of a light source.

Cathedral glass Transparent coloured sheet glass.

Celadon Soft ceramic iron glaze, valued by the ancient Chinese for its resemblance to jade.

Celsius Scale of temperature where freezing point is 0°, as opposed to Fahrenheit scale where freezing point is 32°. (*cf.* Centigrade.)

Cement For mending china. There are various commercial cements available; the manufacturers' instructions should be followed. Enamel or white relief mixed with a little flux may be painted onto two matching broken edges, held together and fired low. The piece to be mended may need support during the firing.

Centigrade Celsius temperature scale. *See* CELSIUS.

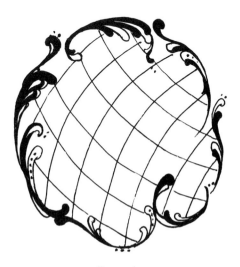

Cartouche

Centre of interest The focal point or that part of a design which should leap to the fore when first viewed.

Ceramic 1. Generic term to cover various clays. **2.** Pieces composed of clay slip and poured into a mould, dried and fired. These pieces are usually finished with a high gloss glaze and/or decorated with engobe, slip, enamel, carving, painting, and are suitable for most of the decorative advice given in this book. Some pieces may have to be fired a little lower than the suggested temperature because of the high flux content of the original glaze and also because imperfections may occur on the surface.

Ceramic à froid A solvent based ceramic liquid colour which may be applied to a porcelain or ceramic surface or to other surfaces such as glass, metal, leather, wood, etc. It is not fired, however, it has the appearance of fired porcelain. It will set hard in 24 hours. There are many colours which are intermixable. WHITE SPIRIT is used as a diluent. The ceramic paint may be applied with a brush, by the print method or, for a very effective decoration, a few drops of various colours may be floated on the surface of a basin of water. The colours will mix and swirl together and create complex patterns. The object to be painted is dipped into the solution, withdrawn immediately and allowed to dry. It takes a little experimenting but the results are a lot of fun.

A clear glaze, a filler undercoat and a thinner may be obtained to go with these unfired ceramics.

Ceramic à l'Eau A water-based ceramic liquid colour similar to Ceramic à Froid but which may be hardened at 200°C (400°F). There are 10 colours which are diluted with water.

Ceramic fibre Insulation material composed of alumina and silica from which ceramic blankets, felt and vacuum formed shapes and moulds can be made. *See* Thermal Ceramics, page 125.

Ceramic glazes Glazes are composed of elements and oxides. The majority of glazes contain lead and other toxic substances and care should always be taken to read the label for complete information and product safety. Most ceramic glazes for food utensils these days are almost free from lead. If they are fired at the recommended temperature, most of the lead content will be leached out in the firing. The majority of glazes may be treated with the techniques suggested in this book, e.g. painting,

enamelling, printing, firing temperatures. Some specialist glazes, however, may require experimentation to attain maximum benefit. Unfortunately, there are far too many varieties to to list them all here. (The Duncan catalogue alone carries sixteen types of glaze, each with many varieties of colour, texture and character.)

Ceramic paints There are many commercial paints on the market for painting on glazed or unglazed surfaces.

Acrylic paints: May be used on ceramic surfaces. Once painted the article should be left to dry and then coated with two coats of a polyurethane varnish.

Car duco or spray paints: These paints contain lead and therefore are *not suitable* for food and drink ware. A wide range of colours is available in spray containers; immensely suitable for stencil designs. Paint with polyurethane varnish for durability.

Enamel paints: These contain lead and therefore are *not suitable* for food and drink ware. Very durable; a wide variety of colours is available.

Onglaze paints: Available in a variety of colours in powder or mixed form. They may be applied to the surface with all the care and detail of an oil or watercolour painting before firing the piece at the required temperature according to the manufacturer's instructions.

Solvent based cold ceramic paints (Ceramic à froid): Paints in which the solvent will evaporate leaving the coloured design. These paints can be removed with a solvent and will scratch and mark with use. They may be protected with a decorative glaze or polyurethane varnish.

Stencil paints: Paint, allow to dry and paint with several coats of polyurethane to make washable.

Underglaze paints: Colour pigments available in either powder or liquid form which are applied to bisque or unfired ware, fired and then glazed.

Vitrified paints: Colour pigments with a base of (usually) silica, borax and other additives. Available in either powdered or ready mixed form, they are applied to the surface and the piece is fired at the required temperature according to the manufacturer's instructions.

Waterbased ceramic paints (Ceramic à l'Eau): Become fixed when heated. Colours are bright and can be mixed with each other. Should not be diluted too much. Apply paint to either glazed or unglazed surface, allow to dry for a day (or longer for thick paint), place in cold oven and bake at 200°C (400°F) for 30 minutes. (Time depends on colour and thickness of paint, drying time and oven temperature variation. It is wise to test fire the colour first as it may discolour if over-fired.) Overlays of colour and intricate patterns should be fired between applications.

Ceramic Solutions, Victoria All Australian development and manufacturing firm providing underglazes, glazes, acrylics, sealers, earthenware leaded 'food safe' glazes, satin glazes, clay mender, casting clay and painting medium as well as seminars on their use. See Product Information, page 98.

Ceramic spray sealer A clear coating to protect unfired coloured objects. It comes in a range of glossy to matt finishes.

Ceramic tiles/shapes Usually have a softer glaze than the hard porcelain or china glazes. They may be painted, printed, stencilled, have glass melted onto them; several may be used to compose a complete picture or scene. The backs may be used as a bisque surface for flooding enamel. It is possible to make your own tiles or slabs, from many of the available clays.

Ceric oxide A pale yellow/cream coloured powder used to polish glass.

Cesco Australian manufacturer of ceramic products, including brushes, underglaze colours, glazes, casting slips and clay bodies.

Chalk Faber-Castell chalks may be used to colour bisque ware. Multiple layers may be applied by rubbing colour onto the clay with a cotton bud or fingertip and spraying lightly with porcelain sealer. Allow to dry and apply colour again to create shadows and a range of colour combinations.

Chamois May be used for padding and for rubbing gold with sand.

Champlevé Enamel flooded into shallow depressions carved into a leatherhard clay or bisque surface, in a free form or traditional design, and fired.

Chelsea paper Art paper for oil painting. To paint on Chelsea paper, coat first with medium and rapidly paint design. Dry and paint again, two or three times. May be cleaned with turpentine. Spray with Chelsea Spray.

Chiaroscuro The exaggerated treatment of light and shade as contrast in art. (From Latin *chiarooscuro*: bright-dark.)

China General term applied to white porcelain ware. May be Japanese, European or American.

European china may be Limoges, Bavarian or Caverswall bone china from England.

China clay Kaolin, a fine white clay used as an absorbent and filler in ceramics.

China mist Onglaze paint in an aerosol can in a range of colours. Used to tint a surface by spraying lightly and firing at Cone 018 or 715°C (1385°F). Several applications are used for darker background work as heavy coats will chip off. May be used for bisque and glass; however, with glass, use light applications only and fire low as for glass between each application. May be sprayed over fired Liquid Bright Gold to matt it with any one of several colours.

Chinoiserie French terminology for Oriental style work.

Chroma Intensity or brightness/dullness of a colour. A greyed colour loses its chroma or intensity. The brighter the colour, the greater the impact and therefore to be used with caution.

Chromatic colours All colours other than black, white, grey.

Chrome colours Blues and greens.

Chromium oxide An oxide which normally produces green colouring; however, in some lead glazes it will produce reds and yellows; brown with zinc oxide; pink with tin oxide; and in lead glazes with a soda content, a brilliant yellow will result with the addition of 1% chrome.

Circular lines Applied by:
- Using a banding wheel.
- Holding the pencil in the normal grip, hold one finger against the edge of the blank as a guide and rotate the piece. The pencil automatically marks the circle. The innermost line is drawn first if more than one is required.
- Using a length of cotton or string attached to a pin embedded into plasticine or Blu-Tack positioned in the centre of the plate with a pencil attached to the other end. By varying the length of the string, the lines can be spaced as desired.
- Using a small tool, roughly triangular in shape, with carefully positioned holes and a hooked end which holds the tool to the edge of the plate.
- Around a vertical piece, using a pencil attached to an upright ruler or a wooden block with depressions and/or holes to hold the pencil or loaded brush.

Cire perdue French terminology for the LOST WAX process.

Classical art Art based on the Greek and Roman principles of art. Characterised by a controlled rational observance of the accepted rules and styles.

Clay Stiff, viscous earth consisting mainly of aluminium silicate which, when mixed with water, forms a pliable paste. It is formed by the decomposition of feldspars, a component of granite. Kaolin is an example of pure clay. The main characteristics of clay include:

Porosity: Sand or grog is mixed with clay to allow the water to evaporate.

Shrinkage: The clay particles form a tighter bond with the evaporation of water.

Vitreousness: The clay is rendered impervious to water by exposure to high temperatures.

Plasticity: Clay is pliable and may be moulded at the direction of the artist. The degree of plasticity is determined by the water content, the presence of organic matter and the size of the clay particles.

There are three main types of clay used by ceramists:

Earthenware: A comparatively low-fired porous clay.

Stoneware: A hard dense ware which may be fired higher than earthenware and because of this is quite vitreous.

Porcelain: The hardest and finest of the clay products.

The sequence of texture in the clay is as follows: Initially the clay is malleable and may be formed into a shape. If left to dry, it becomes leatherhard and may still be gently coaxed into slight changes of form or carved and trimmed. It eventually becomes bone dry and may no longer be adapted without cracking or breaking although it may still be carved or etched. If it is then fired low enough to simply harden but still remain porous, it is termed bisque and will accept an application of glaze. It is also called bisque if it is fired to maturity and left unglazed. The final steps are to glaze and decorate the ware and fire to maturity.

Clay body That portion of the object underneath the glazing and decoration.

Clay carbon Carbonless transfer paper for applying designs to a clay body.

Clay glazing To form, glaze and fire an object in the one stage.

Clock divider A pattern to divide a clock into equal segments.

Cloisonné Traditional design outlined in metal, usually silver or gold, and flooded with enamel, on a metal base. It is possible to create an interesting facsimile using enamel pastes and gold penwork. If the outline is done in water-based medium, it forms a barrier over which the enamel will not flow.

Closed A term used to describe a fast drying medium as opposed to an open or slow drying medium.

Clove oil An oil which slows the drying process of the medium and keeps it open.

Coating cement Coating for fibre moulds and kiln floors, usually composed of colloidal silica and a fine clay.

Cobalt carbonate Produces a weaker blue colour than COBALT OXIDE in glazes. A smooth blue which will vary from a pink mauve in a dolomite glaze to bright blue in an alkaline glaze and a very dark blue in a feldspathic glaze.

Cobalt colours Dark blues.

Cobalt oxide Deep blue pigment used to colour glazes and glass. Deep blue in lead glazes, a vivid blue in alkaline glazes and purple with magnesium.

Coefficient of expansion The percentage of change in length per degree Celsius change in temperature.

Coil pottery Forming an object with layers of clay coils.

Cold painting Application of colour to glassware without subsequent firing. Vitrail, Email Vitrail are common materials, usually transparent, which dry very quickly. They may be diluted with alcohol. These paints are flammable and contain liquid hydrocarbons.

Colemanite Calcium borate, a natural frit used as a flux in glazes to reduce crazing.

Collage Additional decoration of various materials which are attached to a (previously painted) surface.

Colloidal silica A suspension of finely divided silica particles in a liquid medium used as a bonding agent in cement.

Colour Colour is subjective and a way of expressing our thoughts. It is made by light waves which are composed of the prismatic colour spectrum yellow, red, orange, violet, indigo, blue and green. An object absorbs some of the colours of the spectrum and reflects others, e.g. leaves absorb all the colours except green and yellow, which they reflect. Colour has three dimensions—*hue, value* and *intensity. Hue* is the name given to a colour, *value* is the lightness or darkness of a colour and *intensity* is the brightness or strength of a colour. A colour which is lightened by the addition of white is called a *tint;* a colour darkened by the addition of black is called a *shade.* A tint has a lighter value than the hue used to make it. *Cool* colours are usually blues and greens and *warm* colours reds and yellows. However, each *hue* may be given a warm or a cool appearance by the addition of one of the primary colours, e.g. a blue green is cool whereas a yellow green is warm.

Monochrome colour: The various tints and shades of one hue.

Analogous colours: Neighbouring colours on the colour wheel.

Complementary colours: Opposite colours on the colour wheel.

Split complementary colours: One colour plus two colours which are adjacent to its complement.

Triadic colours: Any three colours equally distant on the colour wheel.

Sympathetic and harmonious colours: A primary colour with some adjacent colours.

Colour is not isolated but takes on reflections from surrounding colours. An area can appear larger or smaller depending on the colours involved. e.g. a yellow square set in a purple background will appear larger than a purple square set in a yellow background. Try it! The introduction of a small flash of a dominant colour such as red, yellow or orange can be exciting, but a large splash of the same colour will probably be overwhelming.

Colour contrast Usually colours opposite each other on the COLOUR WHEEL, e.g. yellow/violet; red/green; orange/blue.

Colour elements for glass Glass may be coloured by the following additives—chromates for green, cobalt for blue and manganese for purple. The green of bottles comes from oxidised iron and brown is the result of a combination of iron and sulphur. The addition of gold produces ruby glass, and red glass can be made by adding copper or selenium.

Colour perspective Distant colours should be greyer and lighter, while close colours should be brighter and more intense, to enhance the effect of perspective.

Colour scheme Combination of colours which allows interaction with shape and form.

Colour spectrum Violet, indigo, blue, green, yellow, orange and red.

Colour wheel A colour chart showing primary, secondary and tertiary colours and the various colour combinations which are traditionally most pleasing. There are accepted colour wheel combinations other than the traditional one with which we are all familiar. See ANALOGOUS COLOURS, DIRECT COMPLEMENTARY COLOURS, *etc, etc.*

Combing A technique whereby layers of coloured glass are heated to 900°C (1700°F) until liquid, then 'combed' with a wooden-handled metal instrument to form a wave or zigzag design, with a rake to prduce feathering or with some other tool for an abstract design. Alternatively, coloured glass threads may be applied to the surface of molten glass, MARVERING the threads into the glass and pulling them with a special comb to form a pattern. A wooden rod or broom handle with a nail or screw in the end is an inexpensive tool. *Extreme care* should be taken with these techniques, as the kiln is very hot when opened at this temperature and dangerous if contact is made with the elements. A wooden-handled tool is essential and the kiln must be turned off before combing. Goggles should be worn to protect the eyes from excessive heat. If the glass cools before the combing is finished, the door may be shut and the kiln turned on again and reheated. This technique was originally used by ancient Roman glass blowers.

Comma stroke A useful brushstroke in the shape of a comma which, executed with a square shader, surrounds, cuts in and places backgrounds and, with a liner, creates scrolls.

Compass Drawing tool principally for circles and arcs; may also be used to indicate the distances between lines in the design, e.g. the eyes in a portrait, the width of matching windows.

Compatibility Glass pieces must be compatible if they are to be fused together. It is wise to test fire glass pieces before fusing and if possible to use the same types of glass together. A basic compatibility test is to place two 1 cm by 12 cm (3/8″ x 5″) pieces of glass one on top of the other and warm them with a blowtorch or a gas jet, holding the glass with a pair of pliers at each end. As the glass softens it can be pulled to form a thin thread. If the thread remains straight on cooling, the glass is compatible. If it bends, one piece of glass has contracted more than the other and the glass is not compatible.

Complementary (direct complementary) colours Colours immediately opposite each other on a colour wheel: red and green; blue and yellow; and orange and purple. *Double complementary colours:* Two pairs of colours on a colour wheel. Black and white are complementary.

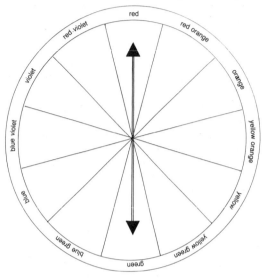

Colour wheel: direct complementary colours

Composition The formation of a pattern or design which should harmonise with the blank to give a pleasing result. There is usually a theme which has a focal point, with supporting design and a gradual blend with the white or neutrally coloured background. There should be variety in form, colour and design to provide interest. There should always be a suggestion of 'surprise', usually an understated echo of the theme which attracts the eye of the viewer but does not detract from the focal point. General rules are that the lines of the design should follow the outline of the object being painted, the main portion of the design should be contained within a triangle, and 'three' is the order of the day. Three main flowers in a floral design, three major points of intense depth, three areas of design: focal point, secondary supporting group and tertiary area or background. Three areas of colour: small, medium and large; and three shades of colour. These are conventional guidelines and, as always, there are exceptions. Obvious faults are lines at right angles to a curve, too busy a design, background features dominating the scene. A good test is to walk away from the painting and return to it

later. If your eye immediately goes to a part of the design other than the focal area, that part is usually at fault in some way.

Compressive stress Caused by contraction.

Concave Indented or curved inwards.

Conceptual arts Where the concept or idea is more important to the artist than the final article.

Conceptual colour Colour, other than the realistic, used to express an idea or meaning.

Conditioning brushes Brushes, like good cooking utensils, have to be conditioned in order to work efficiently. The first time you use a brush each painting session, initially dip it into your medium almost to the ferrule. Using your tile as a surface, work the oil through the hairs of the brush by drawing it along the tile and fanning out the fibres. Re-shape the tip with your fingers and gently press all the oil out of it with one of your fingers against the tile. Re-load the brush by dipping it into the medium approximately half the length of its hairs, wipe the excess oil off on the edge of the jar and gently press any further surplus out before loading the brush with paint.

Cones Cones are small white pyramids of clay to which flux has been added and which melt at varying temperatures. They are used to give you the time/temperature curve of firing time when using your kiln. They may also be used to test the heat and accuracy of your kiln. The time taken to bring your kiln to a certain temperature is important to the reaction of the paints and other substances painted on or adhered to the glazed surfaces. The longer a kiln takes to reach a certain temperature, the less heat is required to mature the paint; a cone will indicate this more accurately than a thermometer which merely indicates the internal temperature of the kiln. That is to say, the longer your kiln takes to fire, the lower the temperature at which the cone melts. When exposed to heat for less time in a rapid fire the cone needs a higher temperature to cause it to bend. The length of time taken to reach a desired temperature in the kiln is frequently governed by the amount it contains or the efficiency of the power supply. Cones give a truer reading of the effect the heat has on the clay body of the pieces being fired. The melting point of the cones and the rate of degrees per hour is indicated by the manufacturer on the container in which they come. The scale below is therefore only a guide. *See* diagram on page 61.

Cone	Fahrenheit	Centigrade
022	1110	598
021	1135	612
020	1175	635
019	1260	682
018	1320	715
017	1375	746
016	1455	790
015	1475	801
014	1540	837
013	1560	848
012	1620	882
011	1640	893
010	1665	907
09	1690	921
08	1750	954
07	1800	982
06	1845	1007
05	1915	1046
04	1940	1060
03	2000	1093
02	2040	1115
01	2080	1137

Confetti glazes Trade name for a Crystaltone glaze.

Confluent colour Graduated colour.

Contour drawing To draw an object or model by pencilling in the outline without lifting the pencil. This may be achieved by looking at the subject and drawing it or by touch, feeling the contour and drawing with eyes closed.

Contrast Striking difference. The use of contrast in painting adds interest and relieves boredom. Check the following areas to see if you have contrast and with it curiosity for your viewers in your painting: lights against darks, straight and curved lines with wide and narrow areas, distinct regions and blurred 'out-of-focus' regions, clear colour and greyed colour, the obvious and the suggested, contrast in form such as well defined shapes and suggested shapes, rough and smooth areas, full face and turned blossoms, painted or positive areas for opposition to negative space or vacant areas. Keep in mind that the opposites on the colour wheel will heighten the impact of each other when placed side by side. Do not overlook the strength of a sharp, clear design on pure white porcelain or the richness of a ground border with a delicate pattern.

Contrast varnish A water-based organic colour solution painted on a dark surface to show up transparent lustres and Liquid Bright Gold as they are applied. It fires off in the kiln and does not affect the gold finish.

Conventional design Traditional semi-stylised naturalistic design.

Conversion formulae for temperature To convert °C to °F multiply by 1.8 and add 32; or multiply by 9, divide by 5 and add 32. To convert °F to °C multiply by 0.55 and subtract 32.

Convex Outwardly curved.

Cool colours Blues, violets and greens which give the appearance of cool, receding and background colours. A wash of blue over a dominant secondary feature will force it into the background. Yellow greens are in the warm range of colours.

Copaiba (balsam of) Viscous fluid from tropical trees of South America. A fast drying medium used with onglaze paints.

Copper carbonate Green colouring agent. When used in glaze recipes will produce a pink colour in dolomite glazes, red in reduction conditions, green in lead glazes and turquoise in alkaline glazes.

Copper enamel May be used with caution on glazed surfaces. It is best used on a prepared surface, such as one from which the glaze has been removed or to which one of the texture pastes or structural substances has been added. Very small amounts of the powdered enamel sprinkled onto the glaze will not chip off; however, larger quantities may chip off, if not in the cooling process then at an embarrassing later date. There are several types of copper enamel available: a powder form which is either opaque or transparent, and solid rods and shapes of coloured enamel. All these forms come in a range of colours which may be mixed together. The powder form may be mixed with any of the oil-based mediums, glycerine or water-based mediums, milk or simple syrups such as cola. If applied with flux it will melt more readily and flow onto your work. As with most of these substances which have many variables, the result is quite unpredictable and almost always interesting, although it could be unattractive if overdone. Moderation in all things!

Copper oxide Pigment used to colour glass which will give a turquoise hue and many bubbles as it frees the oxygen. The more copper oxide used, the more bubbles. Colouring agent for glazes; apple green in oxidising conditions and a copper red, known as *sang-de-boeuf*, in a reduction kiln. Copper will increase the leaching properties of lead and should not be used for food utensils.

Copyright Where does it begin and end? Copyright protects against the unlawful copying, selling, distributing, publishing or use of work in other media. According to the *Legal Guide for the Visual Artist*, every artist should place copyright notice of their work prior to sale but need not register the copyright until there is an infringement. There are many rumours about what one can or cannot copy and a good lawyer could probably prove every one of these right. I really think pride and integrity are the important factors—pride in your own individual creative ability and integrity in giving credit where credit is due. If you want to use another artist's work or photograph as a study or exercise to learn a particular technique, do so by all means. Learn as much as you can from every available source. Then create your own interpretation of what you have learned— and that does not mean paint it another colour or change a detail or two. You learn so that you will develop and improve.

Core forming A vessel made by trailing molten glass around a shaped core of clay and sand, the core being removed after annealing.

Cornelli scrolling Snail-like trailing over the surface of the object being painted, usually in coloured or gold penwork, raised paste or enamel.

Cornish stone (synthetic) Replacement for natural Cornish stone which is no longer available commercially. Cornish stone has all the ingredients necessary for an earthenware glaze and, with the addition of flux, for a stoneware glaze. Synthetic Cornish stone is a blend of minerals which does not contain fluorine and which may be used as a flux in low temperature glazes.

Corolla The cup of petals which forms the inner, and usually most colourful, part of a flower.

Correction of fired errors There are a number of ways to correct, hide or disguise errors or bad workmanship fired into your work. Ingenuity!

Chipped edge: Incorporate a pattern of textured design into the area and build-up the broken space gradually with one of the more reliable textured pastes in a succession of low firings, then paint the area with either gold, platinum or one of the metallic powders. Another idea is to frame it with a slightly smaller mat which covers the offending defect, within a larger frame.

Too busy a design: Portion of the design may be covered with one of the texture pastes or acid look, or the glaze chipped away with glass excising. Or accentuate the design with a dramatic background, fire and dust the whole area, leaving some of the original area lightly covered and pen the outline and part of the background. The remaining design becomes shadows. Use Rustiban to remove most of the design, lustre and penwork to develop and highlight what is left. Pen and flooded enamel is sometimes helpful. If you consider the piece is already ruined, experiment!

Covercoat 1. Water-soluble liquid which dries to form a plastic film which is used to protect or mask an area of your painting surface. It peels off easily once it has served its purpose. **2.** Cellulose coating for decals. **3.** Trade name for opaque underglazes used for complete coverage.

Crack filler Filling for cracks which occur in bisque ware. Fill crack firmly and allow to dry. Re-fire at bisque temperature prior to glazing.

Cracking Cracks in the fired clay body are usually caused by overworking the clay, uneven or rapid drying of the clay or firing too fast, too early. To overcome, do not handle the clay any more than necessary in the forming of the object as your hands will dry out the clay; dry the ware more slowly, wrap in plastic, invert if possible as soon as possible when dry enough, use sharp tools, and slow down the initial firing to 300°C (570°F).

Crackle Cracks in the glaze which may be accidental, purposely made or caused by exposure to the elements (of the weather, not the kiln).

Crackletone glazes Trade name of glazes which fire with a finely crazed pattern.

Craft knife There are many uses for this handy scalpel-like tool. Cutting into resists for sharp detail, cleaning up gold (before it has been fired) which has extended beyond the desired line, and cutting out plasticised clay for moulding are just a few of the obvious ones.

Crank A support for tiles, plates and other flat objects.

Craters Miniature explosions on a glazed surface, usually caused by impurities in the glaze or in the body of the clay.

Crawling Where the glaze has pulled away from the body of the clay and formed into little heaps. Probably caused by the glaze being applied to unclean bisque. An interesting effect when deliberately caused with texture pastes. Texture mixed with oil and combined with more texture mixed with water will repel each other and cause the glaze to crawl.

Crazing A network of fine surface cracks which appear in a glaze or in glass. Occasionally caused deliberately by the manufacturer but usually caused: **1.** By a bad 'fit' between the glaze and the body of the clay. **2.** By the glaze and body of the piece expanding at different temperatures and causing stress fractures in the glaze. **3.** By exposure to harsh elements, such as direct sunlight.

Crest Coat of arms.

Crisseling (crizzling) A defect in glass consisting of a network of fine cracks. Usually caused by a faulty balance of ingredients in a batch. The addition of lead oxide was used as a remedy.

Cristallo A type of soda glass which is very soft and pliable in its molten state; made with the ashes of sea plants.

Cross-hatching Application of paint with brushstrokes which cross over in a grid or diamond pattern. These may be straight or curved to show a contour. The applied paint is then feathered and blended into a smooth, even application with the lighter and heavier patches of colour giving variation of tones and values. Highlights are left in place and look quite natural.

Cross-section The view of the interior of an object when it has been cut through.

Crucible A ceramic pot in which glass is melted. Normal clay may be used but a durable crucible can be composed of alumina, kaolin clay, fine and coarse grog and ball clay.

Cryolite Sodium aluminium fluoride. Natural source of sodium used to obtain alkaline colours and secondary fluxing agent

Crystal Fine very transparent glass with a high lead oxide content. Crystal will lose its shape when fired at more than 600°C (1110°F).

Crystal Clear glaze **1.** Trade name for a Crystaltone glaze for ceramic pieces. **2.** Onglaze use—white powder which contains flux, used to 'dust' onto a piece of painted porcelain to give it a high gloss. It can be used to restore the glaze to a piece which has been cleaned with Rustiban. It will eat out some colours, particularly reds, so caution is advised when using it. Colours will be more reliable if the glazed piece is fired at a lower temperature.

Crystalline glaze Made from zinc silicate, this glaze has patterns of crystals which form in the firing.

Crystals Coloured glazes which have been fired and then ground to various proportions.

Crystobolite Used to make casts for crushed glass.

Cullet Scraps of broken and waste glass for remelting.

Cut glass Glass is cut with a wheel of iron or stone to decorate it with facets and grooves.

Cutting board For cutting stencils and designs. Very inexpensive self-healing cutting boards marked with measurements are available.

Cutting glass Place glass on a flat surface. Using a metal ruler as a guide for the glass cutter, place it flat on the glass. Push down the glass cutter and pull it towards you with a continuous flowing movement. The scratch need only be light but should be unbroken. The glass is then grasped with thumbs and forefingers, either side of the scratch. It should snap apart with a little pressure.

D

Dalle de verre Thick glass slabs approximately 25 mm (1″) thick.

Damar varnish For use with raised paste to facilitate the making of long scrolls.

Decals Transfers with designs to be applied to china and glass ware. Porcelain, ceramic or glass paints are applied, usually by offset or screen printing with the aid of an oil-based medium, in a design or shape to a special waterslide paper, allowed to dry and then covered with a cellulose material and also allowed to dry. Wet the decal for a few seconds, remove backing which should just slide off and position cellulose with design. Remove any bubbles, taking care not to stretch the cellulose, and allow to dry. Fire at a medium temperature, 780–820°C (1440–1500°F). During the firing process the film burns off and the design is left to adhere to the glazed surface. (*Note:* Water-based mediums are not suitable because of soaking the decal.)

Decal medium There are several oil-based mediums suitable for decals. They are usually thicker or more viscous than painting mediums and turpentine is used as a solvent. Follow manufacturer's instructions.

Decorate To embellish or enhance, hopefully, aesthetically. Porcelain is traditionally already beautiful with its pure white translucent glaze and rounded forms. The coloured clays of ceramics often suit a more contemporary decoration.

Decorative design A design applied to enhance and decorate an otherwise plain object.

Deep cleanup tool Long-handled ceramic tool with a curved blade which is sharpened both sides; used to clean up the inner areas of a deep vase or urn.

Deerfoot blender Stippling brush in graduated sizes with an angled base.

Deflocculate 1. Make slip by adding sodium silicate or soda ash to clay thus causing a suspension of the particles. **2.** To make a smooth mixture by dissipating lumps when mixing a product.

Degussa *See* Degussa Products, page 113.

Dehydration During the initial firing of clay, the water is drawn from the clay in the firing range 150–600°C (300–1110°F) and it is necessary to vent the kiln to allow the steam generated to escape. Firing should be slow during this period to prevent a build-up of steam resulting in cracking and perhaps explosion of the clay bodies.

Deka paints Transparent glass paints which do not require firing. Colours may be mixed with each other and pastel shades are obtained with the addition of a colourless extender. The solvent used is Deka Thinner. Not suitable for eating utensils and not dishwasher-proof. Colours are fade-resistant and may be washed in cool water.

Delft Tin glazed earthenware from Holland, usually blue and white but may be any colour.

Demi-relief Relief may be high or deep, low or bas; demi-relief is midway between.

Demonstrate To show how something is done. Frequently we are asked to demonstrate to a group of people and there are one or two points which will help both the audience and the demonstrator. Firstly, choose a sufficiently large surface on which to paint or demonstrate so that all may see it. A piece of white perspex makes an excellent 'canvas' for glaze artists. If you are standing in front of your audience, do not clutch this surface to your chest. Try to learn to paint either from the side or literally with the back of the plate or tile to your chest and your painting hand in front and to the bottom, so that your fans can see what you are doing. If you are sitting at a table, do not hunch over your work. Describe and discuss your subject first and when it is time to paint, do so slowly, explaining why you are doing what you are doing, how you are doing it, which colours and tools you are using and what you hope to achieve. Try to keep talking all the time, even when you are also trying to concentrate, and remember to use stronger colours and heavier loads if in a large room with a large audience. Try not to be boastful, remember, people can actually see how good you are! Do not discuss other teachers and teaching methods in a derogatory fashion and if things are not going well do not look for excuses. Try to assess the reactions of your group and do not be disconcerted by latecomers or the woman asleep in the front row! Audiences have a limited attention span so try to think up some surprises to relieve any monotony. Try to answer all questions; however, do not be afraid to say you do not know but that you will find out. You might like to ask that all questions are held until towards the end so that you will not lose your concentration. Keep in mind that people have come to see you, not to criticise you.

Depth Field of depth or distance from front to back of your design, a three-dimensional effect created by perspective, depth and shading.

Design Sketch or plan for a work of art. The elements of a good design are *line, direction, shape, value, colour, texture, size* and a lot of intuitive sense. *See* ART FUNDAMENTALS. The circular shape is one of the most difficult to design. The line of design is usually an S or C curve, or reverse of these, and this line should take into account the shape and form of the piece, and be proportionate in size. There should be large, medium and small areas of mass with the subject matter in series of uneven numbers (threes, fives, and so on) and covering no more than two-thirds of the area. This leaves at least one-third *negative space*, which is also broken into interesting areas of differing sizes. All design rules may at times be broken and as always there are happy accidents. The guidelines for design are just that—guidelines to be followed where appropriate. So the following are suggestions only. Place the focal mass on the largest area of of the surface, slightly off centre with the centre of intere also to one side of the mass. Design lines should curve round so that if an imaginary line is followed it will lead back to the focal area. Lines should not lead into corners, into the centre of the frame, or divide the area in half. No two lines should cross at right angles.

If the design is floral, no two flowers should be face to face or back to back, nor should any two or three form a row. The flow of design indicates the direction the eye should follow. The focal point is emphasised by the more subdued supporting and surrounding areas. No area should completely encircle another.

Once your design is complete, rotate it. It should be pleasing from all angles. Faults in design are sometimes obvious in a mirror and often more obvious after leaving the painting for some time to return—usually that which is most obvious does not fit or suit. One can frequently become so involved with each individual portion that it is impossible to see the whole.

Design aids There are many practical aids to design in the form of studies, circular and flexible rulers, plate dividers, banding wheels, school dividers, instruments which grip the edge of your plate and allow you to draw borders, car detailing tape, blocks of wood with holes bored at various heights to take a pencil to make vertical marks or simply a pencil taped to an upright ruler. Many of these can be made out of scraps at home. A good design course with practical experience and constructive criticism is invaluable.

Design Coats Trade name of underglazes suitable for greenware and for bisque.

Devitrification Glass will crystallise and become milky if held at a temperature slightly below the point when it becomes liquid. This will mar the surface of the glass.

Diaper All-over surface decoration in a simple repeat pattern of squares or diamonds.

Dichroic Showing different colours when viewed by transmitted or reflected light.

Diffraction Deflection of light rays passing through transparent glass or plastic.

Diluent A liquid used to dilute or thin down a substance.

Dimension values Length, breadth and thickness or depth creating the illusion of depth and realism.

Dimension textural glazes Trade name for opaque, matt textured glazes with gloss crystals which create a two-dimensional effect; suitable for either greenware or bisque.

Diminishing glass Viewing apparatus composed of concave lenses used to see a reduced version of a design or to see it as a 'whole'.

Dip 'n Done glazes Trade name of glazes used for rapid production.

Dipping or immersion A. The act of submerging the object you are painting into a solution. **B.** Coating an object with a liquid glaze by completely submerging it in the glaze container.
• A freshly painted porcelain, ceramic or glass object is dipped into lukewarm water, causing the paint to separate, usually into bubbles of various sizes. Alternatively, interesting patterns can be obtained by floating paint or lustre on water and immersing the piece. For best effects, apply a basecoat of a medium to light colour and fire. Apply a fairly strong coat of a darker colour to the fired piece and immediately dip into a prepared container of water. Experiment with the temperature of the water and different mediums to find the right degree of warmth for the paint you have chosen; it will differ slightly depending on the makeup of the paint, the medium and how rapidly you have painted the area.
• Liquid Bright Gold floated on water will provide you with the most delightful patterns and fascinating shapes and designs. The water should be room temperature as too cold will set the gold before it develops its pattern and too warm makes it difficult to control the pattern. Gently pour some small drops of gold onto the surface of the water. Large drops will sink (may be used when the water is poured off for rims or other applications). The gold will disperse into lacy patterns which can be controlled by lightly touching the water with your palette

knife or other object. Holding the object to be painted firmly, lay it on the area of pattern you want and gently lower it into the water. The gold will adhere in the shape it was on the surface. Remove the piece, clean up any excess gold (put it in your gold lavender jar) and once dried, fire.
• Float a small amount of different coloured lustres on water. (Incidentally, it is rumoured that lustres will sink if they are no longer any good, but I have successfully used a sunken lustre.) Submerge a porcelain, ceramic or glass blank and allow the lustres to adhere to its surface. Remove and allow to dry. Fire.
• It is possible to float paint on water when it is mixed with medium with an addition of lavender oil to help its buoyancy. Experiment until the consistency is correct and the paints float on the water. Stir the paints and then dip your piece, allowing the paint to adhere. Movement in a circular motion will help swirls of colour. Effective with glaze paints which are not meant to be fired.
• Submerge into acid to etch. *See* Etching—*caution with acid.)*

Diptych Painting or relief sculpture done in two panels.

Direct complement Two opposing colours on a colour wheel.

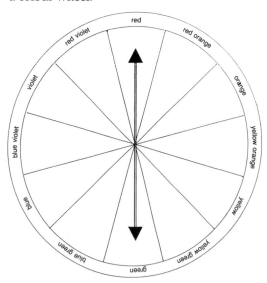

Colour wheel for direct complementary colours

Direction The line of design indicated by the placement of the components of the painting.

Discovery brushes Trade name for a variety of Duncan brushes.

Dishwashing detergent Powder paint mixed with detergent produces interesting effects—the bubbles leave an unusual pattern and the paint is matt when fired.

Dispersing agent Deflocculent which increases stability and fluidity of slip.

Disperzon A form of zircon used to assist dispersion in glazes to cause partial opacity.

Dividers A drawing instrument which may be used for accurate measurements. The distance between eyes, lines and other focal points can be measured on the study and checked on your drawing. An invaluable tool for buildings, portraits and wildlife painting.

Doc Holliday Manufacturer of hobby ceramic products.

Dolomite (natural and synthetic) Calcium and magnesium carbonates combined in crystal form or white or coloured granular masses. Used in stoneware glazes or fires at a lower temperature with addition of other fluxes. Synthetic dolomite is an excellent replacement.

Dominance Most influential—the quality of that part of the design which is the focal point. Unfortunately we frequently cause a minor part of the design to be a dominant factor.

Dona's Manufacturer of hobby ceramic products.

Dottle A sponge used for cleaning tall pots.

Dot makers Tools manufactured by Duncan with a variety of tips for indenting.

Dots Dots are used for decoration and may be either penwork or paste. For paste dots, take a nib or stylus and push into a mound of mixed paste so that the paste sits on the top of the tool. Gently touch the paste to the surface to be decorated and lift again, pulling away in a circular motion until the dot is the desired size. Reload each time for identical dots, but for a line of dots diminishing in size, do not reload. *Pointillism* is the art of creating a design or picture by painting it entirely in dots which vary in size, colour and density.

Double complement Two pairs of opposing colours on a colour wheel.

Double image The images you imagine you can 'see' in a drawing or design; something which looks like another subject as well, e.g. faces in rock formations, scenes or objects in water or clouds.

Double spiral tool Double-ended tool with fine spiral bristle brushes at either end for creating

Enamel applied as a painting medium *This painted tortoise is given another dimension by being raised 2–10 mm above the painting surface* (T. Bradford)

Dusting with dry colour *Contemporary designs and modern interpretations of the traditional still life paintings lend themselves to this medium* (T. Bradford)

Bisque fired ornaments *Small platter with gold, enamel, lustre and mask. There are many commercial shapes available which may be used to advantage in the final presentation of a fired piece. Alternatively, porcelain slip poured to flow into unusual free form shapes may be adhered to the porcelain or used as jewellery pieces* (T. Bradford)

Sculpture in porcelain *Sculpture from a deliberately broken porcelain plate (it took three!) with pewter grounding, enamel, gold and mask. The white enamel turned green when fired to create the unusual effect. The original poem introduced yet another element to the piece* (T. Bradford)

and smoothing holes and difficult-to-get-at places.

Double cast Slip of one colour is poured into a mould, left for several seconds only, then poured out. Once the remaining residue is touch dry a second different coloured batch of slip is poured into the mould and left for a longer period (10–15 minutes). The dry walls of the plaster mould absorbed the first slip quickly but will take longer now that the walls are damp. The excess is poured off and the mould left to drain. Trim the rim and keep the casting in the mould until leatherhard, then continue to dry within a plastic bag. After several days, the clay will be mature enough for the outer colour to be carved, exposing the inner colour. The object is then allowed to dry, fired to a low bisque fire (750°C, 1380°F) and may then be wholly or partially glazed.

Double strength glass Thicker than normal window glass, 10 mm (3/8″) and above.

Dovia paper Plasticised paper on which you may paint with powder paints mixed with co-paiba-based or fast drying oils such as eucalyptus. You use the same techniques, etc., except that obviously you do not fire it! May be cleaned off with turpentine.

Draft The depth of a mould.

Drakenfeld bending colours Glass stains which have a firing range of 626–704°C (1160–1300°F).

Drapery The name given to clothing worn by the figures in a painting, fabrics in the background and also to the clothing on figurines. *Lace drapery:* the name given to net or lace dipped in porcelain slip used to dress figurines.

Draping Forming glass over a mould using its own weight, gravity and heat.

Drawing Sketching with a pencil. Doodling is good practice. A few exercises follow which will help you develop an 'eye' and a 'hand'. Have pen and paper always handy and whenever you have a moment, play practice.
• Select an object and do not remove your gaze from it as you reproduce it without lifting the pen from the paper. This is contour drawing.
• Turn an object upside down and draw it. The unfamiliar shape will confuse your preconceived notions.
• Select an object, e.g. an old boot, a contorted capsicum, and draw it as many ways as you can. Draw the negative space and identify your sub-

ject or ask someone else to do so.
• Draw something while you are looking at it then draw it from memory.
• Make a sketch of something which appeals to you every day and keep a record of your drawings.

Drawn glass Glass with an antique or blown glass appearance; formed by vertical pulling using the Fourcault method of drawing sheet glass directly from the glass melt.

Dresden thick oil A pure prepared fat oil medium especially suited to European style painting.

Dresden A fine hard bodied porcelain manufactured in Germany in the town of that name. The technique used in painting the porcelain is normally the application of bright pure colours forming a myriad of stylised fantasy flowers on the white porcelain background. Dresden is best painted on hard paste fancy white porcelain without flaws and with a smooth glaze. Florets or flowers should suit the blank. Paint with a fast drying medium in brilliant colours that will not fire out.

Dressing To make the surface of a mould waterproof so that the plaster will be ejected freely.

Dry brushing The light application of paint or glaze with a very dry brush.

Dry clay To prepare generally; to every kilogram of dry powder add approximately 280 ml of water; in a strong plastic bag, secure and knead until thoroughly mixed. Age at least 24 hours. (Read the manufacturer's instructions as all clays differ.)

Dry footing The unglazed base of an otherwise glazed object. Will be porous unless the object is glazed internally.

Dry gold Pure powdered gold.

Drying time Time taken to allow paints or enamels to dry prior to the next step. Weather plays an important role in the length of drying time as does the thickness of application and the medium used to mix paints and apply them.
Enamel: Some enamels require several days drying time before firing, otherwise they will chip off at a later date.
Dusting: A fast drying medium usually requires a day or so to dry sufficiently in normal circumstances. Damp or cold weather will prolong the drying time.
Fat oil: Layers of paint may be applied one on top of the other without an interim firing if

using this medium, provided they are allowed to dry between applications.

Dry strength The strength of a material after it has dried and prior to being fired, or the capacity of an overglaze to bond to a given surface.

Duncan Enterprises Designers and manufacturers of ceramic art products which are readily available. They include mould design and production, fired glaze and non-fired colour production, kiln manufacturing, catalogues, teaching instruction and many outlets and hobby shops all over the world.

Dunting 1. Crazing of the glaze, usually caused by removing from the kiln while still hot or by gusts of cold air cooling the glaze too rapidly. Often done deliberately. May be caused by exposure to the elements, such as sunlight. **2.** Breakage during firing caused by trapped air or a foreign body.

Dust Natural enemy of all painters. Palettes and work should be kept covered when not in use and clean at all times. Do not wear woollen garments while painting.

Dusting A method of applying dry powder paint to the glazed surface. The usual method for dry dusting a painting is to paint your design normally, using a fast drying medium, then allow the painted object to become 'touch dry—that is, you can touch the paint and feel it dry but with a very slight pull or tack. Using the dry powder colours that you originally painted with, sieved or squashed between layers of greaseproof paper (waxed paper is porous) with the handle of your palette knife, and a ball of cotton wool, start with the lightest colours first and gently deposit the powder over areas of the same colour with some infringement onto the other colours used. When you have powder on all the areas you want to dust, gently pad then rub the colour into the painted surface, once again starting with the lightest colour and blending all the colours at the edges so that you do not end up with little circles of separate colour. Brush off excess powder and fire. The end result should be a pretty painting with softly blended colours and a high sheen. For an area of solid colour a little softer than a grounded area, the same method may be used. A word of caution: Too much powder will adhere to wet looking areas and after firing the paint may well blister and crack. It would be better to start again.

Drying powder paints Occasionally it is nec-essary to dry out powder paints because they have absorbed moisture from the atmosphere so they do not react well with the oil-based mediums. Spread thinly on paper on a tray and place in an oven at 80–100°C (175–212°F) for approximately 45 minutes.

E

Earthenware Coarse porous clay which is very absorbent. It is fired low and therefore soft bodied. It is usually glazed with soft glazes which normally contain lead or, as in the case of Delft or faience, tin.

Efaplast modelling material Self hardening, air dried modelling material which is composed of 95% clay and 5% binding and hardening components. There is approximately 3% shrinkage when dry. Slow drying at low temperatures provides the best results and drying time may take several days.

Eggs Decorated eggs are popular. They come in bisque ware, glazed china and earthenware or it is possible to paint on real eggs. (Emptied of their contents, they will keep indefinitely.) Simply pierce both ends of the egg and blow through one hole to force the contents through the other. Allow to dry and paint with normal onglaze paints and techniques. Spray with art varnish or fixative. A basket of painted eggs makes an inexpensive and delightful gift for Easter.

Eglomisé The application of gold or silver leaf to a glass surface which is then engraved. Usually applied to the reverse side of the piece and protected by glass or metal foil.

Elasticity The ability to regain a former shape after deformation. The ability to stretch.

Electrolyte Deflocculant; compound which dissociates into ions in solution.

Elements Coils of resistant wire through which heat passes to raise the temperature of an electric kiln.

Elements of design The shape, size, colour, tone, line, direction of your painting and visual and tactile texture. *See* ART FUNDAMENTALS.

Elephant ear Fine sponge.

Embossing Raised impression produced by stamping or the application of enamels and textures.

Emery paper Fine emery paper or wet and dry sanding paper is used to rub painted pieces lightly to smooth the surface after firing, as particles of kiln dust will have adhered to the cooling glaze. There are several commercial preparations available from porcelain, pottery and art suppliers for this purpose; as well, the humble Scotchbrite pot scourer is effective as is a nylon stocking on leatherhard greenware.

Enamel A shiny, semi-transparent vitreous substance applied to porcelain, ceramics or glass to give a raised effect or textured design in relief. The traditional enamelling techniques *cloisonné, champlevé, bassetaille* and *pliqué à jour* are ideally suited to objets d'art. Enamel can be hard or soft (contains more flux) and should be used on the appropriate hard or soft glazes otherwise it will chip off. May be obtained in powder form and mixed with special enamel medium, your normal painting medium or a number of other products such as water-based mediums, glycerine, grounding oil, copaiba, turpentine or milk for various consistencies and effects. It may also be purchased in a pre-mixed state. Enamel powder is more versatile than pre-mixed enamel and more tolerant of successive firings. It should be allowed to dry thoroughly before firing between 780–820°C (1435–1510°F); fire lower for successive firings. Some white enamels may be coloured with a small amount of dry powder paint, 1/8 to 1/6 of the enamel powder used. Enamel coloured this way may be darker after firing as the white powder becomes transparent when matured in the kiln. Darker enamel colours become a shade or two lighter after firing. Enamel may also shrink a little during the firing process. Prepared enamels may be thinned with turps or a small quantity may be left in the open air to thicken. Once fired, enamel may be painted or lustred and such additives as coloured glass fragments, beads, shards, beach sand, semi-precious gems or stones (some of which, like amethyst, lose their colour at normal firing temperatures) may be included. Most modern enamels will stand several fires and some may be fired as soon as applied. Always test fire a new enamel to see how it reacts to added colour and firing in your kiln. In spite of all our care, sometimes a scroll or jewel will pop off. To repair it you can cheat with a little colour added to transparent Araldite which can be persuaded into the shape of the original piece on the porcelain as it dries; alternatively, you can mix some enamel with fat oil or pine oil and colour it to match the original. This can be applied to the porcelain and will eventually set hard. Neither of these two remedies may be fired but will withstand being washed. An interesting design technique is to apply a thin coating of enamel to a paper shape or template, traditional or contemporary, and press it to a solid colour fired surface (matt is good), e.g. the shape of stylised fish, birds or leaves pressed against a solid red or blue matted background. Allow to dry and remove paper. Alternatively, smear enamel onto plastic wrap and place against glazed surface. Remove wrap, leaving an irregular application of enamel to texture the surface. Fire and gild, allowing some of the white to show through. Alternatively, leave plastic wrap in place and fire.

Enamel colours Metallic oxides, usually copper, iron and manganese, blended with powdered glass, for the decoration of metal, glass, porcelain and china.

Enamelware glazes Trade name for a variety of Crystaltone Glaze.

Energy regulator Switch to govern the heating of a kiln.

Energy Saver Kilns Trade name for a type of Duncan kiln.

English bone china Made from soft bodied clay with a comparatively low fired glaze. Should not be fired above 820°C (1508°F).

Engobe A coloured slip applied to clay bodies and fired high.

Environmentally friendly The environment is important to us and care should be taken to protect what we have. Where possible, alternatives like Kevlar have been found for such products as asbestos, other fluxes instead of lead, etc. Burnishing gold preparations no longer contain mercury and procedures such as chemical fire gilding are no longer being carried out. Other damaging elements and practices are being controlled or replaced, while the hydrofluoric and hydrochloric acids we use are too heavy to be a source of concern for the ozone layer.

Equilibrium Balance of the fundamental elements of art in a design or composition.

Eraser pencil There are several types of eraser pencils available. Soft tipped, firm, broad and narrow. Their uses are innumerable. What did we ever do without them? Use to draw in the wet paint, for sharp clear outlines and wipeouts, to apply pastes and enamels and so on.

Esquisse The preliminary or thumb nail sketch to compose the layout of a design.

Essence grasse Thickened turpentine or fat oil.

Essential oils Substances extracted from plants which are the basis for many art mediums and cleansing agents: oils of cloves, lavender, rosemary, etc.

Etchall cream Commercial preparation of acid in cream form for etching glass and china. Available from glass suppliers.

Etched look Product which, when applied to glass, has the appearance of etching. There is also a Matt Etched Look. *See* Josephine's Products, page 122.

Etching Matting and lowering the surface of the glazed porcelain by eating into it with acid. *Etching with hydrofluoric acid (caution with acid):* Sketch a design the size of the required etching and transfer it by tracing with the aid of graphite paper onto the glazed surface. Using asphaltum, paint the area *not to be etched,* completely covering all the surface not to be etched including the back or base of the piece. The asphaltum may have to be thinned from time to time to keep it flowing. Allow to dry a day or so and then, wearing protective clothing, place the object into an acid bath of 50% hydrofluoric acid for 1–2 minutes or until the etching is deep enough. Remove, and wash under running water to neutralise the acid. Wash with kerosene and then with hot soapy water to remove all traces of asphaltum and fire to further clean the piece. Please read more detailed instructions for etching than these if you wish to etch with acid. *See* T. Bradford: *Porcelain Art in Australia Today,* Kangaroo Press, Sydney 1984.
To etch with etching cream: Proceed as above until asphaltum has completely dried and then apply etching cream thickly over the areas to be etched. Leave for 12 to 24 hours, testing occasionally the depth of the etch. Clean as above. Etchall Cream and similar commercial preparations available from glass suppliers should be treated with *extreme caution* as burns will result from the cream just as from the solution. If acid comes into contact with your skin wash immediately in soda, soap and water to neutralise the acid. If severe, seek medical attention.

Exhibition standard The standard required for exhibitions is high. This is not to say that newcomers should not enter exhibitions and competitions. They should! Competitive entry will make you strive a little harder and extend yourself. The piece should be recently painted or formed, entirely the work of the artist and the quality should be your best. The work should be spotlessly clean and well presented. Try to be original in your presentation even if the work is in a traditional style. *See* JUDGING.

Expressionism Movement in art seeking to express emotional experience and reactions to reality.

Extruding Shaping clay or paste by passing it through a hollow lumen or canula and forcing it out at the other end through a shaped opening, or pressing the clay through a sieve or wire strainer.

Eucalyptus oil Fast drying light oil which is difficult to use but which allows crisp wipeouts.

European style Traditional designs and techniques of the European porcelain factories.

EZ Stroke Trade name for concentrated, translucent, underglaze colours used for fine detail, linework and colour washes.

F

Facilitator A thinner for use with Liquid Bright or Roman Gold.

Fahrenheit Scale of temperature where freezing point is 32° and boiling point is 212°.

Faience Tin glazed pottery. Faience is the French name for the Italian town Faenza, which has produced faience earthenware since the sixteenth century.

Fat oil Turpentine which has been evaporated and thickened and is used for mixing paints. The pigment is placed on a mixing tile or glass slab and mixed with oil of turpentine until a thick liquid is obtained. A drop or two of fat oil is added and thoroughly mixed in. Turpentine left in a shallow dish or open glass jar will evaporate until the desired strength is attained. *Caution—toxic if swallowed.*

Fauvism Art movement typified by wild colours and emotional forms. A form of expressionism.

Faux-marbre Representational painting of marble achieved either by painting freehand or with the aid of the commercial preparation, Marbelising Fluid.

Faux painting The art of creating an illusion, e.g. painting a realistic outdoor scene on an interior wall to give the impression one could walk into it. Intricate designs can give impressions of perspective and depth. To make a realistic rendition of something, such as the various semi-precious stones. Gilberton Gallery, Adelaide, has kits and complete directions for painting malachite, turquoise, sodalite, amethyst. Marbleising is a good example of faux painting. (From French *faux*: false.)

Feather 1. To gently blend the wet paint on the object being painted with a broad square shader. **2.** The outer covering of a bird.

Feldspar (felspar) Group of minerals, such as potassium, aluminium, silicate, usually white in colour, occurring in crystals and granite, which is used in the making of porcelain, ceramics, enamels and glazes. Natural frits. *See* Kaolin.

Feldspar potash Potassium alumino-silicate.

Feldspar soda Sodium alumino-silicate.

Ferrule The metal grip which holds the hairs or bristles to a brush.

Fettling To remove and clean up a seam in a cast clay piece formed in a mould using a fettling knife.

Fettling knife Used to clean pour-holes, clay deposits on the outside of the mould and the clay object itself.

Fibre board Flat refractory slab used to line kiln walls and to make moulds.

Fibreglass brush Used to burnish gold. Made up of lengths of glass or fibreglass fibres tied together with a cord which is gradually undone as the glass fibres become worn. Care must be taken to use the brush away from the painting area as minute particles of glass can contaminate the paints in the palette or fall on pieces waiting to be fired, causing scarring as these minute specks of glass melt in the kiln. The fibres also penetrate skin and cause irritation. Wear cotton clothing so that the fibres will not adhere easily.

Fibreglass brush

Fibre paper Alumina silicate fibre paper that may be used as a fusing surface. Will give glass a subtle matt finish. May also be used for making moulds. Shapes (geometric forms, letters, animals, fish, etc.) may be cut out of the fibre paper, placed under the glass and the glass slumped. The imprints of the fibre paper will be indented into the glass.

Fibre softening point The temperature at which glass starts to 'melt' or change shape. To find this point an unweighted glass fibre is placed in a special furnace in which the temperature increases at 5°C (9°F) per minute. The fibre softening point corresponds to an elongation rate of 1 mm per minute.

Filigree Glass (or metal) threads forming a fine lacy or network pattern.

Filler Substance added to a mixture to increase its volume or rigidity.

Filter 1. To carefully blend the applied paint while still wet with a square shader, to obtain a soft finish with no distinct divisions of colour. **2.** To separate one substance from another.

Fimo Self hardening modelling material similar to clay in appearance. Harden in domestic oven for 10–20 minutes at 130°C (265°F). Hardened Fimo may be carved, sawed, filed, cut and painted.

Findings The settings for jewellery pieces.

Fine design Intricate detail is best achieved with a partial fire of an application of paint. Paint entire area, fire to 300–400°C (570–750°F) and remove from kiln. Alternatively, place in the kitchen oven at 300°C (450–500°F) and leave for fifteen minutes or until paint will not move when touched but will scratch off. An intricate design may be drawn or traced onto the partially fired surface and scratched out with a nib or stylus. Clean thoroughly and fire again to desired temperature to mature paint.

Finger A very useful tool. Wrapped in a small square of silk it will 'wipe out', blend, pad or lighten. Wrapped in a tissue or latex surgical glove it will clean, define edges, make strong lines, stems, shapes and outlines. Discover its uses!

Fired Antique Trade name for underglazes used for antiquing and shading.

Fire clays Refractory clays used as additives to produce open texture and reduce risk of cracking

Fire gilding The commercial application of gold

using a chemical process to paint the surface with gold and mercury and evaporating the mercury with heat is no longer practised because of the toxic mercury fumes.

Fire polishing (fire glazing) The practice of directing flames or radiant heat at a glass surface to cause a surface flow and 'polish' the glass.

Fire out Fade or disappear in the firing process. Colours such as cadmium or selenium reds, colours applied over a heavily fluxed glaze and pen and pencil guidelines will fire out.

Firing The process of applying heat to a clay body for the purpose of vitrification or to allow the glaze to accept further decoration. Porcelain, china, glass, etc. are fired at sufficient heat to melt or soften the glaze so that it will absorb the paint pigments. The paint should be absorbed deeply enough to allow the glaze to be even and shining. Metallic paints remain on the surface and do not sink into the glaze. Oils and impurities such as grease pencil marks, graphite, etc. burn off in the kiln during the firing. Some ballpoint pen inks will not fire out at comparatively low heats. The lowest part of the kiln is usually the coolest; however, individual kilns have different hot spots. These are usually known or soon discovered by the owner. Most onglaze paints require a range of 720–900°C (1330–1650°F) and the temperature selected should suit both the clay or glass ware to be painted and the paints which are to be used. There should be a free flow of air in and around a stacked kiln during firing. Air vents should be open initially to allow fumes to escape when burning off. Glazed surfaces should not touch one another. If fired too hot, the colours will fade and sink deeply into the glaze, the glazed surface may craze, blister and roughen, particularly with soft glazes like some of the English and Belleek china. Some pinks will turn purple and some greens will turn brown; reds will turn brown or fade completely. Yellow tends to become more intense and reds and oranges fade or become a dirty colour. If not fired high enough the glaze will be uneven with some matt areas and some colours, such as blue, will rub off. The first fire should be hot enough to attain a good even glossy glaze. Colour may be added later. If you realise that as you apply colour you are also adding more flux, you will be aware that you will not need as high a temperature for subsequent firings. It is possible to fire fast without damage; however, a slow fire is safer

and more sure, particularly with large pieces and tiles. The normal procedure recommended by the kiln manufacturing firm, Tetlow's, is to switch on the kiln at a low setting for an hour to evaporate any water or dampness, leaving the vent open to allow the steam to escape. Then switch the kiln to a medium setting of 50 to 70 on the energy regulator and leave for another hour with the vent in position before switching to the highest setting. The vent should now stay closed until firing is complete. At this stage gas bubbles may escape through the glaze layer, leaving craters; if firing is rapid there may not be enough time for these craters to repair themselves in the softened glaze before the kiln is switched off. Once the kiln is switched off most of us leave it to do its own thing; however, there is another word of advice from Tetlow's. This information mainly applies to the initial application of glaze to the clay body but could affect later applications of paint as well. If the kiln takes too long to cool down to 750°C (1380°F), glossy surfaces may become dull. In contrast, matt glazes require a comparatively slow cooling period. Cooling may be accelerated by the partial or complete removal of the vent plug which should then be replaced for the later stages of the cooling process. The kiln should be allowed to cool slowly until the temperature drops to approximately 130°C (265°F), when the process can be speeded up again by the removal of the vent plug and the progressive opening of the door. Kiln furniture is available for stacking a kiln. It is safest to stack plates, plaques and tiles on their edges. If plates are stacked one on top of the other the weight may cause breakage and the stilts may penetrate the glaze. (The only accidents I have had have been with plates stacked on tripods or stilts. Never again!) Do not stack tiles against elements as the uneven heat may cause breakage, and do not cram or wedge pieces in as there is need for expansion. Glazed surfaces should not touch although the unglazed surfaces and rims may do so.

The manufacturer's instructions should always be followed, but a general rule of thumb would be to fire your kiln for half an hour or so on low, with the vent open to allow fumes to escape, a further 30 minutes on medium and then high until the desired temperature is reached. For large tiles or a partially filled kiln, slow the rate of firing if necessary. To fire glass, place it on a shelf, lifted off the floor of the kiln, with space all around.

Firing chamber Space within the kiln.

Firing diary Recording of firing processes, times and temperatures.

Firing down To reheat the kiln slightly once it has started its downward trend to slow the cooling process.

Firing schedule Diagram of firing plan, times and temperatures for fusing, annealing.

Firing tree Kiln furniture designed to hold ornaments, beads and eggs, etc. Will not fire high but suitable for onglaze temperatures. Made of NICHROME WIRE and obtainable from ceramic stockists.

Fit A glaze should fit or completely cover the entire body of a clay object.

Flairs Trade name for glass particles used for decoration. Fired at Cone 22 or 600°C (1110°F). Balsam of copaiba or mineral oil is brushed onto the otherwise completed and fired piece and the flairs or frosts are sprinkled on. Firing at a higher temperature may cause the particles to pop off. See FROSTS.

Flaking As for glass excising.

Flameware Glass which will not crack when subjected to direct flame.

Flamework Glass worked in the direct flame of a blowtorch.

Flash casting The practice of cleaning a mould by pouring a thin casting with an alternative slip to collect residue of the last used clay slip.

Flashed glass Two different coloured layers of glass fused together, one usually thinner than the other. A bubble of molten glass is dipped into a crucible containing molten glass of another colour. When sandblasted or etched, designs and shading can be obtained.

Flat enamel painting The application of flat enamel similar to the enamel paintings of the Limoges factory. The difference between enamels and onglaze paints is that enamels are opaque, have body and sit on the glaze as relief work whereas onglaze paints are flat (or should be), transparent and are embedded in the glaze during firing. Try it on a shard first as it is important that your enamel expands and contracts with the glaze (do not use a tile to test as the glaze on a tile is usually softer than on a utility piece). First tint your piece with the colour that is to be left on any exposed porcelain or other glazed surface. Fire and pen in your black (mixed with a little of another colour to soften it) or gold outlines. Fire again. If you use a water-based pen oil there is no need to fire prior to applying the enamel. Mix your enamel with fat oil or Dresden thick oil (I have used Base for Raised Gold with a copaiba-based medium) to a thick paste, add a little flux powder and thin with lavender oil to almost liquid, with enough body to flatten and smooth itself out without running all over the place. Apply with a soft brush smoothly and evenly, allowing for expansion to the penned lines. If it overlaps the line, quickly and carefully wipe back. The aim is to produce smooth and even areas of brilliant colour. Fire the enamel only once and as low as it will tolerate, to prevent chipping. Enamel will adhere more readily to a bisque surface.

Flat tint A wash of colour over the surface that does not vary in tone, depth or intensity.

Fleur-de-lis An iris of conventional design used in heraldry.

Flint Hard stone of almost pure silica.

Flint china Hard dense earthenware, similar to ironware.

Float process Molten glass floated on the surface of a bath of molten tin will spread into a sheet of uniform thickness. Most window glass is made like this.

Floating Spreading enamel or paste to cover an area such as a geometrical shape, petal or leaf. The edges are usually left slightly raised.

Flow Fluid movement of a glaze, enamel or paint.

Flow on enamel or glaze To flood enamel, paint or glaze onto a surface with a well loaded brush, keeping the brush from touching the ware.

Fluorescent light Light is produced by the passage of electricity through a metallic gas encased in a tube. Photographs taken in a room lit by fluorescent tubes will have a yellow cast. A fluorescent filter obtainable from camera shops minimises this yellow tone.

Fluorite Calcium fluorite, used as a flux in glazes for ceramics and porcelain.

Fluorspar (fluorite) Natural calcium fluoride. A transparent/translucent mineral which comes in various colours. Used as a source of calcium in glazes. May cause bubbling or craters in low temperature glazes because of the volatility of fluorine.

Fluting Rounded or mitred parallel grooves.

Flux Substance composed of borax, calcium, potassium, soda, lead and sand, used to facilitate fusion. The pigments in powder paints and glazes are all mineral, fuse at different temperatures and require the addition of flux to help them melt at a uniform temperature. Colours with too much flux appear semi-transparent and cloudy. Some colours such as blues work better with the addition of a little flux to the dry powder prior to grinding with oil. Colours which have been fluxed will mature at a lower temperature and have a high glaze. Crystal Clear is a clear powder paint consisting of a great deal of flux which may be used for dusting an object which has been painted and fired and which will give it a high gloss. It should be fired at a lower temperature than normal. Too much flux will destroy or 'eat' some colours and it is difficult to replace them because of the amount of flux in the glaze. Roman Gold may be purchased both fluxed and unfluxed. Unfluxed gold is for use over painted areas where the paint already contains flux.

Foam plastic Strong lightweight material in which air or gas bubbles have made holes which vary in size. Has many uses for the onglaze painter such as pouncing, applying colour and visual and tactile texture. Rigid plastic such as polystyrene may be used to form the template for a plaster mould for glass.

Focal point The area which should dominate the painting. It may be a single feature or a group of objects placed in a well balanced position in the design, usually one-third in, one-third up or one-third down.

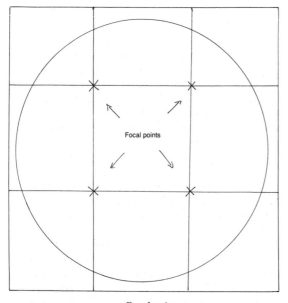

Focal point

Foil Aluminium foil may be used for visual texture on paints and glazes. Copper foil is used with glass and comes copper backed, black backed, silver backed, and silvered both sides.

Foot The base of a vase, pot or urn.

Foreground That part of the design which is closest to the viewer. Detail is clear, sharp and 'in focus'. There is no clear dividing line between fore and middle ground. One area blends gently into the other.

Foreshortening Exaggerated perspective applied to single objects or figures.

Form The external shape or appearance of an object.

Formula 10 An odourless all-purpose open medium suitable for mixing, painting and brush conditioning, which allows for a heavy application in one-fire work (take care not to use too much oil as it will run in the kiln) or a light application for washes.

Found line Obvious separation in design, such as the edge of light against dark objects, e.g. dark ball on white paper. Opposite to a LOST LINE, where values and colours are similar and the division is difficult to see.

Foundry sand A refractory sand composed of silica, alumina and clay that is capable of withstanding high temperatures.

Frame Construction to surround a painting, holding it in place and enhancing its appearance. A variable sized frame may be made from two L-shaped pieces of cardboard to frame a scene or portion of a design.

Free blown Glass formed and shaped by blowpipe alone.

Free form Having no recognised shape.

Free hand To make a drawing of a subject without sketching aids.

French antique flashed glass Handmade mouth-blown seedless glass.

Fresco The method of painting with powdered pigments mixed with water applied to plaster walls or ceilings before the plaster is dry.

Fret Carved or embossed work in decorative patterns, often interlaced or intersecting repetitive designs.

Frieze Decorated band, usually around walls.

Frisk film Masking film used by commercial artists as a resist or stencil. It is lightly tacky and easy to peel off, clean and re-use. Comes in sheets which may be cut into any shape or design. A temporary substitute can be made from the tacky perfume pages in magazines but this is a once-only use. Contact is another substitute.

Frit **1.** Vitreous composition from which soft porcelain is made. **2.** Calcined mixture of sand and fluxes prepared for melting to form glass. **3.** A recipe for glazes using such glazing materials as flint or silica sand, that has already been fired and ground finely, for use as low and medium fire glazes. **4.** Soluble or toxic materials melted together with insoluble materials, cooled rapidly, fractured in cold water and powdered to render highly toxic materials less toxic. *Lead frits:* The inclusion of lead frits in glazes enhance the colour and brightness when used with various oxides, and colourants. *Borax frits:* A substitute for lead frits for food and beverage utility ware. *Alkaline frits:* High soda and potash content and good expansion rate.

Frosts Trade name for glass particles—as for FLAIRS.

Froth Trade name of a glaze.

Frottis A French term used for a wash of colour or glaze.

Fugitive Elusive nature of a material, colour or effect that is difficult to control or remain the same.

Fugitive colours Colours in which the pigments react to those in other colours or to the heat of the kiln. Yellows and reds are a good example, as are colours which fade with age or exposure.

Full brush The hairs of the brush are loaded with oil so that it acts as a 'tank' to carry the paint.

Full load A fully loaded brush is an oil-filled brush loaded with paint right across its width.

Furnace Apparatus containing a chamber capable of continuous intense heat.

Furnace product The product of a process to mature colours by roasting at varying degrees of temperature according to the pigment content.

Furniture For the kiln—the shelves, shelf props, tile and plate racks and stilts, etc. which are used in the process of firing.

Fuse In the case of glass or glazes, to melt with intense heat and join together.

Fused silica Melts at a higher temperature than normal, has great purity, excellent optical transparency, high temperature and chemical durability and extreme resistance to thermal shock. Used for commercial containers with these requirements.

Fuse-to-stick To fuse two pieces of glass at the lowest possible temperature so that they retain their individual characteristics.

G

Gallery Opaque Glaze Trade name for a variety of opaque glazes.

Gallipot Originally a small tumbler-shaped porcelain container used to hold medium.

Galvanometer Apparatus for measuring the strength of electric currents.

Gare One of the major brands of hobby ceramic products available in Australia. (The other is Duncan.) Gare provides educational and teacher training programmes along with a wide range of products including moulds, colours, brushes and tools. Catalogues are available from distributors.

Gare Bark Glaze Special effect glaze which has the appearance of bark or cracked leather. For best results apply several coats of Gare clear glaze, drying between coats, and then three coats of white bark glaze, once again drying between coats. Fire at Cone 05–06 (1000°C, 1830°F).

Gare Bead Glaze Opaque glaze which separates and crawls during the firing process. Several coats may be applied prior to firing at Cone 05–06 (1000°C, 1830°F).

Gasket Even kilns may have one! The seal on a kiln door to prevent the escape of heat.

Gather A mass of molten glass attached to the blowpipe or PONTIL prior to forming an object.

Geometric abstraction Abstract designs made up of squares, rectangles, circles and triangles. Try it!

German Desag glass Imported antique machine made and mouth-blown glass in a wide variety of colours and styles.

Giffin grip Apparatus to centre and hold unfired clay when it is almost dry or leatherhard.

Gild To paint with gold.

Glad wrap *See* PLASTIC WRAP.

Glass (brief history) Glass was used in Egypt prior to 3000BC. Making glass was perfected around 1500BC and glass blowing around 50BC in Phoenicia. In the eleventh century in Bohemia ash from plants was first used as a raw material to give glass a lower melting point. The Venetians added manganese to oxidise impurities, clarify the glass and remove the green or brown tint caused by the reduced state of iron. By adding lead, borate and more soda, the temperature range was increased, enabling thinner blown glass, finer enamels and more intricate shapes. Crystal was developed in the late seventeenth century with purer raw materials, oxidation of iron and the addition of lead, leading to more transparent glass. (Source: *Grolier Electronic Publishing*.)

Glass Non-crystalline solid substance, usually transparent, which provides us with a similar surface to glazes on which to paint. Especially manufactured glass paints which mature at a lower temperature more suited to glass objects are available; and the same techniques are used to apply the paint. Extreme care is needed to blend the paint and eliminate brushstrokes because, when lit from within or behind, every brushstroke, speck of dust and paint build-up seems to take on enormous and obvious dimensions. There are many decorative ways to paint glass, which will take a thicker application of colour than a glazed surface. Before buying expensive glass try painting on a cheaper piece such as a jar or sturdy drinking glass. You may use your low-firing onglaze paints or add flux; however, you will probably achieve better results if you use glass paints. Use a fast drying medium, not an open medium or a mineral oil. Fire at 600°C (1110°F). It is a good idea to paint a kiln wash over the shelves of the kiln to protect them. Place the painted objects well apart on a shelf about the lower middle of the kiln. Fire slowly for the first hour with the kiln ventilated, then gradually bring the temperature to maturity. Allow to cool in its own time. Glass objects tolerate repeated firings if fired correctly.

Glass beads *See* GLASS SAND. Available from onglaze suppliers.

Glass blowing The process of shaping molten glass by blowing air into it through a tube.

Glass chipping *See* GLASS EXCISING.

Glass cutter There are many types available. Each has a diamond point. A pneumatic cutter works well.

Glass cullet **1.** Coloured glass used as decoration on flat surfaces by firing into the clay

or pooling in shallow concave areas. Temperature range 850–1100°C (1560–2010°F). **2.** Powdered transparent glass which may be used as glazing flux. **3.** In glass blowing, small pieces of glass which form at the neck of a bottle and are knocked off. **4.** Refuse glass used to replenish crucibles.

Glass decoration For decorative purposes, small pieces of glass, clear or coloured glass beads, frosting, etc. are adhered to porcelain with the aid of flux mixed with a medium (almost any will do) and fired at a suitable temperature. There are so many types of glass that it is impossible to state a definite heat. As a general rule glass pieces fired under 750°C (1380°F) will retain its shape but lose sharpness—over 800°C (1470°F) they tend to become smooth and rounded. A subsequent fire to colour the glass after it has been fired onto the glazed surface should be as low as possible as the glass may chip off with further firings. It is a good idea to fire a lot of glass beads, shapes and glass shards on a kiln washed shelf and keep them for future applications when needed. Pieces of coloured glass or beads may be embedded in texture paste and coloured with a lustre on the upper surface of the glass in the final fire. The threading holes in glass beads may be filled with smaller beads (for animals' eyes or some modern designs). Because of all the factors involved in firing glass, i.e. the type, thickness, size, position, the various mediums which can be used to adhere it to the porcelain, the drying time, the length of time individual kilns take to reach a temperature, actual temperature, cooling time and the human element, it is impossible to accurately forecast the results.

Glass etch An acid-based cream which will matt the surface of glass in three minutes. Sketch design and apply cream with brush or sponge to desired area. A thicker application will etch more deeply into the surface. Leave in place for at least three minutes, then wash off well with water. (*Caution acid—please take all precautions required for acid.*)

Glass excising To remove the glaze from the glazed body of an object with glass sand, glass beads or excising beads. Resist that part of the surface which is not to be excised and paint the area from which the glaze is to be removed with a mixture of flux ground with medium to a liquid, keeping away from plate and vase rims. (Excising close to the rims of objects may leave a sharp edge.) Pour the glass sand or excising beads onto the wet area and press as many as possible into the flux mixture, using as much glass as the mix will absorb. Clean rims carefully and remove masking lacquer and any beads of glass on clear part of the glazed surface. Fire high. As it cools the glass will contract at a faster rate than the glaze on the piece and should be able to be flaked off easily or with the aid of a sharp flat tool. Beware of flying glass chips and wear protective glasses or goggles, heavy gloves and protective clothing. If some of the glass is reluctant, simply refire until it eventually comes off. It may look interesting where it is, however, it will eventually pop off with the natural contraction and expansion of the glazed clay. Excising is a perfect way to disguise a marred, chipped or badly painted surface. To make your own ground glass choose old bottles, or soft glass which is not plasticised or hardened, as this is difficult to remove.

Glass gold A gold preparation for use on glass to be fired at comparatively lower temperatures.

Glass lamp painting Before buying an expensive glass lamp try painting on a cheaper piece. You may use your low-firing onglaze paints or add flux, but you will probably achieve better results if you use glass paints. Use a fast drying medium, not an open medium or a mineral oil. Glass objects will tolerate repeated firings if fired correctly. The disadvantage is that lightly applied paint does not penetrate the glass at low temperatures and will eventually wash off in a dishwasher or wear off with constant use. Obviously if the piece is for decoration only, this is not a problem. Mix your paints with the medium and apply paint to glass surface with a brush or sponge. Place the painted objects well apart and fire slowly to the desired temperature of 580–600°C (1075–1110°F). The glass molecules begin to move at approximately 600°C (1110°F) or lower if there is a lead content, and the glass will change shape and slump. It is a good idea to paint your kiln shelves with a kiln wash to protect them. Allow to cool gradually and do not open the kiln door until the temperature has dropped to equal the outside temperature. Paint lamps as porcelain, taking care with brushstrokes and dust particles as every flaw takes on major proportions when lit from behind.

Glass painting There are many ways to apply paint or lustres to glass and as glass can tolerate heavy applications your options are greater than with a glazed surface. Many of the following suggestions came from Barbara Dimitri of The Glasswork Shop in Melbourne:

- Paint or pen as you would on a normal glaze.
- Place several parches of paint, no more than three colours, mixed to cream consistency onto a piece of glass, place another piece of glass on top and slide the two layers together to form a good design or pleasing array of colour. Pull apart carefully and fire when dry. Try the same technique with lustres.
- Mix dry powder paint with methylated spirits, pour onto glass and blowdry with hairdryer to create streams and rivulets of colour.
- Mix a phial each of two colours and a metallic with a small amount of water based medium and fill with methylated spirits. Shake well and draw into separate slip trailing bottles. Decorate the glass by drawing, throwing, dribbling, dropping or drying with a hairdryer to form a myriad different designs. Great fun to play with.
- Thin gold with a little thinner and sponge lightly onto a piece. While still wet, gently touch with plastic wrap. The wrap can be used to apply its retained gold to another piece of porcelain.
- **1.** Apply gold as above, and dab until smooth. Drip methylated spirits in small drops for interesting patterns. **2.** Do as above, fire, paint the back of piece with a dark colour and fire again. **3.** Apply a colour, fire and then do as above and fire again. **4.** Work back into fired design with penwork and enamels.
- Airbrush using stencils, masking fluid, mesh, or any other resist. *(Use a mask when airbrushing.)*
- Airbrush and when dry, cut back design into paint.
- Lustre dipping.
- Glass may be coloured with small amounts of high firing enamel powders, ceramic oxides such as cobalt oxide, iron oxide, manganese oxide and copper oxide.
- Mix powder and/or metallic paints with methylated spirits and roll around the inside of a vase. The spirits will evaporate and the paints will remain in place, if undisturbed, until fired.
- Mask out a design and apply paint with a plastic sponge.
- Pour paint onto the glass surface and 'print' with an object.
- Apply paint and scratch out a design.
- Use your imagination.

Glass palette Small square of heavy roughened glass on which to grind paints. It should not be used as an ordinary palette as the tooth of the roughened glass will damage the hairs of a brush very quickly.

Glass sand Fine particles of glass which may be applied to a glazed surface with the aid of medium and flux and fired to remove the glaze. Take care not to leave particles of glass on the areas you want to remain smooth as they will leave marks on the surface. It is available in coarse, medium and fine particles and the resultant pattern left on the clay body depends on the size of the particles, type of porcelain or other clay, thickness of the application of glass sand or beads, heat of the kiln, length of the kiln cycle of firing time, amounts of medium and flux, and many other variables.

Glass slumping *See* SLUMPING.

Glaze The chemistry of glazes is a very complex. These vitreous (glass-like) substances are made up of three types of material—fluxes which lower the melting point; amphoteric materials which give body to the glaze; and acidic oxides which are the glost components. Basic compounds such as alumina and silica and such derivatives as barium, boron, calcium, lead, lithium, magnesium, potassium, sodium, strontium, white lead and zinc, fix the glaze by fusion to the clay body or bisque to give it a smooth gloss surface. The glaze may also be coloured by agents such as antimony, cadmium, chromium, cobalt, copper, iron, manganese, nickel and selenium and opacifiers such as tin, titanium and zirconium. Confused? Artists may well add local properties such as wood ash, local clay and granite to individualise the glaze.

The following information is courtesy of Walker Ceramics of Victoria and relates specifically to their own glazes; however, generalities may be applied to most glazing techniques and practices:

Some glazes may leach lead and other toxic elements when in contact with acids and Walker Ceramics have used frits which have a very low lead solubility to comply with health standards; however, a glaze may become unsafe by the addition of small amounts of other materials such as copper, or the use of incorrect firing temperatures and techniques. Cadmium/selenium glazes should not be used on the inner surface of utility ware and if there is any doubt only leadless glazes should be used on inner surfaces

of cooking and eating utensils.

Powdered glaze—mixing: Sprinkle powder into suitable container of water and stir to mix. Allow to settle overnight and pour off surplus water. Sieve through fine mesh and bring to desired consistency to suit porosity of bisque with the addition of water if necessary. A flocculent or 'anti-set' solution may be added a few drops at a time to glazes which settle or require constant stirring. Too much may cause the glaze to dry slowly or crack and crawl during firing. A 10% solution of Calgon may be added to glazes which have a high clay content or contain raw zinc oxide, magnesium carbonate and talc and which have a creamy feel, dry slowly and crawl during firing. 'Anti-set' and Calgon may act as antidotes for each other under certain conditions. For brushing Walker Ceramics have a Paint-On Medium, which will not deteriorate on standing and which is non-toxic, to mix the powdered glazes which are then stirred with a paint stirrer or cake beater and put through a fine sieve. Follow manufacturer's directions for correct proportions.

Liquid glaze: Ready for use but should be shaken well and stirred thoroughly prior to use. If still thick a little water may be added.

Prior to glazing: Bisque ware should be wiped over with a damp sponge to remove dust. Refrain from eating, drinking or smoking as the surface may be contaminated with grease or food particles and prevent the glaze from adhering.

Dipping: Use a suitable container, bucket or glaze wok. Transparent glazes should be thinner than opaque glazes and require diping only once; rutile glazes once or twice for colour variation. If double dipping, dip the top two-thirds twice and leave only a single cover on the lower portion to prevent a glaze build-up which may run onto the kiln shelf. The use of glaze tongs will eliminate patches where the piece of ware has been handled.

Brushing: Fully load the glaze brush by immersing it into the shaken and stirred glaze to the ferrule. Apply an even coat with the fully loaded brush to the bisque, allow the wet look to disappear and then apply a second coat in the opposite direction. After the wet look has disappeared again a third coat is applied in the direction of the first coat.

To glaze the inside of a narrow necked piece: Brush-on glazes may be thinned to be rolled around the inner surfaces where a brush cannot reach before you paint the external surface. If adding water, a rough guide is to use 1 part water to 3 parts liquid glaze. Place lid firmly on the container and shake and stir thoroughly. Pour the glaze into the ware, roll to cover the entire inner surface and pour out slowly, making sure the whole internal lip is covered. Invert the piece and allow to drain for five minutes.

Brushes: Square or oval hake, camel or ox hair brushes are recommended as these carry a good load of glaze and colour.

Glaze Crystals Trade name of crystals which are compatible with Duncan glazes.

Glaze hardener Used to increase adhesion and strength.

Glaze saw A tool capable of grinding fired glaze and bisque ware. *(Caution—always wear protective goggles.)*

Glaze suspender Prevents clay slip from settling out.

Glory hole A furnace for re-heating glass on a blowpipe or PUNTY during the shaping process

Glost Glazed—a glost fire is to fire ware to glaze it.

Glue To use glue as a pen oil, mix your powder paints with a couple of drops of mucilage and thin with water to running consistency. The mixture dries quickly; it is possible to use normal paints mixed with oil with and over the glue penwork.

Glycerine May be used as a water-based medium to mix paints and adhere the paint to the porcelain surface.

Gold chasing (patterned gold) To chase gold requires several fires. Firstly paint the design in gold and fire. Polish with a glass brush and wash well afterwards to remove any glass particles. Paint again with gold, fire and rub with burnishing sand for a brilliant finish. Outline the design, taking care not to mark the gold. Put in detail, such as veins on leaves, highlights and shading, etc. with fine penwork and fire again. The previously painted gold will have a beautiful finish and should be left. The latest application is then chased or rubbed with a pointed pencil-shaped agate. Every line is polished, highlights rubbed, and details such as veins of leaves and shading are polished to accentuate the design and emphasise the linear separations. The whole design is then softened with a fine glass burnishing brush.

Gold colours Colours which contain gold, usually the roses, rubies and purples, which are fired high in order to reach maturity. Should not be used for glass which requires a low firing temperature (unless slumping or fusing). The addition of one or two drops of Liquid Bright Gold to gold colours is reputed to enhance the colour.

Gold eraser Hard substance used primarily for removing the purple smudges and finger marks left by careless cleaning. Will remove gold and lustres if the rubber is applied diligently.

Gold printing Pressing an object or a textured material such as a sponge or the veined side of a leaf which has been coated with gold, onto a prepared surface.

Gouache 1. To matt colours. **2.** Opaque watercolours.

Graining To simulate a wood-grained effect by the application of: **1.** Specific glazes such as Woodtone glazes. **2.** Suitable onglaze colours which are applied with cloth or tissue. **3.** Using a comb to make grain marks in the paint or the unfired body of the clay.

Graphite Element of carbon which used to be called *plumbago* or *black lead*. If used to draw on a glazed surface the grease content will act as a resist. Alternatively it may be used to adhere the paint in a thin line.

Graphite outline Trace your design with black or coloured graphite paper and dust the outline with powdered paint of your choice, preferably to suit the painting, e.g. pale or flesh colour for portraits and pale outlines, darker colours for scenery or penned outlines. Clean the surrounding surface and fire.

Graphite paper A type of carbon paper used for tracing.

Graphite pencil A pencil capable of writing on glaze. The lines drawn will burn off when fired.

Graal glass Pattern cut and/or etched onto coloured glass which is returned to the furnace to make the design more fluid before being encased in clear glass.

Grease pencil A coloured crayon, often in a peel-off paper wrap, used to draw and write on a glazed or plasticised surface. Will almost always fire off in the kiln in a normal fire. Could act as a resist to applied colours, lustres and metallics. Alternatively, colour applied over the pencil outline will adhere to the grease and fire on.

Green earth A greenish coloured clay occurring mainly in Cyprus and Central Europe.

Greenware Raw clay not yet fired. May be etched, carved, painted and, depending on the state of dryness, shaped.

Greenware drill Small tool with drill shaped point for drilling holes in leatherhard greenware and, with care, in bone dry greenware.

Greenware preparation Remove seams and scars and smooth surface of leatherhard greenware.

Greenware saw Serrated edged tool for cutting greenware.

Greenware seam cleaner Synthetic rubber tool with a curved metal blade for cleaning the seams of poured, unfired clay objects.

Grey scale The scale of achromatic tonal values from black to white.

Greyed colour Another colour is added to lower the intensity of a hue. A primary colour may be greyed to paint some area of the background so that the general tone of the design is repeated throughout.

Grind To grind the powdered paint pigments to a toothpaste or thick cream consistency, start by tapping the base of a phial of powder on a flat surface to settle the contents and avoid spillage when the lid is removed. The fine powder, if spilled, could land anywhere, on the surface you are painting, in your palette or on the work of the person sitting next to you. Place some powder onto a tile or ground glass slab and with your cleaned palette knife remove some grinding oil from its container and place it on the slab as well, but away from the powder. The oil you use to grind the paints can be a commercially prepared grinding oil, one of the open or slow drying mediums, paraffin oil or other oil of your choice, which will keep your paints workable for several weeks or longer (although they will have collected a lot of dust by then). Alternatively, you may use a copaiba-based medium which produces a less slippery result than the open oils; with this, however, the paints will harden in just a few days. Take some of the oil with the palette knife and, using a circular motion and the flat surface of the knife, mix oil and paint powder together. Take more oil if necessary but do not add it all at once (if you add too much you will then have to add more powder). Continue mixing until it is well mixed and there are no grainy particles left. Some colours require more mixing than others because of their gritty nature and may well be helped by first grinding with a little methylated spirits or turpentine.

Grinding To smooth the edges of glass or etch glass by abrasive action. The glass surface is crushed by the high pressure of the abrasive substance on a wheel. Water is used to prevent the glass from overheating, to increase the grinding rate and to keep the abrading surfaces free from particles of glass.

Grinding oil Oil which has been commercially prepared to mix onglaze paints.

Grisaille 1. Brown paint made from iron oxide, fused onto glass and used to define details in stained glass windows. **2.** Decorative painting in shades of grey, occasionally used to simulate relief sculpture. **3.** A tonal underpainting over which, once fired, colours may be applied.

Grit cloth Abrasive cloth or pad.

Grit sponge Sponge with abrasive surface on one or two sides.

Grog Crushed or ground fired clay particles which are added to clay bodies to reduce shrinkage, increase strength and add texture.

Grosing pliers Used to assist in cutting glass and removing uneven edges.

Grounding (Used as both noun and verb.) Application of a rich, usually solid colour to an area, e.g. a ring or irregular border or part of a contemporary design, to a piece of porcelain, ceramic or glass. The surface is cleaned well and the area not to be grounded is protected with masking lacquer. Mix a little of the powder paint you intend to use with the grounding (not *grinding*) oil, and paint the area to be grounded, making sure the entire area is covered as it is almost impossible to repair. The small amount of colour in the oil will let you see where you have applied it to the surface. Allow the grounding oil to dry for a few minutes and then pad with a silk cloth or fine athletic support bandage wrapped around plastic foam to smooth and even out the oil. The area will be ready to apply the powder paint when the oil feels tacky on the fabric and makes a sticking sound as it is padded. There will be a slight pull on the pad. Prepare your dry powder by crushing it between sheets of greaseproof paper and return it to its phial. Place a piece of stocking over the top of the container and fix in place with an elastic band. Sprinkle the powder over the oiled area, covering it entirely but without touching the surface. Use a large dusting brush and gently press the powder into the oil, then with a circular motion work in as much of the powder as the oil will absorb without touching the oiled surface with the brush. It should look dried and matt. When you are sure it will take no more colour and has an even matt appearance, brush the superfluous powder off and leave for an hour or so. Check then to see if any damp patches have appeared; you may apply more powder to slightly damp areas. However, if these damp areas are very oily, the wise thing to do is to take it all off and start again, as too much oil will absorb too much powder and the result will be chipping and crazing. (This is not the case with glass which can accept more colour than a glaze.) Remove the masking lacquer and clean any stray bits of powder from the rest of the surface, including the back, the base and inside. Use methylated spirits, as this will not run into the grounded area as mineral turpentine does. For a multi-coloured ground sprinkle various colours onto the prepared surface and press the powder into the oil; alternatively, the paint may be applied through a stocking or strainer. An interesting effect may be obtained by grounding a surface, allowing to dry and, with a selection of sharp-pointed tools, both thick and thin, scratching out a 'penwork' design. This is easier if the grounding is dried in your kiln or kitchen oven to 300–400°C (570–750°F) before scratching out a design. *See* HALF-FIRED.

Grounding oil Heavy, fast drying oil used for grounding.

Grounding with water-based solutions A solution of 60% dried fat-free milk powder or Coffee-Mate and 40% powder paint may be mixed to a thick cream consistency and applied to the area using fine athletic support bandage wrapped around sponge. It is essential to work quickly as the milk dries quite rapidly, particularly in warm weather. However, if you apply a fine layer of the solution, removing all the bubbles, evenly over the surface, you will have a hard area which is difficult to damage and you will be able to paint over and beside it using an oil-based medium and apply any paste work and penwork all prior to firing. To remove a portion of the design simply dampen with a wet cotton bud and to remove it all (prior to firing) just wash the article with water.

Grozing iron A tool used to cut off the raw edge of a piece of glass.

Gum acacia tragacanth Gum from small shrub of the pea family used in glazes, slips and colouring pigments to aid adhesion.

Gum arabic May be used to assist the fluidity of glycerine as a medium; 2 parts gum arabic to 1 part glycerine may be used to mix enamels or to adhere foreign bodies such as glass, stones, etc. to the glazed surface. Also used as a binder for glass paints and, in ceramics, to adhere glaze to a clay body and increase plasticity of the clay.

Gypsum Hydrated calcium sulphate. The mineral from which plaster of Paris is made by de-hydration.

H

Hake brush Natural fibre brush used in many art applications; perfectly suited for applying shelf primer because of its retentive and absorbent qualities.

Half-fired or partial fire A surface may be painted and fired to approximately 300–400°C in your kiln or 500°F for 15–30 minutes in your kitchen oven or for several minutes in your microwave oven if it has no metallic paint on it. Remove when the paint is dry enough to touch without marring it. It is then possible to draw a design onto the surface, 'print' a pattern onto the surface, scratch into it or remove paint from it. It is possible to obtain a very precise and intricate pattern in this way and is also a clever way to clean up a complicated painted design that would be in danger of being destroyed if the wet paint were accidentally touched.

Half tone 1. Area leading away from light source. **2.** The description given to a dot screen process to produce a positive (as opposed to a negative) film for screen printing and making decals.

Halo effect 1. When part of the design is completely encircled by a single background colour or mix of light colours. To avoid this, first select three areas where you can 'cut in' with a dark colour for depth, usually a division of petals or deep shadow area, not necessarily equidistant; next, load your brush with a medium to light shade and place some background against the dark portions of the design, then load with medium to dark colours for placement adjacent to the lighter areas. Then load your brush with colours which will 'reflect' other parts of the design. This should give you a variety of background colours which will blend together to show depth under the area, provide contrast and draw in the rest of the design for support. Always use each colour in a design more than once, otherwise that colour will look very lonely. A rainbow effect is almost as bad as a halo effect. (You can't win, can you?) Keep your applications of colour varied in size and shape and avoid repeating the order in which you apply colours.

Hancock's Glass Paints and Stains Range of colours for painting on glass.

Hancock's Raised Paste Yellow powder for raised paste under gold.

Hancock's Raised Paste Medium Medium for mixing Hancock's Raised Paste.

Handrest A simple handrest is built by attaching two corks or small blocks of wood to the underside of each end of a flat ruler.

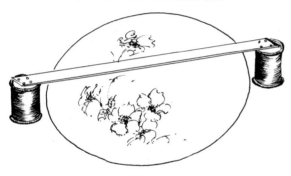

Handrest

Hanovia Cerama-pen Liquid Bright Gold pen for penwork or decoration. To start, remove cap and depress tip on piece of paper. Hold until gold appears on tip. Write slowly and evenly to allow adequate flow of gold. If tip wears down before gold is depleted, replace it by inserting the spare tip stored in the top of the pen. Recap tightly to prevent possible evaporation. Fire as you would for ordinary Liquid Bright Gold.

Hanovia gold and lustres Brand of gold and lustres.

Hard glaze porcelain Japanese, French and German porcelain clays are usually considered as hard glaze porcelain bodies which are capable of taking a high fire (860°C, 1580°F and above) although there are some exceptions.

Hard spots Areas which are difficult to coat

with glaze or colour which are usually caused during casting, by overworking greenware or by greenware becoming contaminated.

Hard paste Refers to true (high-fired) porcelain clay body.

Harmonious colours Colour combinations of several hues which have a good relationship. Specific names are given to the most commonly used combinations.

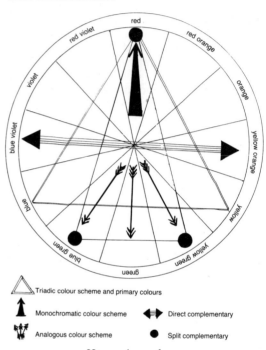

Harmonious colours

Harmony Achieved by the elements of good design; colour compatibility and direction play the most important roles.

Harrison-Bell Manufacturer of hobby ceramic products.

Hatching Shading with fine close parallel lines. Light and shade are suggested by the number of lines, how closely set they are, and how thickly the lines are drawn.

Health hazards There are a number of serious health hazards which the glaze artist should know about.

Paints and glazes: Many products may be harmful if swallowed, inhaled or used carelessly over periods of time. Paints are composed of oxides (some of which are not very good for you) and salts of elements, and they must be fired at a

Lustre decorated glaze on glaze vase
(Greg Daly)

Porcelain bowl, glaze on glaze
(Greg Daly)

Lustre decorated platter, glaze on glaze (Greg Daly)

ABOVE: *Detail of lustre platter decorated with gold and silver leaf and enamel* (Greg Daly)

RIGHT: *Porcelain vase, glaze on glaze* (Greg Daly)

temperature sufficiently hot to mature them, which in turn requires the use of a flux to react with and assist in dissolving all the particles. One example of a flux is *lead oxide*. Some of the other elements with which we paint, besides lead, are *cadmium, cobalt, copper, gold, iron, manganese, silica and zinc*. These can all be dangerous if inhaled or taken into the mouth in quantity. Precautions to be taken include wearing a suitable mask when decanting powdered colours, dusting or grounding. Do not shape your brush by putting it in your mouth. Do not prepare or eat food or smoke if your hands still have paint on them. Note the lead content of paints and avoid using paint with a high lead content on food utensils (in fact, this is *against the law* in many parts of the world). Fire paints which contain lead at the correct temperature otherwise the lead will leach out into the contents of the container.

Acids: An acid burn is horrific. It is not merely superficial but continues to penetrate the tissues deeply even after the surface is neutralised. Please take all the precautions necessary with acid use. *Caution with acids*. Wash with soap and water or baking soda and seek medical attention if the burn is extensive.

Glass excising: This can be dangerous if precautions are not taken. Wear protective glasses and gloves when chipping tglass from the clay body. *Allergies:* This is a concern for the individual. Avoid using any product to which you are allergic. There is bound to be an alternative.

Because of the complete involvement the glaze artist has with the arts there are compensations for the health hazards in the form of therapeutic value. Most painters seem to have the ability to shut out the rest of the world, with all its material cares and worries, while they are painting. Loneliness becomes a thing of the past and the main need for company is the desire to paint with others in order to share and benefit from the combined stimulation and ideas generated in a group situation. The only hazard caused by this is lack of understanding from the rest of the immediate family.

Heavy oil Fast drying oil such as oil of copaiba, grounding oil and fat oil.

Heat Physical form of energy generated by combustion, electricity, chemical action and friction. Measured in calories or BTUs (British Thermal Units). Used to fire kilns and conduct some conversations.

Heat soak Maintaining a desired temperature in the kiln for a period of time to allow the heat to penetrate and mature that which is being fired.

Highlight That part of the design which is the focal point of the light. The area closest to the light. Because of the brightness suggested, the subject should not be in great detail in that area.

History of origins of porcelain The use of clay as a utility vehicle for cooking and water originated in very early times. Ancient historical and archeological discoveries have proved that the Egyptians used glass as a glaze as early as the Fourth Dynasty and tin glazes were used for wall tile pictures as early as 500BC. Metallic oxides were used for decoration by other civilisations of that era. Turquoise blue was derived from copper by the Assyrians and Babylonians. Civilisation was mainly concentrated around the eastern Mediterranean area and technology developed in one country soon found its way to another, with minor changes in decoration. Porcelain is distinct from pottery in that it is translucent and, when broken, displays a clean smooth fracture. Pottery is opaque and the break is rough. The word is derived from the Chinese terms *kaolin* and *petuntse* and means 'hard paste'. Artificial porcelain is known as 'soft paste'.

Hard paste contains only the natural elements of china clay and feldspar, whereas soft paste porcelain is made up of combinations of clays, animal and mineral ingredients. The terms 'hard' and 'soft' refer to the degree of firing required by the clay bodies to vitrify them.

Pieces of porcelain from China first appeared in Britain in 1506, although there are stories of pieces being brought across land from the Orient earlier than that. It was not until the early 1700s that the secret of porcelain manufacture reached Paris and Sèvres. Porcelain factories were able to commence production in Europe and porcelain began to replace the tin-glazed pottery from Majolica and other popular ceramic factories.

There are pieces of porcelain from Italy which date back prior to the early 1700s, such as the Medici porcelain and porcelain from Venice, but these were not produced in commercial quantity and the secret of their production was very well kept. The first true hard paste porcelain produced in Europe was made in Saxony in 1709; also in 1709, the Meissen factory commenced production under the direction of

Bottger. In England, factories commenced production around 1745 with Worcester, Bow, Derby, Rockingham and several others all being founded in the next ten years.

Hobby ceramics Underglaze and onglaze painting on cast slip models. There is a huge array of models and moulds from which to choose and an equally bewildering range of paints and glazes. Most of the techniques described in this book are suitable for these blanks, although it may be necessary to fire at a lower temperature in some cases, due to the high flux content of the high fired glazes.

Hobby Colorobbia Tips for glazing: The glazes, Christmas Red and Strong Yellow, are cadmium selenium colours and can only be mixed with each other. For best results, apply four coats. Fleeing White is a special glaze which has a beaded, broken and uneven finish, determined by the thickness of application. The heavier the application, the more textured the surface. The only glazes not overglaze compatible are Caribbean Sea in which the overglaze and glaze slightly discolour, Oxide Silver where the overglaze goes matt and discolours slightly, and Mirror Green in which the overglaze discolours.

Hogarth curve Line of design in the shape of an elongated S.

Hollowware Concave or scooped out vessels or objects (as opposed to flatware).

Horizon A horizon line is needed in most paintings and designs, even if it has to be imagined. It should never be in the centre to 'cut the design in half', but a little to the top of or below the centre. Once again, rules may be broken.

Horn knife Horn or bone palette knives are useful for mixing gold and other metallics. Not readily available now but easily made from the handles of old cutlery for the purist painter.

Hot glass Kiln fired glass.

Hue Name given to a colour.

Hump mould Positive form over which to press clay or slump glass. Also drape mould and mushroom mould.

Hybrid hard paste porcelain Hard paste porcelain with the addition of magnesite and quartz.

Hydrofluoric acid *Caution:* Very dangerous acid which should be used with extreme care to etch glazes and glass. This acid will continue to eat into your tissues, should it come in contact with them, long after the surface has been neu-tralised. For those people conscious of damage which may be done to the ozone layer by the use of chlorofluorocarbons, it is not possible to produce these light substances from heavy hydrofluoric and hydrochloric acids through the actions of etching and leaching as described in this book.

I

Ice glass The outer surface of the glass resembles cracked ice; made by plunging the white hot glass briefly into cold water, then reheating and reblowing, or by rolling the hot glass in splinters of glass prior to reheating it to fuse the splinters to the glass.

Icon Originally conventional paintings of Christ and the Saints of Grecian design. Now used for any image in art.

Idealised fusing cycle Simplified firing of glass in six stages, two for heating (initial heat and rapid heat) and four for cooling (rapid cool, anneal soak, anneal cool and cool to room temperature).

Ilmenite Iron and titanium oxide in powder or sand form used in conjunction with rutile to develop rutile break in glazes.

Illusionism (faux painting) The art of creating an impression—an example is extending an indoor scene into the outdoor area with the use of painted windows, doors or archways and scenes beyond, taking advantage of perspective and foreshortening, light and colour.

Imari Japanese ware and style of design, usually geometric designs in black, dark blue and red, outlined in gold with simple stylised flowers, animals, fish or small scenes.

Imbricate To arrange to overlap (like fish scales).

Immersion (dipping) A freshly painted porcelain, ceramic or glass object is dipped into lukewarm water causing the paint to separate, usually into bubbles of various sizes. Alternatively, interesting patterns can be obtained by floating paint or lustre on water and immersing the glazed piece. For best effects, apply a basecoat of a medium to light colour and fire. Apply a fairly strong coat of a darker colour to the fired piece and immediately dip into a prepared container of water. Experiment with the temperature of the water to find the right degree of warmth for the paints you have chosen; this will differ slightly depending on the contents of the paint, your medium and how rapidly you have painted the area.

Impasto Raised decoration in enamel or slip on ceramics. Thick paint may not be applied to a glazed surface, however, the impression can be given with visible brushstrokes and shaded edges.

Impervious Unable to be penetrated (waterproof) in reference to clay ware and glazes.

Impressionism Method of painting ascribed to French artists who painted the momentary or transitory appearance of things, particularly the effects of light and atmosphere as opposed to form or structure.

Impressionistic Not an exact reproduction of the subject but rather an artist's impression.

Incandescence The emission of visible light by a hot object.

Incandescent light Light source created by a filament heated by electricity (or a flame). Colours appear different under various types of lights, such as incandescent or fluorescent.

Incising To engrave or cut into the surface. May be done manually with a tool or chemically with a solution.

Incising paste A commercially prepared paste which is applied to the porcelain or other glazed surface and covered with a specific type of glass or incising beads. During the firing process the glass fuses with the paste and glaze, causing the glaze to crack and chip off during the cooling process when the glass contracts at a faster rate than the glaze, to expose the body of the clay. Because of the variables involved, i.e. the amount of paste, type and size of the grains of glass, glaze and body of the object, length of firing time and temperature, it is impossible to predict the resulting pattern. The exposed clay body may be painted with paints, lustres, liquid bright gold or metallic paints.

Inclusion Any foreign body enclosed in glass. A leaf or some other object may be slumped between two layers of glass. Because air trapped with the encased object expands, a bubble will usually form in the top layer of glass. This can be very interesting and beautiful but is usually very fragile.

Incompatible colours Colours which would react adversely if used together because of the imbalance of their chemical components.

Indian ink A design may be drawn in Indian ink, and painted over without being moved; the ink will disappear as it is burned off in the firing process.

Individuality That which is specifically you—the artist. The individual style and character which makes your work unique.

Infinite switch A temperature control which governs the 'on' time of the elements to control the level of temperature in the kiln.

Initial heat The first stage of a simplified glass firing during which the kiln is heated slowly (to avoid cracking the glass) from room temperature to just above strain point. *See* STRAIN POINT.

Ink Thin fluid used for penwork or writing text. May be made up from pen oil and powder paint mixed to ink consistency. A quick alternative is to add a little turpentine to mixed paint from your palette.

Inspiration The stimulating ideas we all have from time to time. Write them down—NOW! They are precious. Sources of inspiration are everywhere—nature provides the leaves, wood and bark of trees, seeds and pods, flowers, shells, patterns in semi-precious gems, photos of and from space, etc. Man produces fabric patterns, gift paper, cards, old wall paper books, Oriental carpets, building shapes, geometric designs, and so on. The cracks in a worn pavement, cultural designs, doodling, earlier styles such as Art Deco, Art Nouveau, Vienna style, Tiffany—even a selection of children's paper cut out shapes randomly scattered onto the painting surface provide colour and shape. Isolate portion of a design or shape and take what you need from it. Look at a kaleidoscope. Look around you.

Insulation brick (or firebrick) Used for walls of kilns.

Intaglio Incised design or carving. Paste may be applied to the painting surface to synthesise a sunken design.

Intensify To strengthen colour with further applications or to strengthen a design with contrasting depth or detail.

Intensity Brightness of colour value.

Intercalaire To apply two layers of decoration to a glass surface, the first one covered with a glass skin which acts as a surface for the second layer.

Interpretation Everyone views a subject differently. Each artist puts his or her own interpretation or ideas on a subject into the design.

Ions Electrically charged particles.

Iridescence Multicoloured effect on a glass surface caused by: **1.** Weathering. **2.** Lustres.

Iridising solution Solution of metallic salt in diluted hydrochloric acid which is sprayed onto the surface of very hot glass to produce rainbow like colours similar to lustre preparations. Stannous chloride is the most successful metallic salt; other metallic salts may be added to it to vary the range of colours. Variations occur depending on the type of glass and strength of application. Good ventilation is essential and a mask should be worn as the vapours are dangerous. The recipe for stannous chloride solution is: 1 part stannous (tin) chloride crystal, 1 part muriatic acid (swimming pool acid) and 2 parts water. Ferric chloride may be added to stannous chloride to produce blue, green and silver; strontium nitrate, barium chloride and stannous chloride will produce blue over amber glass; zinc oxide and stannous chloride gives opalescent misty white. As with all mixes—experiment!

I-Relief Substance introduced from Denmark to add structure. It is a ceramic composition which may be used on porcelain, china and tiles and on the body of the clay once the glaze has been removed. It can be mixed with a variety of solutions, oil-based mediums, water-based mediums, simple syrups, milk, etc.—almost anything to bring it to a thick cream consistency. It should be thick enough to hold its shape and may be applied with a stylus, brush, sponge, or other applicator to obtain the effect you want. Such additives as powdered paints (in small quantities, i.e. 1/8), enamel paints of the copper enamelling variety, sand, glass fragments, etc. may be included in the mix. After firing it may be coloured with liquid bright gold, lustres, paints etc. It will fire at a wide range of temperatures, being more glossy and rounded with higher temperatures, while holding its shape and having a semi-matt finish at lower temperatures. As with most structural substances it will not tolerate successive hot firings happily and should only be fired at the lowest temperature suited to mature the lustre, gold or paint requiring the further firing.

Iron colours Red colours containing iron oxide which are usually fired at a low temperature 720–760°C (1330–1400°). Iron colours do not mix well with yellows, although some recently developed colours are more adaptable.

Iron chromate Colouring agent producing brown, black and grey.

Iron oxide Pigment used for colouring paints, glazes and glass—a rich yellow colour on glass. Iron or ferric oxide will produce a wide range of colours from a yellow to dark shades of brown. Black iron oxide is stronger than red oxide; synthetic red oxide also produces interesting results. Iron oxide may cause some glazes to run as it can act as a flux.

Ironstone Hard dense earthenware from Staffordshire, similar to Spode stone china.

Ivory The powder paint colour ivory contains a high gloss and may be used to repair a glazed surface cleaned with Rustiban. The hydrofluoric acid in Rustiban removes the gloss from the porcelain surface; if this area is lightly dusted or lightly grounded with ivory the gloss will be restored. Once repainted, however, it should be fired at a much lower temperature, or the paint colours will be faded or 'eaten out' by the flux in the grounded surface. *Take care not to let the Rustiban or any other acid touch your stainless steel sink. It will be permanently marked and scarred by the acid.*

Ivory vellum Cream coloured powder which, when dusted onto porcelain and fired, gives a creamy matt surface similar to bisque finish. May then be painted with matt colours or other onglaze paints and enamels.

J

Jack Device on which to mount a profile to shape moist plaster.

Japanese bone china A clay body made up with approximately one-third calcined bone or bone ash. It is able to take a higher firing than English bone china, which has a higher content of bone ash.

Jayma Mallory Manufacturer of hobby ceramic products.

Jewelling Enamel applied to look like jewels.

It can be coloured before application or painted afterwards. True jewelling will sit above the surface in the shape of a sphere, as opposed to a flat-based dome.

Jigger Machine used to form utility ware from batts of plastic clay. A profile is attached to a spinning mould and a moveable arm simultaneously shapes the inner and outer surfaces of the object.

Jolly Turning head of a jigger.

Judging When your work is judged professionally, the judge looks for the following: Originality, composition and colour harmony, proportion, technique, finish, firing and attention to detail. The initial impact or first impression is of utmost importance and the viewer frequently does not know why he or she likes or dislikes a painting. Art is very much a matter of personal opinion; however, it is the judge's opinion (which should be objective as opposed to the artist's which is usually subjective) and the value placed on the judging points which count in this case. With regard to porcelain, usually the judge awards a point score for each of the artistic requirements, such as 6, 7 or 8 out of 10 and then totals the result which provides a fair and accurate grading. Hobby ceramics have a manual for training judges for Australian shows.

Originality: The work should be the original work of the artist—even copies of the Great Masters will lose marks for lack of originality.

Composition and colour harmony: The composition or design should be balanced and the viewer's eye should go immediately to the focal point or centre of interest. The lines of the design should then lead the viewer's gaze around the supporting features and not off the painting. There should be a balance between painted design and negative space and the groups of design should also balance in size (that does not mean they should be the same size) and relate to each other in position and in the way they connect with one another.

Colour harmony: Colour combination that does not glare and fight with itself. The colour scheme should be pleasing to the eye, well balanced and have a variety of values to give the painting a third dimension. Colour gives a very important first impression! Many unlikely sales have been made 'because it matched the curtains'.

Proportion: Relative size of subject matter.

Technique: Suitability of application of design, quality of brushwork, penwork, additives such as enamelling, glass, gold and grounding, etc.

Finish: Attention to detail, cleanliness and presentation. In fact, presentation is often half the battle.

Firing: A smooth evenly glazed surface with no flat spots or chipped or crazed areas is the desired appearance. An uneven application of paint will leave shiny and dull patches. If your paints are guilty of containing varying amounts of flux which can be responsible for patchy work, several light washes of colour will bring the work to exhibition standard.

K

Kakiemon Asymmetrical designs from Japan.

Kaleidoscope Tube which makes symetrical patterns with the aid of coloured glass when rotated. There are many beautiful and expensive models on the market but it is possible to make your own from inexpensive kits. A great source of designs.

Kanthal wire Wire which can withstand high temperatures.

Kaolin China clay used in making porcelain, formed by the decomposition and weathering of feldspar in granite.

Kemper pen For fine line drawing with liquid gold solutions. The pen consists of a handle with a small tank that has a funnel-shaped outlet. The tank is filled with gold liquid and used with a normal writing motion. Must be kept clean at all times. If it does become blocked, soak in turpentine; if the little stylus becomes lost, try fuse wire to clean the funnel.

Kemper pen

Kevlar Strong fibrous synthetic fibre, resistant to high temperatures, which is used in place of asbestos for heat-proof gloves and other protective garments.

Keys Locking devices for joining surfaces of a mould.

Kick A cavity in the base of a glass vessel, ranging in size from a small indentation to a deep hollow.

Kiln Furnace for drying and maturing clay and paints, glazing, and painting and slumping glass. Not all kilns are calibrated to the temperatures they read; every kiln should be tested for accuracy occasionally with cones if you do not already use cones to fire. Most kilns in Australia are electric; to work out the cost of firing your kiln multiply the amps by the voltage, which will give the number of watts used; multiply this sum by the current cost of a kilowatt hour and adjust by the number of hours it takes to fire your kiln. There are a number available and it is a matter of personal taste, convenience and finance when you make your choice. The one most commonly used by onglaze artists is an electric kiln with an inner chamber measuring 32.5 x 32.5 x 32.5 cm (13" x 13" x 13") with built in temperature control which automatically turns off when the desired temperature is reached. These kilns are 240 volts, 10 amps and 1 phase which plug into any household power outlet. Kilns of 15 amps and larger, preferred by ceramic artists, should be professionally installed. Most kilns are fitted with an energy regulator to control the rate of temperature rise, a warning light, a safety switch which turns the kiln off should you open the door, a spy-hole in the door, and a vent in the roof. It is possible to obtain smaller kilns, larger kilns, round kilns, gas kilns, kilns which are not automatic, custom built kilns with digital readouts and kilns for your microwave.

The following information was provided by various manufacturers and in places has been condensed; more complete information would be available on application from the firms or from your retailer:

CROMARTIE KILNS LTD Prior Industries NSW Pty Ltd, PO Box 918, Bankstown NSW 2200 and PO Box 276, Acacia Ridge Queensland 4110. Top-loading kilns available in various sizes and both round and oval with an approved interlocking lid, safety switch, lockable lid catch, adjustable lid stay, heat resistant handle, lockable castor wheels, easy to change elements, mains 'on' warning light, energy regulator/s, plug in control socket, choice of temperature control system, ventilation plug/s in lid. The construction is of a mirror finish stainless steel jacket surrounding a lining of 75 mm (3") fuel efficient lightweight bricks backed with a thick layer of ceramic fibre. The kiln load is supported by an all brick floor and the lid is lined with ceramic fibre. Capable of 1300°C (2370°F). There is a range of temperature controls available such as a pyrometer which is either analogue or digital, kiln sitter with limit timer, electronic controllers ranging from a simple soak/cut-off feature to a highly sophisticated multi-ramp, multi-dwell digital computer.

B.W. & L. TETLOW PTY LTD 12 George Street, Blackburn Vic. 3130. An extensive range of kilns is available and Tetlow recommends that kilns used for porcelain be clad in stainless steel for maximum life expectancy. It is possible to get highly corrosive acid as a by-product during the normal firing process which may shorten the life of a mild steel kiln. There is a comprehensive manual available with all kilns which is most informative on all aspects of firing.

The bricks used for electric kilns are of the refractory insulation type. All kilns are fitted with an energy regulator complete with a pilot light which switches on and off automatically as the

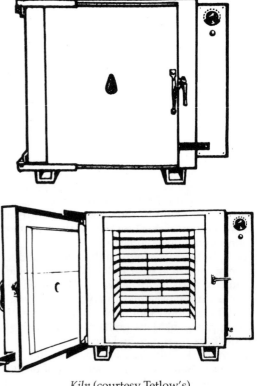

Kiln (courtesy Tetlow's)

energy regulator switches the current to the elements on and off. The most common elements used are Kanthal Al which are made from alloys of iron, aluminium chromium and cobalt and operate to a temperature of 1300°C (2370°F). Before any kiln is put into use, it should be fired slowly, preferably over two or three days, to a temperature no higher than 100 or 200° below the maximum firing temperature for which it is designed. This slow firing will remove any moisture from the brickwork.

RAPID FIRE KILNS Available from Deirdre Fewell Studio Supplies, 6 Kurramatta Place, Cronulla NSW 2230. The concept of a 'plug in–go any-where' kiln is revolutionising the trauma of owning a heavy, immobile, time-consuming apparatus for firing small items. The benefits, of course, have to be weighed against the advantages of long and thorough soaking. With these small, energy-efficient kilns, several fires may be completed daily. In this range there is a Woodrow kiln which will fire to 680°C (1255°F) in 10 minutes, 730°C (1345°F) in 15 minutes, 800°C (1470°F) in 18 minutes and 1220°C (2230°F) in 55 minutes—ideal for decals, onglaze paints, glazes and greenware; the Quick Fire Kiln is 6″ x 6″ x 6″ and weighs 7 kilos, and the Microwave kiln EZ5 is 7.5 cm (3″) in diameter and perfect for small glass, ceramic and porcelain pieces and jewellery. The kiln sits in a microwave oven and the inside of the kiln becomes red in in minutes as the heat is trapped within the silicon carbide lining. The outer shell is made of a porous, heat-resistant ceramic fibre that does not get hot. Firing time is 3-5 minutes, depending on the article being fired.

Accessories

Energy regulator: Used to control rate of temperature increase. Controlled by a knob which is calibrated from 1–100%. If 50% is selected the electricity supply to the elements is stopped for half of a given time, e.g. on for 5 seconds and off for 5 seconds, on again for a further 5 seconds, and so on.

Door switch: Mechanical contact which interrupts the flow of electricity to the elements when the door is opened.

Time clock: Timing device which allows one to pre-set the time at which the kiln is activated by setting one of the hands to the commencing time, with another hand or pointer set to the finishing time. Some clocks have day control as well as hour control.

Pyrometers and pyroscopes: Pyrometers measure temperature and pyroscopes measure heat work. Pyroscopes are indicators made of ceramic mixtures based on silicates which bend when heated to a certain temperature.

Cones are commonly classified as pyroscopes and come in two sizes, standard 6.35 cm (2½″) tall and miniature 2.5 cm (1″) tall. They are made of carefully controlled mixtures of ceramic smaterials designed to give a graduated scale of fusing temperatures at approximately 20 degree intervals. The cones will melt and collapse when they have been subjected to a certain temperature or rate of temperature increase for a length of time. That is to say, a temperature attained rapidly will not have the same maturing effect as the same temperature reached slowly. It is important to mount the cones correctly and it is usual to use three cones for each firing; one about 20° C below the desired temperature, another indicating the temperature at which the ware is to be fired and the third about 20°C higher.

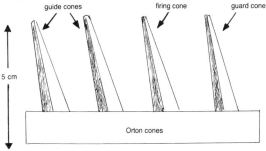

Orton cones

Kiln shelves or 'bats': Each bat used as a shelf in the kiln should be supported at three points to prevent rocking, which may occur if the bat is supported at each of its four corners. The supports should be placed in the same position for each shelf inserted so that the weight is distributed in a downward column. The shelves should be painted with a commercial kiln wash or one made of a mixture of alumina and china clay or zircon and china clay mixed with water. The shelves and props are usually made from sillimanite or a mixture of similar materials. For a bisque fire pots may touch, however, allowance should be made for shrinkage. All clayware placed in the kiln must be dry, as damp ware is likely to crack and may explode as a result of steam pressure building up inside as it heats up. Ware placed in a kiln for a glost fire must not have glazed surfaces touching.

To fire: Remove the vent plug and if desired the spy-hole may be left open as well. Set the energy regulator at a fairly low setting to evaporate any surface moisture. After 30–60 minutes increase the setting to about 50 to 70% and leave for a further hour. The vent plug should be in position during this period and should remain in position until firing finishes. Complete firing at 100%.

Kiln care Vacuum your kiln occasionally. Dry your kiln before initial use and after prolonged disuse by heating for a short time.

Kiln furniture The shelves, posts, stilts, plate and tile stands used in firing.

Kiln sitter An optional extra for a non-automatic kiln which will turn it off once it has reached the desired temperature.

Kiln ventilation system An exhaust system from Woodrow which removes the fumes with the aid of an exhaust pipe.

Kiln wash A wash composed of dry powder and water which is applied to kiln furniture and the floor of the kiln to protect the firebricks against dripping glazes and paints.

Knop A bulge of varying size and shape on the stem of a glass.

L

Lace May be sprayed with glue and adhered to a glazed or glass surface. When dry, 'paint' with a sponge dipped in paint from your palette; the paint may need a little thinning with turpentine (or glycerine if water-based). There are many patterns and grids available.

Lace drapery The name given to net or lace dipped in clay slip and used to dress figurines. Only cotton fabrics should be used as synthetic nets melt in the kiln rather than burn.

Lace draping tool A wooden-handled tool with a fine needle at one end and an angled blade at the other for impressing and lifting clay to form 'lace'.

Laminate To join layers of glass and other materials with fusion or glue.

Laminated safety glass Two sheets of float glass with a sheet of plastic sandwiched between them with the aid of heat and pressure.

Lampblack A black powder used for reproducing patterns/designs. The powder is placed in a soft cloth and tied into a pad. A design is drawn onto tracing paper and pinprick perforations are made along its outline. The paper is attached to the piece to be painted and gently padded with the lampblack pad so that the powder penetrates the holes and reproduces the pattern.

Lampworking To shape glass with the aid of a flame or torch.

Latticinio Opaque white glass threads embedded in clear glass to form a filigree pattern.

Lattimo Milk glass, opaque white glass or glass decorated with marvered bands of opaque white glass.

Lavender oil Oil used to keep medium open and usable for longer periods of time. Lavender oil is also used to paint on bisque and for cleaning gold utensils.

Lawn A sieve of fine mesh, usually stainless steel.

Laying in colour Filling in the shape of the object being painted with a flat well loaded brush. It may or may not be outlined.

Leach To draw out or purge part of a substance. Some lead is leached from paint during firing by the action of heat and some may be leached from glaze by fluids, particularly acids such as lemon or vinegar, during domestic use.

Lead Heavy, soft, easily fusible metallic element which can be absorbed into the system causing lead poisoning.

Lead in glass There is a high content of lead oxide in crystal which causes it to have a lower melting point than other glasses and it will change shape at less than 600°C (1110°F).

Lead in paints and glazes Most colours and glazes have a certain amount of lead in them as it acts as a flux; these days manufacturers state on the label the lead content in percentage form. Liquids and especially liquids containing acids (fruit juice, soft drinks, wines, vinegar, tomatoes, etc.) draw out the lead from the paint even after it has been fired, which is why it is not wise (and in most places, illegal) to use a paint with a heavy concentrate of lead on food or utility vessels. Should not be used in conjunction with cobalt or copper as these destabilise the lead in the frit. In Australia, the National Health and Medical Research Council recommends that the sale of utensils used for food and drink be prohibited if there is a chance that lead may be released from the vessel and be hazardous to human health; that glazing formulas containing lead be labelled with a warning; that amateur potters do not apply lead-bearing glazes to the inner surfaces of food and drink utensils and that acidic foods and beverages not be stored in pottery containers. Lead volatilises during the firing process and the atmosphere around the kiln may constitute a health hazard if it is not well ventilated. If the articles are fired at the correct temperature most of the lead will be leached out during the firing process. It is therefore important to follow the manufacturer's directions if a temperature range is suggested. When using paints, care should be taken not to transfer the paint from hand or brush to mouth, or with dry powder, not to inhale the particles of paint dust.

Lead flower Term given to main flower in floral design.

Lead glaze A reliable low-fired flux commonly used. Lead glazes have a relatively low melting point and a wide softening range. Their low surface tension and viscosity cover minor imperfections on the clay body. There is usually sufficient reaction between the molten glaze and the clay body to form a bond which relieves stress and gives a high resistance to crazing and devitrification. Should not be used in conjunction with cobalt or copper as these destabilise the lead in the frit.

Leading lady Term given to main flower in floral design.

Leadlight (stained glass) Small segments of glass joined together with solder to form a picture or design. Coloured glass may be used or the glass may be coloured by the artist.

Lead oxide Red oxide of lead, used in pigments and in glass making.

Lead silica Low-melting mineral for use in lead crystal glassware.

Lead solubility The solubility of glazes with a lead content in a solution of dilute hydrochloric acid.

Lehr A long tunnel-shaped oven with a continuously moving belt or rollers, designed for annealing, sagging, slumping or for firing enamels or lustres on glass.

Leatherhard Describes a clay body not yet fired but dried to the stage at which it can be further shaped and carved.

Legends *Dogwood:* The Dogwood used to be a huge strong tree, but when it was used for the cross on which Jesus was crucified, the tree was so upset at being used for this purpose that it decided it would never again be big and strong. Its blossoms are in the form of a cross, two long and two short petals. In the centre of the outer edge of each petal there are 'nail' prints, brown with rust and stained with red. In the centre of the flower is a crown of thorns.

Rose: One day Chloris was walking in the woods and came upon a dead nymph. She decided to turn her into a flower, but thought her too pretty to be an ordinary flower and asked the other gods for advice. Dionysius donated nectar, the Three Graces bestowed charm and elegance; Aphrodite, goddess of love and beauty, gave these as gifts. The result was so beautiful that they made the flower the Queen of Flowers and named it the Rose. (My daughter wants to know who donated the thorns.)

Pansy: Once there was a widowed woodsman living with his two daughters, who married a widow who also had two daughters. He was worried because there were only five chairs. The widow had ideas of her own, however, and took command. She sat at the head of the table and because her beautiful skirts were so wide she sat on two chairs. She placed her daughters who were almost as well dressed and always in the same colours either side of her. The two plump daughters of the woodsman sat at the end of the table on the remaining chair. If you study the pansy you will see that the full-skirted petal sits on two sepals, the two colourful petals next to it sit on a sepal each and the two large petals (daughters of the woodsman) share a sepal at the top of the flower. And the poor woodsman? Well, if you look under the flower you will see a trumpet-shaped spur which is for water storage. This is the basement of the cottage and the woodsman sits down there with his feet in the water to keep warm.

Another pansy story to help paint these flowers: There was a lady who lived in a tent who had two favourite daughters who were always by their mother's side and who always wore the same colour dresses. There were also two fat twin stepsisters who always dressed alike. The tent is the inverted V which is the first part of the pansy to be painted. It gives both position and direction. Next the mother in her full skirt with the two daughters, one either side in the same colour and finally the two large petals, often a different colour from the rest of the family or flower but always the same as each other.

Lepidolite Lithium-based material with lower fusion point than most fluxes. May cause pitting due to presence of fluorine.

Light Without light we could not see. The artist must create the illusion of light in a painting.

Highlight: Where light from the light source falls directly on the subject.

Diffused light: Light which is softened and widespread.

Filtered light: Light which is patchy where it is obstructed by objects in its path.

Reflected light: Light thrown off one object onto another; carries the colour of that object with it.

Transmitted light: Light rays shining through an object.

Light box Container usually lit with fluorescent bulbs under an opaque glass cover. Used to trace, follow a pattern, e.g. glass backed with adhesive paper is placed on the box with a design underneath the glass. The light behind clearly shows up the design. In an emergency, a temporary lightbox may be made from a cardboard box, covered with a sheet of white or clear perspex and lit with a strong torch.

Light source Direction from which light falls on subject.

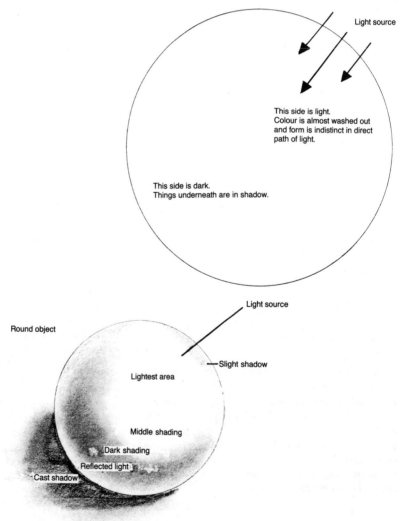

Diagrammatic representation of light source

Limit timer A device used to switch off a kiln at a desired temperature.

Limited palette A palette consisting of a maximum of six or seven colours for all your requirements.

Limoges Town in France which is famous for making porcelain from the large deposit of fine porcelain clay found nearby.

Limoges enamel Realistic and naturalistic designs painted on porcelain or metal which has been given a prior coat of white enamel and fired. A product of the Limoges factory.

Line (of design) The line of design is the path where all the action is. All lines have direction which the viewer's eye will follow. A line leading away from the design should be curved in such a way that it leads the eye back again. Lines may be straight or curved, complete or broken, thick or thin, light or heavy, single or multiple, short or long. Line plays an important role in penwork, the variety of marks making the whole picture.

Linear Pertaining to lines.

Linear perspective All parallel lines close in upon vanishing points. Parallel planes retain shape but diminish in size with vertical lines remaining vertical and horizontal lines remaining horizontal.

Liner A fine pointed brush used for detail work such as lines and branches, etc.

Liner

Lint *Enemy!* Comes off cloths used to clean, clothing, especially woollens, from hair and rugs or carpets and just from the atmosphere. Look at a shaft of sunlight! Found everywhere (dust and lint, that is, not the sunlight): in the paint, on the painted surface, etc. The oils we use attract it! Lint and dust particles landing on a wet area where no further work is to be done before firing usually burn off in the kiln and so are best left alone. While the painting is still being worked these particles gather colour and paint and do cause unsightly marks. Be scrupulously clean with all the tools of trade at all times.

Liquid Bright Gold for Glass Similar to Liquid Bright Gold for porcelain but matures at 600°C (1110°F).

Liquid Bright Gold Liquid gold lustre to colour and decorate; available in varying strengths or percentages from 6% to 30%. However, for painting, a 12% gold content is recommended. The contents of an opened jar will thicken with exposure to air or if it has been stored for some time. This increased viscosity makes the gold more suitable for relief surfaces or rims, as it does not run as easily as the thinner solution. It is possible to thin the liquid gold with gold thinner or lavender oil if it becomes too tacky. Try to pour from the bottle only enough for immediate needs. To be used with care on almost any clean surface. It is a bright, high shine metallic colour which may be dulled by applying over previously fired pastel coloured paints or onto a matt surface such as one of the dull texture pastes, bisque or the body of the clay where the glaze has been removed. Apply the gold as evenly as possible as thicker concentrations may be obvious after firing (however, it does seem to sort itself out and a slightly uneven coat is not serious). A lower percentage gold solution may be applied a little more thickly than a higher concentration. It may be painted over glazes, fired enamels, texture pastes, structure substances, glass, semi-precious stones and water based paints and products. If the surface is not clean the gold will fire black or marked. It may be mixed with some lustres to give different effects and also with some paints. If mixed with the gold rubies or gold purples it gives a much richer colour. Keep a separate brush for gold at all times and clean it in lavender oil. A jar of lavender oil kept solely to clean your gold brushes, and applicators such as toothpicks and satay sticks, will soon contain enough gold to use. If this lavender oil solution is painted onto an unpainted surface, it will fire a delicate mauve, the intensity of which is dependant on the amount of gold in the oil. Firing should be in a well ventilated kiln up to about 300°C (570°F) and then the vent may be closed. The oils and the liquid gold solution burn off in the form of fumes and resins which can impair the brilliance if they are not vented from the kiln. Too high a temperature can affect the gold, causing cracking and dulling. Too low a temperature will allow the gold to be rubbed off. *(See Degussa Products, page 113.)* Lustres over Liquid Bright Gold produce interesting variations of colour. Liquid Bright Gold, and other metallics and lustres, are not absorbed into the glaze (unlike paint) and will come off in a dishwasher or with abrasion. For pieces requiring a low temperature, e.g. for a textured surface that you do not want to fire high again, use Liquid Bright Gold for Glass and fire at 600°C (1110°F). Delightful and interesting free form designs are created when Liquid Bright Gold is floated on water and the porcelain or glass dipped carefully into the water so that the design adheres. *See* DIPPING.

Liquid Bright Palladium Similar to Liquid Bright Gold and used in the same way. Silver in colour.

Liquid Bright Platinum Similar to Liquid Bright Gold. Silver in colour; does not tarnish.

Liquid Burnishing Gold A liquid gold paint which must be burnished after firing.

Lithium borate Alkaline metal used as flux in glazes.

Lithium carbonate Alkaline metal used as strong flux for alkaline glazes. Has lower rate of expansion than either sodium or potassium. When replacing either of these materials it produces a more stable glaze without affecting either gloss or colour.

Lithium manganite Red-brown powder used as glaze colouring agent.

Lithographic pencil Used for drawing on porcelain. These lines will fire off or disappear with the heat of the kiln.

Loading a brush A brush should be conditioned before use by working oil well into the hairs. Pull the brush along the tile, fanning it out a little. If there is not enough oil on the brush it may 'split' or separate. A square shader should be flat when loaded with oil. Load with colour by working into the edge of the pile of mixed paint in a circular or C stroke. This will give you a shaded load with an even distribution of paint across the brush, more intense on the left side if you are a right handed painter, fading to the right.

Local clay May be used in glaze recipes. It should be completely dried, broken up and soaked in hot water for several days. The mix is then sieved and stood to settle once again for several days before the water is poured off and the clay allowed to dry out. This clay may have to be milled in a ball mill for three to four hours before it will melt at around 1200–1250°C (2190–2280°F).

Local colour Actual colour of object.

Lo-Sheen Glazes Trade name for glazes which are matt or semi gloss.

Lost line The separation or division within a design which is lost because of the common value and tone of two objects, e.g. a white moth on a cream flower.

Lost wax A shape is carved in wax and a mould made. The wax is then melted and poured out of the mould and replaced by molten glass. Also called *cire perdue*.

Lustre Solutions of mineral pigments in organic solvents which give an iridescent glaze when applied to porcelain, glass or ceramics. During the firing process the organic solvents volatilise, leaving a very thin layer of metal oxides fused to the glass or glazed surface. Lustres are either transparent or opaque.

Transparent lustres are mostly coloured; the opaque lustres include Liquid Bright Gold, Silver, Copper, Platinum and some colours which contain gold such as Ruby, Purple Violet and Dark Blue. These liquid metals are not absorbed into the glaze during the firing process; instead, they remain on the surface as does gold. Prior to firing, almost all of these colours appear brown and are hard to distinguish one from the other. Lustres should be stored in a cool dry place in well sealed bottles. They should be used as soon as practicable as some deteriorate rapidly. When using lustres, cleanliness is essential as every speck of dust and moisture will cause a mark on the finished transparent surface. Even humid conditions can adversely affect the result. Care must be taken not to contaminate one colour with another or with other products as they will lose their individuality and all turn out the same grey. Take care not to mix or confuse the lids of bottles and to replace the lid on its original bottle as soon as possible to prevent the lustre collecting dust or spilling. The surface to be painted should be cleaned with methylated spirits or acetone, not turpentine, and dried with a lint-free material. Don't use a grease pencil for sketching on a design when you are working with lustres, because it will act as a resist and prevent the lustre from adhering where the pencil has been used. Use a separate brush, cotton bud or sponge for each bottle. An economical method of applying lustre over a large surface is to wrap a piece of sponge or plastic foam in plastic wrap, then cover with fine athletic support bandage to prevent the lustre seeping into the plastic sponge and being wasted. Thickened or jellied lustre may be thinned with lustre thinner or lavender oil, preferably in a small dish rather than in the bottle, but this is not always successful. To use a lustre, pour a little into a small dish or saucer. (Never return leftovers to the bottle.) A thin coating is all that is required for each application; thick coats may blister and brush off. If you use a brush to apply the lustre, the brushstrokes should not overlap. If penwork is required in the same firing, use an agglutinate mixture of sugar and water or gum arabic and glycerine, as oils will affect the lustre. Enamels and pastes can be applied over the unfired lustre but may take on some of the colour, particularly around the edges. To tint the inside of a cup or bowl or box, pour in a few drops and rub with a small pad. When applying lustre with the aid of an airbrush, thin it a little first. Take care not to touch the unfired lustre as fingerprints can easily be seen. Tissue will stick to the wet lustre, as will plastic foam as the lustre becomes tacky. Moisture from a sneeze or a cough can mar the finish. Firing temperatures usually range from 700–800°C (1290–1470°F).

Bisque painted with lustre has a rich appearance. Fire in an initially ventilated kiln so that the fumes from the oils and resins in the lustre do not mar its brilliance. Colour combinations will give dramatic effects but are subject to many variables such as the amount of each lustre used, heaviness of application, firing time, condition of the lustres, etc. Some common combinations:

Copper over Pearl = a peacock blue
Liquid Bright Silver with Ruby or Purple = maroon
Yellow Pearl over Liquid Bright Silver = bronze
Blue over fired gold = a gunmetal colour
Light Green over Copper Bronze = iridescent green
Yellow over fired Orange = auburn
Pearl over ordinary black paint = satin black

Lustre painting

Some suggestions:
• A marbleised effect may be achieved by applying different lustres to a porcelain or glazed surface and dribbling or dabbing a little turpentine or lavender oil onto the wet lustre with a sponge.
• Select two or three, no more, compatible lustres, pour a few drops into small individual containers and thin with lustre thinner to the consistency of water. Pour the contents of one or more of the containers onto a platter, leaving some areas of white and, holding a powerful hair dryer close to the lustre, turn it full on. Hold in place until the lustre in that area is dry before moving on to another area. Continue until all the lustre is dry. Remove any unwanted areas and fire. It is difficult to control the design and impossible to predict the results, which can be very dramatic.
• Apply a coat of opaque lustre, fire and apply a second coat of opaque or transparent lustre. While this coat is still wet, wrap or dab with plastic wrap. Remove and fire again.
• Reverse the order of opaque and transparent lustres above. Alternatively, use light and dark lustres.
• A blank piece may be dipped into lustres floating on water.
• The wet paint area may be dabbed with crushed plastic, foil, tissue or other print object.
• Spray with an aerosol can of hairspray, ironing spray, water.

Lustre resist Several preparations are available from porcelain suppliers: a thick substance resembling poster paint which is water-soluble. Apply to white porcelain, glazed clay body or over fired lustre. Do not apply over a painted or fluxed surface as it will not come off easily. Sketch design onto surface and apply lustre resist to areas to be resisted, e.g. the petals of flowers, some leaves and stems or geometric shapes taken at random from a modern design. Allow to dry. Apply a pale shade of lustre to the entire surface, including the resisted areas. Fire low (700–740°C, 1290–1365°F) as the resist is difficult to remove if fired high. Block in some more flowers or shapes with the resist over the pale lustre, allow to dry and apply a further coat of a darker shade of lustre. Fire again. Repeat the process until you have three or four gradually deepening coats of lustre. After the last fire, wash off the resist with methylated spirits or water. You will have flowers or other elements in your design ranging from white through the lustre colours you have used from light to dark.

Luting The joining together of two pieces of clay with the aid of a tool which joins the two sides together from the inside.

M

Magnesium carbonate 1. High temperature flux for glazes. Up to 10% for a smooth surface, in higher concentrations a semi-matt glaze; if used in excessive amounts, crawling and pinholing may result. **2.** In low temperature glazes magnesium carbonate reduces fluidity and if used in conjunction with cobalt and manganese it will produce interesting colour effects.

Magnesium sulphate Silver white metallic element (Epsom salts). Used to aid suspension and thicken glazes.

Majolica Porous vitreous earthenware or faience of Hispano-moresque origin; frequently decorated with brightly coloured opaque glazes.

Majolica technique Design painted in underglazes over an unfired glaze. Once the piece is fired the design becomes a permanent feature of the glaze.

Malti Italian glass tile.

Manganese oxide Used to make glass and colour paints, glazes and glass—a dark purple in colour.

Manganese carbonate Colouring agent producing pinks and brown colours. In glazes, colour tones will be pink and mauve in alkaline and dolomite glazes and brown in feldspathic glazes.

Manganese dioxide Will produce purples and plum colours in alkaline glazes. In combination with iron, browns will be produced and with cobalt oxide a deep violet will result.

Mannerism A sophisticated and sometimes artificial style of art that evolved from an emotional reaction to the classical rules of the Renaissance.

Marbleising Application of paint to give the appearance of marble or an artistic interpretation of it. Various commercial preparations or oils can be applied to obtain the variety of colours available in marble (but it is a good idea to see how many colours you can see in a piece of marble before trying to imitate it). There are, however, many other methods which can be used to obtain this effect. Start with the lightest colours and work up to the dark veins.
Paint the area with a variety of light colours and blend edges well together so that there is no distinct line marking a colour change. While wet, draw uneven streaks through the paint with a liner brush loaded with turpentine and darker colours. The darker paint will run/bleed into the lighter colour depending on how much turpentine your brush is carrying. Light 'cracks' in the marble are made with a wipe-out tool, and the edges softened.

Solutions of oil, turpentine, dispersing solution for lustres or acetone may be dribbled onto a wet painted or lustred surface and the piece turned every which way to enhance the running of the paint. Experiment with a variety of solutions on the tops of jewellery boxes. Wipe it off if you do not like it.

The wet painted area is dabbed with crushed plastic, foil or other print object and the resulting lines and marks enhanced.

Marbleising liquid Commercial preparation which is dribbled on, touched to, and otherwise applied to unfired paint.

Marker pens Available in many colours, water-soluble or permanent ink. Will disappear in the firing process. Ideal for applying design to glazed surface and for colouring in areas which are difficult to identify.

Marinite A high duty refractory insulation board sometimes used in place of a kiln shelf.

Martelé Decorative technique producing a multi-faceted surface with a hammered appearance similar to the surface produced by glass incising.

Marver An iron or marble table on which the gather is rolled into an even mass.

Marvering The controlled forming of viscous glass on a flat metal table (marver). Used in the making of colour bars and in glass blowing.

Masking lacquer A cellulose coating or resist which is used to protect areas of the painting surface. Spirit-based (usually green for use with water-based mediums and Rustiban) and water-based (usually pink for use with oil-based mediums). Paint the area required with the solution and allow to dry. Ground or dust the exposed area and lift off the resist. For intricate designs it may be wise to take a tracing first so that you know where all the resist is when you come to lift it off as it is sometimes hard to see where you have applied small areas. Coloured nail polish is a good substitute if you are simply removing part of the design with Rustiban. (*Caution—acid*.)

Masking tape Ideal for straight edges and masking areas to be left alone. Place a strip where required or place several strips side by side, draw a design on top and remove excess tape with a craft knife.

Mask 'n Peel Trade name of water-soluble resist solution used to protect areas of greenware or bisque.

Mass A coherent body of matter of indefinite shape.

Matt A dull or satin finish.

Matt china To matt china, use either Ivory Vellum, Matt White, Matt Ivory or add a small amount of Zinc Oxide to your powdered paints. Best results achieved by dusting or grounding on.

Matt paints These paints fire with a satin or matt appearance. Used on bisque porcelain or on surfaces which have been dulled with an application of acid, Ivory Vellum or have had the glaze removed. Available at porcelain suppliers. It is possible to matt normal powder paints with the addition of zinc oxide. The normal ratio is 4 to 1; however, some powder paints contain a lot of flux and may require more zinc oxide. Liquid detergent used to mix paints will also matt them. Overworked paints will lose their gloss.

Mature Term used to describe the colour, tone, state of enamel, glaze, etc. intended by the manufacturer after firing in the kiln. A glaze or enamel is considered overfired if firing too high results in washed-out colours, and underfired if firing too low results in patchy colour which will sometimes rub off.

Maturing point Required temperature to fire clay, glaze or paint to its full potential.

Mayco Manufacturer of hobby ceramic products, available in all states of Australia.

Medium 1. The method in which the artist works—oil, watercolour, painting on porcelain, forming and painting glass, pouring ceramics. 2. Oil used to apply the paint to the painting surface. There are a great number of oils used and even more with which to experiment. The medium should evaporate or volatilise before the glaze melts and the kiln should be well ventilated to prevent the vapour settling on the painted porcelain. The medium should also be able to retain its viscosity as the heat increases until it evaporates, otherwise it will boil and run before the heat has caused the glaze to melt and absorb the paint, which would then flow over

the surface with the boiling medium.

Fast drying medium: One which dries quickly and is best suited to the rapid painter. *Not* for use in seminars unless a few drops of an open medium are added or the teacher requests it. Main ingredient is usually copaiba.

Slow drying medium/open medium: For painters who like to take their time and for seminars.

Anise oil: Slow drying, lightweight oil used for penwork. If too much is used, it may cause the paint to run during the firing process.

Balsam of copaiba: Base used for most commercial mediums.

Oil of cloves: Slow drying, added to faster drying oils to retard the drying process. If too much is used, it may cause the paint to run in the kiln during the firing process.

Eucalyptus oil: Fast drying thin oil, ideal for Sgraffito.

Fat oil of turpentine: Fast drying oil used in European techniques and in earlier painting methods. Will give body to a medium recipe. To make, place a small amount of turpentine in a flat dish (and cover) or in a small jar. Leave in a dust-free place to evaporate until thick and viscous. Time will depend on amount and weather.

Kelp oil: Slow drying lightweight oil used for pen work. If too much is used it may cause the paint to run during the firing process.

Oil of lavender: Essential oil used in some mediums as a drying agent. Used in lustre and gold work as well as for painting on bisque.

Spike lavender: Less expensive than oil of lavender but has similar properties and is used for the same purposes.

Mineral oil: Volatile oil used frequently as a base for open mediums. Can cause loss of colour, chipping and running problems if used too liberally.

Oil of rosemary: Used with lustres.

Paraffin oil: May be used as an open medium as well as to mix paints. Use sparingly.

If a medium is too heavy, add a few drops of either pure turpentine, lavender, clove or tar oil. Other oils such as baby oil, machine oil, olive oil, motor oil, cooking oil, peanut oil, coconut oil, linseed oil, etc. can be successful if used with caution. They are mostly volatile oils and boil in the kiln before they evaporate or are burned off, causing the paint to run, lose some colour or chip off. Use very sparingly! *See* Product Information, page 106, for brand name mediums.

Glycerine: May be used by anyone allergic to various oils or who prefers to paint with a water-based medium, both for mixing paints and as a painting medium. It is possible to use a water-based medium for paints as well as an oil-based metallic such as lustre in the same fire if time is short. A number of commercial water-based mediums are available.

Medium recipes Taken from every source I could find.

Fast drying mediums

1. 2 parts fat oil + 2 parts copaiba + 1 part lavender oil + 1 part clove oil

2. 8 parts copaiba + 1 part clove oil + 1 part lavender oil

3. 8 parts copaiba + 2 parts clove oil + 2 parts lavender oil

Heavy medium

6 parts copaiba + 1 part clove oil

Open mediums

4. 1 part lavender oil + 1 part copaiba + 1 part tar oil + 25 drops clove oil to each 30 g (1oz)

5. 1 part copaiba + 3 parts lavender oil

6. 30 g (1 oz) mineral oil + 60 g (2 oz) clove oil + 7 g ($^1/_4$ oz) lavender oil + 7 g ($^1/_4$ oz) tar oil

7. 500 ml (1 pint) mineral oil + 20 ml (1 tbs) clove oil + 7 ml (1½ tsp) lavender oil

8. Equal parts of lavender oil, copaiba and tar oil + 25 drops of clove oil to each 30 ml (1 oz)

Commercial mediums (Courtesy of Russell Cowan.)

Lakides and *June Kay* mediums are copaiba-based and are reasonably fast drying, making them very desirable in areas which are inclined to be a little dusty.

Jenny's Medium is for the painter who requires a little more time to work on a project.

Dresden Water-based Medium is for one-fire painting and for painters with allergy problems.

Grinding Oils: M30 and *Dresden Grounding Oil* Dresden Grounding Oil dries quicker than M30 and can be ground immediately. It may be mixed with M30 to obtain an intermediate characteristic. Such an oil is M35.

Russell Cowan Pen Oil and *Barbara Dimitri Pen Oil* are both suitable for very fine pen work. They are fast drying pen oils suitable for pen and wash painting and are also suitable for screenprinting.

Meissen Classics A range of colours marketed by Alexanders specifically created for porcelain artists and small kilns. *See* Alexander's Products, page 106.

Meissenware The first hard paste porcelain made in Europe at Meissen.

Mending cement Clean both edges or surfaces thoroughly. Mix mending cement with water and apply to both surfaces. Place pieces together and support with kiln furniture or a nichrome cord (available from ceramic shops—used for firing beads), and place directly into the kiln as the mix does not adhere until fired. Fire to 745°C (1365°F) or Cone 017. Small pieces may be mended in the same fashion using texture paste.

Metallic Flo-Base A solution which is applied to a clean glazed surface over which small drops of Liquid Bright Gold or other lustres or metallics are applied while the substance is still wet. Interesting free form patterns are produced. Tilting and turning the object being painted will enhance the flow of the mix and encourage different patterns to emerge. Brushes are washed out in water.

Metallic paint Powder paint with a frosted metallic appearance. Good for grounding and hiding faults. Try grounding over a painted design and detailing the result after firing, or grounding a base and painting a design on the frosted background. Underfired metallic paint will rub off; if overfired it will lose the metallic sheen. Fire at 750-800°C (1400-1475°F.)

Methylated spirits Ethyl alcohol which has been treated to make it undrinkable. It is a colourless, volatile, flammable fluid used, among other things, for cleaning blanks prior to painting and for cleaning grounding surrounds. May be used occasionally to clean brushes thoroughly; continual cleaning with alcohol will eventually destroy the natural oil in the hairs.

Microwave kiln EZ5 Available from Deirdre Fewell Studio Supplies, Sydney. A very small kiln, 7.3 cm (3″) in diameter, which is perfect for small glass, ceramic and porcelain pieces and jewellery. The kiln sits in a microwave oven and the inside of the kiln becomes red in minutes as the heat is trapped within the silicon carbide lining. The outer shell is made of a porous, heat resistant ceramic fibre that does not get hot. Firing time is 3-5 minutes, depending on the article being fired.

Middleground The area between background and foreground. There is no distinct line drawn between the three areas. Foreground is sharp and clear in detail; background is hazy and indistinct to imply distance; middleground has some broken sharp detail with some indistinct

Pen and wash—suitable for all onglaze and glass surfaces (T. Bradford)

Penwork owl (T. Bradford)

Brushstrokes

Geometric design (Barbara Adams)

Rose plate in soft technique (B. Torkington)

Traditional raised paste work, suitable for most glazed surfaces (T. Bradford)

Onglaze Images (27 Monkman Street, Chapman ACT 2611) reproduces photographs onto a glazed or glass surface

Large (empty) whisky bottle slumped into shape of human form. A glass orb ball was used for the head and the final result painted (T. Bradford)

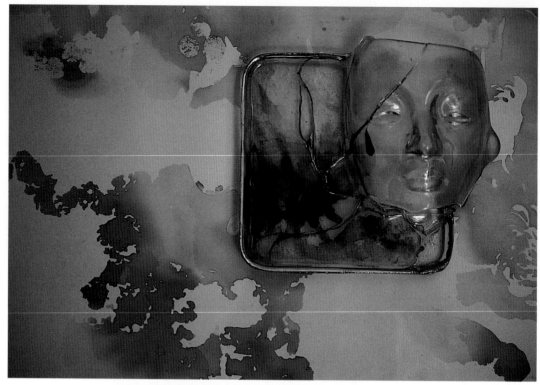

Glass sheet slumped over a porcelain mask
(T. Bradford)

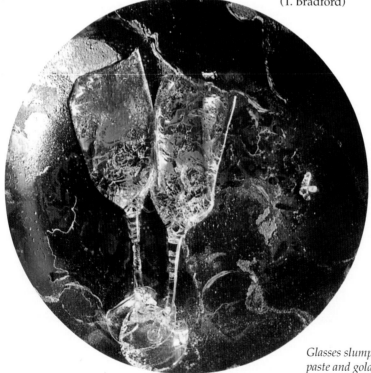

*Glasses slumped onto a platter, with chipping,
paste and gold work* (T. Bradford)

areas and slightly blurred design.

Mildew Dark or black spots which appear in some china. Attributed to bisque being moist when glaze applied. These spots ocasionally fire out when fired very high.

Millefiori Italian term for many-flowered. Porcelain or ceramic clay may be coloured with powder paint and rolled into a multicoloured pattern and cut or shaped into a desired form. (Italian *millefiori*: lit. 'a thousand flowers'.)

Millefiori glass Coloured glass canes intricately arranged, often in a floral pattern, and fused together. Dates from 1st century BC.

Mineral oils Highly volatile crude petroleum oils which 'boil' at a lower temperature than the glaze in a kiln, allowing paint to run before the pigments are absorbed.

Mishima Korean technique of carving, stamping, or otherwise depressing clay and filling the hollows with ENGOBE of another colour. May have a final glaze coat.

Misting To apply paint with an airbrush or spray can.

Mixed media More than one type of painting material or substance used to create a painting, e.g. paints, glass and texture paste, porcelain and glass combined or porcelain incorporated into a silk or paper background.

Mixing colours There are so many colours available that it is seldom necessary to mix them dry. However, it is often a good practice to add a little of the main colour featured in your design to some of the background colours, mixed on the brush, to carry the tone through the painting. For instance, if painting in ruby colours, an addition of ruby will 'grey' the darks and give strength to the painting. Try tipping the greys and greens of foliage with a ruby/grey mix. There are many lists of combinations in the various books published.

Mode Form or style.

Modelling Manipulating clay to form a shape or to simulate a form. In our work, one can 'model' the lights and darks to give impressions of concave and convex surfaces (on a petal or part of a body), or the outline of a leaf or flower to change its shape. Clay can also be formed into an extension of the blank and adhered during firing.

Modelling clay Clay which has been prepared either commercially or by the artist for hand modelling.

Moisture expansion A porous ceramic body will expand when it absorbs water.

Molochite Alumino-silicate refractory aggregate: non-plastic form of kaolin used to reduce tendency of glazes to crawl.

Molten Made liquid by heat; melted.

Monochromatic The use of different shades, tones and tints of one colour only.

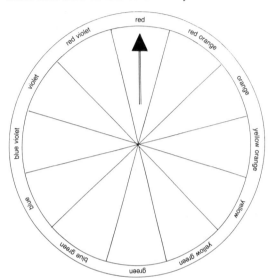

Monochromatic colour scheme

Monochrome To paint the design in one colour or shades and tones of one colour. In onglaze work a monochromatic painting in shades of grey is used to establish form and values. Once the initial painting is complete it may be dusted with normal colours prior to firing or fired as it is and then painted with washes of colour in a second and/or third firing stage.

Monogram Two or more intertwined initials.

Mood May be created or altered by colour. A painting in bright yellows, greens and blues will look modern and happy; the same design in pastels will look traditional and subdued.

Mortar Hard vessel in which paints may be ground or pounded with a pestle. It is customary to use frosted glass with its rougher textured surface for the powdered porcelain and glass paints.

Mosaic A decoration made up of small pieces of various coloured materials or tiles positioned to form a pattern. There are several methods available to the porcelain artist to achieve this effect, the most realistic being to draw your pattern onto the painting surface (the reverse side of a tile, bisque or other unglazed surface is best) and then pencil in the horizontal lines, followed by the vertical lines which form the tiled pattern. Fill each square or rectangle individually with either coloured or white (to be painted after firing) enamel or texture paste, wait until completely dry, preferably several days, and fire to the temperature required by the enamel or paste. Alternatively, apply enamel or paste evenly over the entire surface and use a ruler, string or other object to make the required indents and form the tiled shapes (a credit card is good). Fire and paint. Penwork lines and/or painted shadows around small painted areas would also simulate mosaics. *See:* T. Bradford: *Porcelain Art—The International Collection,* self published, Brisbane, 1994; and Rocio Borobia de Gomez: *An Art Without Frontiers,* self published, Mexico 1996.

Motif Dominant idea or theme of design or composition. A repeated pattern.

Motion (or movement) A design will be more 'alive' if it appears to have movement within it. For instance, a bird or two in a scene will give life and movement to a painting. Flowers will appear more realistic if they are painted in different positions and facing in different, but not opposing, directions. Turning leaves on their side, and the suggestion of forms behind the main focus of the design also helps.

Mould (mold) A form made from any refractory material, including clay moulds and collars from stoneware, earthenware, porcelain bisque, ceramic slip and bisque terracotta; metal, e.g. stainless steel, alumina fibre, ceramic fibre, plaster of Paris and kiln wool. There are many shapes which may be used as templates for moulds. All moulds should be prepared with kiln wash before use.

Mould keys Moulds for pouring are composed of two or more parts, each with a locking device, matching notches or projections to align the mould.

Mould scraper Tool designed to clean the outside of casting moulds.

Mould soap Potash soap used as a dressing when mould making. May be diluted with water.

Mould thumper Synthetic rubber hammer-like object for releasing greenware from moulds reluctant to let it go.

Moulding 1. Forming a shape from clay by hand. **2.** Pouring slip into a mould to form a shape. **3.** Moulding the contour of a petal or leaf with heavy and light applications of paint or with shading.

Movement An illusion created by the artist to give the effect of a living, vibrant scene, figure or blossom.

Muffle kiln A low-temperature kiln used for firing overglaze colours or for refiring glass to fix enamel and gilding. The objects are placed in a fire-clay box to protect them from moisture, air, smoke and fumes.

Muller Rounded stone or glass grinding tool with a flat base useful for grinding grainy paints and pigments, preferably on a ground glass tile.

Mullite Material with a high alumina content which, when fired to 1430°C (2600°F) grows a mullite crystal which is refractory and durable. Commonly used for kiln shelves, it is smoother and has a less porous surface than silicon carbide and will lose heat more rapidly.

Muriatic acid Acid used for swimming pools and *not* for removing fired paint or etching.

N

Nail polish Cosmetic nail polish makes a good resist or masking lacquer when removing part of a design. Paint it over the area you want to keep, allow to dry and use Rustiban (*caution—acid*) to remove the fired paint. Wash off Rustiban and remove nail polish.

Nail polish remover May be used in place of pure acetone to clean brushes and surfaces coated with a spirit-based mixture such as masking fluid. Interesting effects when used with paint, lustres and liquid metallics. Experiment!

Natch Locking device to join two sides of a mould together.

Naturalism Faithful representation of nature or reality.

Naturalistic Artist's realistic impression of nature.

Naturalistic design Nature has provided a wealth of material from which to obtain designs. Vegetables such as capsicum, onion, tomato, enlarged photos of human tissue, flora, landforms and geographical designs and more recently the satellite photos of the planet from space, are all wonderful sources of inspiration.

Needle point Sharp pointed protrusions on the edge of glass caused by over-firing.

Neo-classic Return to, revival or adaptation of the classical.

Neo-impressionism Art theory to make impressionism more precise in form. Pointillism painting technique.

Nepheline syenite One of the feldspathoids, silicate minerals rich in the alkali elements sodium and potassium and poor in silicate. Low melting point is useful as a body and glaze flux when a lower maturing temperature is required.

Neutral Not distinctly coloured.

Neutralised colour Colour which has been greyed; also tertiary colour.

Nib Normal ink nibs used for penwork. A fine mapping pen nib is ideal for fine work while the larger Post Office pen is great for heavier lines. Choose a hard nib and keep it clean. If it has an air hole, this should be kept free of paint.

Nichrome wire Wire which will withstand heat in the kiln. Used for elements, firing objects which are completely glazed, such as beads, or as support for repaired china.

Nickel oxide Colouring agent which produces browns and greens. In glaze recipes will produce pale watery blue with zinc oxide glazes, yellow with zinc oxide and titanium dioxide, pinks and mauves when used in conjunction with barium carbonate and zinc oxide.

Non-moving glazes Glazes which are stable during firing.

Non-objectivism Suprematism. Extreme abstract art based on geometric forms and simple colours.

Notes What you should keep about every piece you paint. It is helpful to have a record of successes you would like to repeat or disasters you would rather not. A notebook (better than scraps of paper) in your box of tricks is worth its weight in gold if you use it. Every time you paint something note the colours used. If you make up a texture paste note its ingredients, and if you use one colour on top of another in a subsequent fire, note that as well. You may want to know later. If you change the temperature at which you fire, make a note. If something 'strange' comes out of your kiln note where it

was positioned. (You will already have a note of what went in, won't you?) Take notes at seminars and workshops and during class discussions (how else can you remember all those jokes!) and date them so that you can locate them easily.

Nuggetting Glass is applied to porcelain with the aid of flux and fired; because the glass contracts at a faster rate than the glaze of the porcelain or other clay body it will chip off easily during the cooling, taking some of the body of the piece with it and leaving a pitted surface. This may then be lustred or coloured. It is a good idea to paint with a lustre before using Liquid Bright Gold. Large pieces of glass placed too close together may cause structural fractures during the firing process.

Nyon designs From Nyon on Lake Geneva. Clear well-defined florets in repetitive geometric pattern on white background.

O

Objective colour A colour named after the object it depicts, e.g. sky blue, grass green.

Objectivism An art theory stressing objective reality. The exact rendering of detail.

Objet d'art Valuable art piece. Your finished article, hopefully.

Oblique perspective Perspective where three faces of an object are visible and there are three separate vanishing points.

Occupational hygiene Workrooms should be vacuumed and mopped regularly, spills immediately cleaned up and vacuumed, a dust respirator should be used if mixing dry powders or glazes. Airbrushing should only be done in well ventilated booths exhausted to the exterior. Kilns should be away from the household environment or otherwise fitted with a hood exhausting to the exterior.

Oil of cloves Used to prevent colours from drying too rapidly or to keep the paint open.

Oil of lavender Used to keep colour open, for gold application and to clean brushes used for gold. Used for painting on bisque.

Oil of rosemary Used to keep medium open.

Oil of tar Mainly used with raised paste for gold to make it more stringy and pliable.

Oil of turpentine A solvent for cleaning brushes and palette. It may also be used for thinning mixed paints and for applying paint to the surface of the china. However, paint applied this way dries rapidly.

One-fire technique 1. For painting on porcelain or a glazed surface. The aim is to obtain the entire design, with full depth of colour, with just one application of paint and one firing only. Using a fairly open medium and a comparatively dry brush, paint the design in rich, fully loaded strokes of colour, making each brushstroke count. Either a wipe-out or paint-in method may be used, with a complete background and sharp accents of depth under the focal areas. Use wet on wet technique to introduce secondary and supporting design. Do not have the medium oil too thick as it will run in the kiln; also the thick applications of paint may not be fully absorbed by the glaze and thus could chip off. A fun exercise to loosen up. **2.** To build, glaze and fire a ceramic object in one stage only.

Onglaze Painting on a glazed surface.

Oozles The results of turpentine dribbled through paint. (Watercolour term.)

Opacifier Substance which makes a glaze opaque, e.g. tin, titanium, zirconium.

Opalescent glass Translucent glass with a milky iridescent appearance.

Opaque Unable to be penetrated by light. We have opaque lustres, colours, glasses and glazes and sometimes minds which are closed to new or different concepts.

Opaque porcelain Hard dense earthenware, similar to ironstone.

Open A medium is said to be open if it is slow-drying. Some will never dry.

Outline painting A simple teaching method. The outline of the flower or design is drawn with a fine liner dipped only in turpentine and mixed paint, the colour usually being of the same tone as the flower, e.g. ruby for cyclamen, fuchsia or clematis, etc., or in the case of white flowers a grey shaded with the tones of the desired background, e.g. blue, mauve or pink, etc. Once the design is drawn, a square shader loaded only with medium is used flat to thin the outline and in doing so bring in enough colour from it to form the shading and moulding of the petals or shapes being painted. Initial lines

should not be too thick or heavy, otherwise too much paint will be carried into the shaded areas, but should be just thick enough to supply sufficient colour to create a light shading. The result should be a soft blending of colour giving a delicate moulding and translucent appearance. Ideal for fragile flowers, skin tones, contemporary designs and shading.

Overglaze 1. Fine ground glass applied to a prefused glass surface to prevent devitrification and to produce a very glassy (glossy) surface. Usually applied as a powder or spray. **2.** Glaze applied over painted design or previously applied glaze.

Overglaze colour Suitable colour for painting on a glazed surface.

Overlays Fused layers of glass.

Oversights The 'nasties' you fired onto your porcelain because you did not check it properly.

Over-tint Application of colour over an already painted and fired area.

Overworked Paint which has been pushed and pulled around the plate will fire dull and grainy.

Oxide Compound formed of oxygen and another element which remains unchanged during ordinary chemical reactions. Metallic oxides used to colour paints and glazes may be harmful if inhaled or ingested. Please exercise caution with all oxides.

P

Padding Blending and softening a design, or smoothing an application of oil for grounding by padding or pouncing with a pad made from foam plastic or cotton wool covered with fine silk or fine athletic support bandage.

Painterly True artistic quality and technical excellence of brushstrokes and application of paint.

Painting Applying paint consisting of pigments or colours mixed with a liquid medium such as oil, varnish, milk, glue or water to a surface by brushing, spraying, a variety of tools, a roller or other padded device. The surface to be painted may be paper, canvas, wood, stone, plaster, plastic, clay or porcelain.

Palette A covered flat box or tray in or on which to keep your paints. Should be kept clean to prevent the dust particles it attracts from marring your painting. Paints mixed with an open medium will stay workable for months.

Palette knife A flat stainless steel blade with a wooden handle and either a round-tipped or triangular blade which is used for grinding paints and may be used for painting and applying enamel. It can be used to make some interesting marks, with either the flat surface or the sharp edge.

Pantograph Drawing device used to copy, enlarge or reduce a design.

Paper doily To reproduce a paper doily pattern, thoroughly paint and pad a plate with grounding oil. Carefully position a paper doily on the surface and dust with dry powder paints. Remove excess and gently lift doily. Doilies may also provide ideas for raised paste, enamel and relief paste work.

Paper, painting on It is possible to paint on various types of paper using oil-based, onglaze, porcelain, or glass paints and mediums. There are commercially prepared papers like Dover paper, but any plasticised paper, oil-painting paper or canvas, waxed surfaces such as the inside of milk cartons, plastic sheeting, in fact, any non-absorbent surface may be used. A fast-drying medium, i.e. copaiba or fat oil based, is essential. Good brushstroke techniques are an advantage, since although it is possible to clean the paper with turpentine or lavender oil, it is not as easy as cleaning a porcelain or glass surface. Once the painting is dry, additional depth, detail and shadows may be added with care over previously applied paint. When finished, the painting should be allowed to dry thoroughly in a dust-free environment and then sprayed with one of the oil-painting lacquers. Water-based mediums and paint mixed with glycerine may be used on various types of paper in the same manner but do not have the same lasting quality.

Paraffin Mixture of hydrocarbons obtained by distillation of petroleum; the least expensive and the least volatile oil. May be used as a medium or to mix powder paint. Use with care as too much oil will cause running in the firing process.

Paraffin wax Used as resist for glaze and colourants.

Paraison The bubble of molten glass formed on the blowpipe after air has been blown into it.

Parallel perspective Linear perspective with one surface facing the viewer.

Parchment Treated animal skin used for painting and writing.

Partial fire Paint entire area, fire to 300–400°C and remove from kiln. Alternatively, place in the kitchen oven at 300°C (450–500°F) and leave for fifteen minutes or until paint will not move when touched. Convenient when the piece has to wait or be conveyed to another place for firing. If there is no metal in the paints, the piece may be placed in the microwave oven for a few moments.

Paste gold Gold in paste form. Mix to painting consistency with lavender oil, gold essence or gold facilitator.

Pat gold A flat smear of gold which is softened with lavender oil, essence or facilitator.

Patch-A-Tatch Trade name for mender for welding broken greenware or bisque.

Pâte de verre Crushed glass, flux and colour fused in a mould.

Pattern Often repetitious design useful for concealing faults and marred surfaces. May be naturalistic, representational, geometric or abstract.

Peduncle Stalk of flower or fruit.

Peephole Hole with plug or bung in door of kiln for observation, not for venting.

Pen and wash A method of sketching in grey, brown or dark green then washing colour over the design. If the sketch is executed in a simple syrup or water-based medium, the wash may be applied with a normal medium in the same firing stage, as the oil-based medium will not move the simple syrup or water-based design.

Pen oil 1. A fine thin open medium for use with pen nibs. Various brands available. **2:** Thin paint mixed with turpentine to ink consistency. Mix powder paints with simple syrup or a sugar-based soft drink such as lemonade or cola, etc. Diet soft drinks, which are not based on sugar, do not work.

Penwork Penning a design with a nib. A mapping pen, an ink composed of paint pigments and a prepared surface are the requirements.

Perfect Pen Porcelain art pen from Deirdre Fewell Studios, Sydney. The brainchild of Doris Ann Johnson (USA), this pen with its refined nib is ideally suited to onglaze paints which are used with any pen oil, a little thinner than normal. The pen is taken completely apart to clean the barrel, trocar and nib.

Perspective The impression of distance and depth.

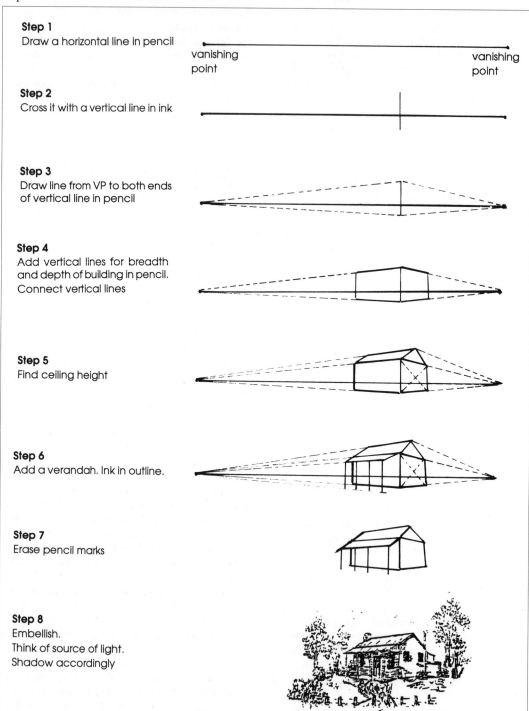

Step 1
Draw a horizontal line in pencil

vanishing point   vanishing point

Step 2
Cross it with a vertical line in ink

Step 3
Draw line from VP to both ends of vertical line in pencil

Step 4
Add vertical lines for breadth and depth of building in pencil. Connect vertical lines

Step 5
Find ceiling height

Step 6
Add a verandah. Ink in outline.

Step 7
Erase pencil marks

Step 8
Embellish.
Think of source of light.
Shadow accordingly

Simple perspective drawing

Petal Each of the divisions of the corolla of a flower.

Petalite Secondary flux in high temperature glazes; also used to lower the expansion of glazes. When used in small quantities, it will heighten colour.

Petit point Painting with texture to resemble tapestry or needlework. Choose a piece of porcelain with a convex surface and cover with a piece of fine nylon net drawn taut, securing with an elastic band or clothespeg. Make sure all the net lines are straight. Apply petit point paste evenly (thinned with turpentine if necessary) with a brush, leaving the net visible. Allow to dry naturally and remove net. Fire to manufacturer's instructions or around 780–800°C (1290–1470°F). Sand gently and paint with matt paints as for bisque. The net may be re-used.

Petit point paste Substance with dull matt finish which gives the petit point texture. Usually pre-mixed. Powdered colour may be added in small proportions. Fired at 780–800°C (1290–1470°F). Porous after firing; note that colours and metallics fire dull when applied over the paste.

Photography Photographing a glazed surface or glass can be difficult and frustrating. There is a wide range of cameras and equipment available and you should familiarise yourself with your own. A good lens will let you get close enough to fill the frame with the object you want to photograph. The background for your porcelain should be uncluttered and not divided by the edge of a table or shelf. I like a dark, almost black drape for most light-coloured pieces, with most of the drape area excluded, otherwise it will wash out the colour on the object. A suitable simple backdrop is a sheet of card in a mid grey tone or a piece of roller-blind fabric. I have found blue intrusive and neutral colours seem to blend too well without giving contrast. If you want to have your work reproduced, transparencies are better than negatives; however, it is a good idea to send a print as well (if only to prevent your work being printed upside down). Try not to use a flash (to avoid reflections) and also be wary of reflections from windows, trees, people and, of course, the photographer. Photographs taken outside in early morning or evening daylight before the sun washes out some of the colour are often successful. Take at least two or three photographs of each object. It is not really advisable to spray your work with hairspray or any commercial variety of spray to heighten the gloss. If there is a gold trim it could be marred, or enamel could be chipped off. It is possible to take good photographs without doing that.

Photo-sensitive glass Photographs can be reproduced within this glass by placing photographic film or mask in contact with the glass and exposing it to ultraviolet radiations and heat treatment.

Pincers Tool used for grasping threading or pinching glass for decorative effect.

Pine tar An additive for enamels and pastes to aid adherence and stringing.

Piece Object to be painted. China, ceramic or glass blank.

Pigment Colouring in paints or dyes.

Pistil Ovulating organ of a flower.

Plaster of Paris White powder consisting of calcined gypsum. Mixed with water to paste consistency to form moulds and to make other shapes. Dries rapidly, but drying may be retarded by the addition of glue or hastened by alum.

Plasticiser Solution added to clay to make it more pliable. Plasticisers may be added to artist's paints to increase fluidity and flexibility; sugar may be added to watercolours and beeswax to oils.

Plasticity Ability of a material to be deformed and to be shaped into another form with ease.

Plastic wrap Plastic wrap has a myriad uses. Apply visual texture to a painted surface by padding with crumpled plastic wrap. Apply paste to a surface and cover with the plastic. Move and swirl the plastic to form a pleasing design. Leave the plastic in position and fire. The plastic will burn off and the design will stay in place. Protect an unfired painted surface by covering container or plate with plastic wrap. Two plates of similar size, covered in plastic and placed face to face, will travel easily.

Platinum A rare metallic element, fusable only at very high temperatures. Treat as you would gold.

Plate divider A pattern or template to divide a plate into sections for a repetitive design. May also be used to segment a vase or urn by continuing the lines up or down the side of the vessel. Photocopy a plate divider pattern and cut out the centre, forming a collar to place around an upright vase or cylinder so that you are able

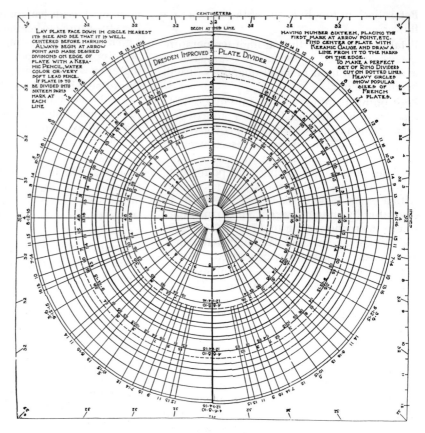

Plate divider, about one-quarter actual size

to continue the lines and segments on a vertical piece.

Plate glass Window glass which usually exceeds 10 mm (3/8") thickness and used for large areas; manufactured by the float process.

Plate quality With reference to glass: the uniformity and optical precision; originally differentiating between fine quality ground and polished plate glass and drawn sheet glass.

Plate rack Kiln furniture designed to hold plates in a vertical position during firing.

Plate stand Several different types are illustrated.

Pliqué-a-jour Enamelling technique resembling miniature stained glass windows. As in cloisonné the enamel is held in place by metal wiring or holes drilled in flat metal sheets, the difference being that there is no metal backing and light is transferred through the enamel.

Pointillism Painting with small coloured dots which vary in size, colour and density. The dots blend when viewed from a distance to give tonal and colour values.

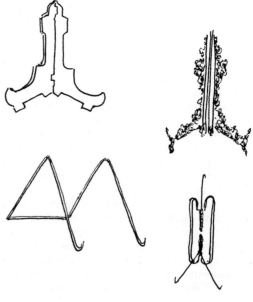

Plate stands

Polarised lenses Two identical lenses used to detect stress in glass.

Polishing **1.** Glass is polished using a rouge (usually ferric oxide or ceric oxide, both in the form of a fine powder) which is applied to a buffing pad of felt, leather or cork. **2.** Metals such as gold, silver, platinum are usually polished warm from the kiln with a commercially available burnishing sand. **3.** Glazes should be polished with a fine wet and dry sanding paper or one of the prepared commercial sanding papers to remove the dust particles which adhere to the melted glaze in the firing process.

Polishing sand Fine sand used to polish or burnish gold. Available from porcelain suppliers. Good results are obtained when work is burnished submerged in warm water. If you use it in a texture paste, it may then be painted with paint, lustre or gold, etc.

Polychromatic Multi-coloured.

Polychrome Multi-coloured.

Polyptych Painting or sculpture in more than three panels.

Pontil A solid metal rod tipped with a ring of hot glass used to remove a blown object from the blowpipe so that the final shaping may be done. The object is knocked from the ring when it is cool and solid, leaving a rough mark, the 'pontil' mark.

Pooling or puddling Glaze which has slipped to the base of the piece during firing.

Porcelain The finest and hardest kind of earthenware, made mainly of china clay (kaolin) or feldspathic clay and flint; fired or baked at a high temperature.

Porcelain carving The carving or sculpting of greenware or a clay body prior to firing. The following technique is taught by Deirdre Fewell of Sydney. The greenware is allowed to dry leatherhard and cleaned of all blemishes with the appropriate tools and finally sanded gently with a nylon stocking. The dry clay is very fragile and must be handled carefully. Sketch design lightly onto clay surface and apply Hi-Lo masking agent to protect all areas which are to remain intact. Dilute 1 tablespoon of Thick 'n Etch with 1/2 cup water and, using a damp sponge, gently wash away the surface of the areas not covered by the mask to form shallow depressions. Remove mask and using a sgraffito tool, detail edges, add additional lines and tidy up design. Some areas may be completely removed to form holes (above waterline for urns, vases, etc.). Smooth roughened surface with damp sponge or brush. Fire porcelain to 1250°C (2280°F), ceramic and terracotta to 1100°C (2010°F). The article may then be decorated with various other products. Gare have a number of pastes and glazes whiach are suitable. *See* GARE.

Porcelain colours Powdered metallic oxides and other pigments used in painting on a porcelain surface, on and in ceramic glazes and for enamelling on metal.

Porcelain enhancer A product for thickening slip; if less is used, it will vary the stabilisation of porcelain slip used for draping or slip trailing.

Porcelain with a Touch of Glass Interesting and creative mixed media courtesy of Fay Robinson of Sydney. Requirements are a good quality glass cutting knife and other tools, moulds which you will make yourself from fibreboard, fibrewool or similar, a kiln or the use of one, and glass—American bullseye, some bottle glass, soda lime glass (float glass) or any other glass which is compatible. It is a wise precaution to use the same sheet for the various sections of each project. Glass may be coloured or painted by the artist with onglaze paints or lustres which fire to 800°C (1470°F); it is also possible to use lower-fired glass paints after slumping is complete. Fay colours her glass, fires, laminates with the colour between and then slumps. A mould is made to suit the porcelain base; the glass is slumped into, onto or around it and the composites put together.

Porosity Full of pores or holes which enable an object to be more absorbent and less watertight.

Portraits The (usually realistic) painting of faces which belong to living subjects. There are commercially prepared portrait colours available, although it is possible to use normal paints with good results. It is probably better to paint with an open medium to allow for corrections. Use a drawing or photograph of your subject and make a tracing for accuracy. Acetate tracing paper is best for clear transparency and a light graphite paper and stylus are helpful for transferring the tracing if you use one. The tracing should show all the main detail lines of eyes, nose and mouth. Another invaluable tool is a compass or divider to measure the various distances, such as widths between eyes, the length of limbs, and other distances, etc. Skin tones should be smooth and rounded. To obtain a good resemblance, carefully and faithfully reproduce the shape of all shadows and highlights. Hold your clear acetate tracing above your painting to make sure your features are the correct size and in the correct place. View your painting and your study upside-down to find less obvious faults.

Posts Supports for kiln shelves; usually round columns which may be painted with kiln wash and used also as interesting shapes over which to fire and slump glass.

Potash Alkaline substance used in making glass and enhancing clays.

Potash glass Hard glass containing potassium carbonate (potash) derived from plant ash, suitable for cutting and engraving.

Potentiometric indicator Used to indicate the temperature (of the kiln) on a digital display.

Potter's plaster Used for making moulds. Mixing ratio 4 parts powder to 3 parts weight in water.

Potter's wheel Revolving wheel driven by hand, foot or electricity on which a ball of clay is centred and 'turned' to form a shape.

Pottery Decorative and utile vessels and shapes formed with clay. Most of the instructions for decoration in this book can be used for glazed pottery, stoneware, earthenware, ceramics, etc. The clays used for these vessels are usually coloured, e.g. terracotta, which influences the final colour of the piece. For dark clays it is wise to use darker or opaque colours. The original glaze is usually fired much higher than onglaze paints and you may have to experiment to find the most suitable temperature for subsequent additions of colour; however, the suggested firing times and temperatures for onglaze are usually sufficient unless the original glaze has a high flux content, in which case a lower temperature will be necessary.

Pottery and ceramic tools You may find the following tools useful, particularly if you work with unfired clay or wish to shape drying enamel. Cleanup tools, spear-tipped cleanup tool, ribbon tool. double drill, lace draper's sgraffito, duster, zigzag saw, wire loop sgraffito, stylus, double-spiral deep cleanup tool, sponge, glaze saw, sabre saw, large zigzag saw, greenware seam cleaner, palette knife, gold applicator, decal squeegee, trim knives, rung cleaner, mould scraper, mould thumper. All available from ceramic and pottery stockists. Many household or studio objects may be used as convenient tools.

Pouncing Plastic sponge or cottonwool-filled silk pad is bounced or moved up and down quickly against the painted surface to blend and soften the colours.

Pouring sprue Excess clay which gathers around the pour hole and which must be trimmed away prior to opening the mould.

Powdered glaze Heavily fluxed powder. Mix with soft pastel colour using any medium and apply to porcelain surface. Pad with silk pad. The more glaze powder mix left on the surface the higher the glaze; however, too much will 'eat' the colours applied. Fire at a lower temperature if you have this problem.

Practise To work at perfecting an ability, like piano playing. If you do not practise, you will not be able to paint well.

Preserving varnish Varnish applied as a liquid which sets on the area which is to be kept white or a previously painted colour while surrounding area is painted, dusted or grounded and which is then removed before firing. If fired it will adhere to the surface as a raised roughened texture.

Pressing 1. To shape glass by applying force to hot glass in or on a mould. **2.** To press plastic clay into a mould.

Pre-tint Wash of colour applied to the painting surface and fired before the design is painted on, to allow an even application of colour and shine and to give the surface 'tooth'.

Pricking Method of transferring a design by a series of dots which are then joined up, or by piercing the outline of a design with a needle and dusting powder through the holes onto the surface to be painted.

Primal heating Initial stage of firing process, from room temperature to strain point.

Primary colours The primary colours of pigmented paints are red, yellow and blue.

Printing Painting a shape or object such as a leaf with paint, lustre (work quickly with lustre), gold or texture paste and 'stamping' the area to be painted with this object.

Product labelling There is no standard in Australia equivalent to the voluntary American ASTM D4236, which is well recognised in the hobby industry, for Labelling Art Materials for Chronic Health Hazards. Ceramic Solutions, Victoria, use a red sticker to identify potentially hazardous material and ask that it be used strictly as directed.

Project finishes Trade name for Duncan mould accessories which are used to complete clay projects.

Prop-it Ceramic fibre used to support clay in the kiln.

Proportion Comparative relationship. Objects within your design should relate in size both to each other and to the blank. All parts of a floral design should match in size. If you are painting roses 7.5 cm (3″) in diameter, all the blooms should be approximately that size, rather than the main one 7.5 cm (3″) and the subordinate flowers 3.75 cm (1½″) because they are less important. In a landscape trees retreating into the distance should be smaller in stature, not the same size as those in the foreground. Pears, apples, oranges should be relative in size to grapes, cherries, etc.

Propylene glycol Clear colourless, non-toxic viscous liquid available from pharmacies which may be used as an open medium.

Prunt Knob of glass used as decoration on a piece, sometimes pointed or impressed with a design.

Publish To submit work to a magazine for publication. If you would like to have your work published there are a number of magazines which will accept articles, especially if you are a subscriber. I know of no porcelain art magazine that will pay you for your article, however, there are some art and craft magazines which do (*Pottery and Ceramics* for one). Your work must be original; if you are quoting an author or including an example of an artist's work you must have their authority to do so, in writing, and credit must be given to that person. If you submit something done in a seminar situation, this also should be stated. Do not send the original piece and do not discredit your efforts with inferior photography. Professional photography is expensive and sometimes an amateur produces better results with a little effort. Send transparencies as opposed to negatives unless otherwise requested, and enclose colour prints as well to help the editor select size and placement, etc. It is always advisable to send a stamped addressed envelope to ensure their return. Use black and white photography only if there is good contrast and clear precise linear work. The photographs should be clearly labelled showing which way is up, the title and your name. They should be accompanied by an explanatory text which should be concise and yet contain all relevant information; your reasons for painting that particular subject on that particular blank, how you went about it, the materials used and the temperature at which it was fired. An article which rambles on will be cut or if too terse may be overlooked.

Puff-On Suede Coloured fibres which gives the appearance of a suede lining when applied to the inner area of porcelain and ceramic (or wood, tin and plastic) boxes. Place the object you wish to coat in a large container and coat the surface evenly with an adhesive which will stay moist for 5–10 minutes. Generously 'puff' on the fibres from the container, holding it about 10 cm (4″) away from the surface. When the piece is thoroughly coated put it aside to dry for 30 minutes or so. Once dry, remove excess fibres by shaking the object; they can be returned to the container. Brushes are washed in water. The suede comes in many colours and may be used for a wide range of objects such as trinket boxes, the bases of vases and bowls, picture frames, cutlery drawers, show cases, displays, shoes, restoration of various objects and wooden boxes (but please seal any wooden surfaces before applying the fibres).

Pug mill Apparatus for mixing and blending clay.

Punty Solid steel gathering rod which is used to hold glass during the fire polishing or finishing processes.

Pure colour Colour without additives.

Pyrex Trademark of Corning Glass Works for a borosilicate glass which has a low coefficient of expansion and which resists thermal shock when subjected to a direct flame.

Pyrometer Instrument to measure the temperature inside the kiln during firing. Composed of three parts: a thermocouple, a temperature indicator (either a galvanometric or potentiometric indicator) and a connecting lead wire.

Pyrometric cones Clay pyramids used to show the temperature in a kiln. *See* diagram of Orton cones on page 61.

Pyrophyllite Hydrous aluminium silicate, used for developing special porcelain and refractory bodies.

Q

Quadrant system Dividing the blank into four sections to plan design; very useful to help identify faults in a design.

Quartz Mineral consisting of silicon dioxide, used as an alternative to flint.

Quartz inversion The rearrangement and changes in volume of quartz crystals when the temperature of a clay body containing silica is raised to 565°C (1050°F). This expansion on heating is reversible on cooling.

Queen's ware Cream earthenware made by Wedgwood for Queen Charlotte.

Quill Pen or brush resembling the quill of a feather. Originally a real feather was used.

R

Radiant heat Heat which is emitted from a glowing source, such as a red hot kiln element. Radiant heat from a red or white hot kiln can inflict severe burns or damage to the corneas of your eyes. Wear goggles if you are raking or otherwise working with glass.

Radmaker's Relief Clay Low-fired clay (720°C, 1330°F) which can be fired several times. May be formed into simple shapes, used as high or low relief or as a binder for glass. Mix and knead with palette knife and water until it stays together in a pile. Glycerine will prevent drying out.

Rails Walls that form the shape of a case mould.

Rapid cool Third stage of a fusing cycle for glass when the temperature is dropped rapidly from the highest point to reach an ideal annealing temperature.

Rapid heat Second stage of glass firing and fusing when the temperature is raised from strain point to the desired fusing level.

Raised enamels Enamel applied to form a relief design. *See* ENAMEL.

Raised paste Paste applied to glazed surfaces in relief as a base for Roman Gold. May be purchased as powder or pre-mixed paste, in white and yellow. The white paste fires with a satin finish, the yellow fires semi-matt. Colour may be added to the white paste (but not to the yellow) and it may be painted after firing. White raised paste is suitable for Liquid Bright Gold, Platinum or Bronze. Yellow raised paste will take these metallics plus Burnishing Matt and Roman Gold. The powdered paste may be mixed with medium for raised paste and turpentine, painting medium, water-based mediums, fat oil and turpentine, and copaiba. Experiment with other liquids for different effects. Do not use grounding oils, glycerine or mineral-based open mediums as these may cause the yellow paste to flatten and crack (unless you are after a unique effect). Oil of tar may be added to give body to the paste and help it to string. Pastes are porous after firing and care should be taken to keep them clean to prevent contamination of the gold when it is applied.

To mix: Place a quantity of paste onto a ground glass slab and divide into 8 even sections. Add 1/8 (the same amount as one of the portions of paste) tin oxide and just enough copaiba medium to hold the mixture together, plus a drop of fat oil. Using a glass muller or bone knife, mix with alcohol and grind the powder until quite dry. Use enough oil or raised paste medium to bind it and add a little oil of tar. The mixed paste should be crumbly, not thin. Moisten with turpentine, heat gently, breathing warm air on it, and continue to stir, testing the stringing ability after five or ten minutes. If it does not string add a little more oil of tar until it does. Paste for dots needs rather less oil of tar. Fire at 780–820°C (1435–1510°F) normally; however, fire only as high as necessary to mature gold or colour if successive firings are required. Damp or rainy weather is not conducive to good results with raised paste as the moisture in the air affects the properties of the paste.

Raw glaze Unfritted glaze.

Rebound To return heat to the kiln from heat stored in the kiln brick, insulation or shelf after the rapid cool stage.

Receding colours Blue and blue green will make your design appear to recede.

Recession Fading or diminishing background such as receding mountain ranges in a landscape.

Red Coats Trade name for true red, orange and yellow opaque glazes.

Red Stroke Trade name of translucent underglazes.

Red Stroke Clear Glaze Trade name for specific glaze to be used over Red Stroke translucent underglazes.

Reduction glaze A glaze which will develop and mature its colour in a reducing or oxygen depleted atmosphere.

Reflected light The light bounced back onto one object from another.

Refractories Materials such as alumina, silica, zirconia, which do not change chemically at high temperatures. Refractory bricks or lining are used in kiln walls, and refractory material for kiln furniture.

Refractory Able to resist high temperature. A heat resistant substance that raises the melting temperature of a glaze eg flint, quartz, tin oxide, titania, chrome, zirconia and antimony.

Register The exact alignment of a design for successive prints using the screen printing method. As each application of colour requires a separate screen block, it is important that the paper remains or is replaced in the same position aided by register guides.

Relief Method of moulding, carving or stamping in which design stands out from plane or curved surface. Low or high relief.

Relief white Powder which is mixed with medium and fires in opaque relief. Some relief whites are porous, others not as porous, depending on the brand. The higher the fire the more glossy the result. Like most relief pastes it does not like repeated firings.

Renaissance Revival of art and intellectual pursuits originating in Italy during the fourteenth century and spreading throughout Europe through the sixteenth century.

Repel To remove and move wet paint around. Water dropped onto a freshly painted surface will 'repel' the paint in that area, as will turpentine, methylated spirits, acetone, vinegar, lemon juice and other solutions. Experiment for interesting results. Try it on a piece you are not happy before you wipe off an unsatisfactory painting.

Repetition Element of design where a motif, colour, etc. is repeated more than once. Repetition of a colour or shape will add to the rhythm and balance of the painting.

Representational art Drawn or painted subjects are recognisable.

Resist Used to cover a portion of the painting surface to protect it from the other techniques used to decorate the piece, e.g. grounding, lustre. There are several substances with different properties available. *See* Product Information, page 106, to find one to suit your needs.

Resizing a design A photocopier with adjustable positions is the easiest method; a pantograph may be used or a grid of squares.

Retreating colours Cool colours, i.e. the blues and violets, which appear to recede.

Reusche glass paints and stains Wide range of vitreous paints and stains which are a mixture of ground glass and a pigment oxide for colour, with a firing range between 565–675°C (1050–1250°F). The powder paints are mixed with water and gum arabic or other medium prior to firing.
Glass stainer colours: 648–676°C (1200–1250°F)
Transparent colours: 565–582°C (1050–1080°F)
Gold base transparent: 565–582°C (1050–1080°F)
Opaque range: 648–676°C (1200–1250°F)
Silver stains: 565–582°C (1050–1080°F)

Reward Manufacturer of hobby ceramic products. Also the satisfaction you have when a piece is successful.

Rhythm Pleasing design with sense of balance and movement.

Rib Tool of wood or fired clay used to press or scrape clay or plaster.

Ribbon tool Wooden-handled, double-ended ceramic tool designed for cutting into leatherhard greenware. One end is a flattened hollow scoop and the other is curved.

Rolled glass Sheet glass formed between two rollers or one roller and a cast iron table.

Rolling consistency Required viscosity of glazes which are rolled around the interior of a pot. Milk consistency for 2-coat glazes, light cream for 3-coat glazes and thick cream for 4-coat glazes.

Rolling glaze Act of coating the internal area of the object. The glaze is rolled around inside the piece and the excess is then poured off.

Roman Gold A burnishing gold paste with a higher concentration of gold than the liquid golds. May be fluxed for use on an unpainted surface or unfluxed for use on a painted surface.

Romanesque Italian style characterised by

sweeping arches and heavy ornamentation.

Rookwood technique The original Rookwood technique was an underglaze design. Today it refers to a highly glazed surface with the design deeply embedded and coloured with overtones of one colour. Briefly, the design is sketched on and painted in a monochrome with stronger contrasts and heavier accents than normal but with care taken to see that there are no build-ups of paint. This is fired and future firings consist of various methods of applying layers of one or two colours over the monochrome painting. Washes of colour and dusting are the most common with yellow and red being the most popular combination.

Rouging As blushing. **1.** A small amount of colour is picked up on the fingertip and rubbed into the design to tint it or give it colour. Dampen the fingertip first with medium. **2.** To apply a glaze with a cloth over a fired base coat.

Rouge The reddish colour of ferrous or ferric oxide gives its name to this powder which is used to polish glass or metal.

Roughing **1.** To make a surface coarse in preparation for the acceptance of another material, e.g. a roughened porcelain glaze will more readily accept texture pastes or glues. **2.** The first phase of grinding glass.

Roulette Wheel with a pattern which is rolled against plastic clay to impress the pattern into the clay.

Ruby colours Very high in gold content and therefore very expensive.

Rung cleaner Synthetic rubber tool designed to clean the rungs and rods of a pouring table.

Running The fluid quality of a glaze at maturity prior to cooling and hardening.

Rustiban *(Caution)* Weak solution of hydrochloric acid (which must be used with great caution) which will remove fired paint from a glazed surface. It is a commercial preparation available from pharmacies and normally used to remove rust stains from clothing. If only a small area of the design is to be removed, resist the surrounding area with masking lacquer, lustre resist, or even nail polish and, using rubber gloves, paint the area with the solution on a cotton bud. Allow it to penetrate the glaze and the colour will gradually be removed. Wash off thoroughly when colour is completely stripped. The area will be etched because the glaze has been removed. A wash of clear or white paint or a coat of Crystal Glaze will help to bring back some of the gloss. If the whole object is to be treated, place in a plastic container of water, add Rustiban (the amount will depend on the size of container and how rapidly the colour is to be removed—half of the Rustiban container to an 18-litre/4-gallon bucket would be a rough measure) and leave immersed in the solution for a week or so. Several pieces may be immersed at once. If you want to treat a tall narrow object, the extra space in the bucket may be taken up with a lidded plastic container full of water or a brick to prevent waste. *Caution:* Wear *protective clothing and gloves* whenever you work with acid. If acid splashes onto skin wash immediately with soap and a soda solution as the resultant burn could be very severe. Seek medical attention if this is the case.

Take care not to let the Rustiban or any other acid touch your stainless steel sink. It will be permanently marked and scarred by the acid.

Rutile Rutile sand/form of titanium dioxide. Common ore containing titanium, iron oxide, chrome oxide and silica used in glazes. Usually reddish brown in colour. In glazes it will produce a range of browns and in a reduction fire will give blue grey. In high lead rutile glazes it usually constitutes approximately 10-15% of the glaze contents. Copper glazes containing rutile may show interesting mottled effects and in high zinc glazes an orange tan colour. Rutile may matt the surface in lead glazes. Similar in behaviour to titanium dioxide. Rutile sand is sometimes used to obtain a speckle effect in bodies.

S

Sabatella Commercially prepared medium used for grinding and painting. Very open and has to be used very sparingly otherwise colours will run and separate.

Saddle Kiln support for firing objects.

Safety precautions The various methods, paints and mediums we use contain many risks and highly undesirable components; the acids for etching and cleaning can burn and blind us, the powders we inhale can cause lung disease, the paints can poison us, glass can cut us, the kiln can burn us—the list is long. Please take sensible precautions for all the methods and products described. Do not eat while painting nor put your brushes and other tools in your mouth; wear a mask when dusting, grounding or decanting powder; wear gloves when using Rustiban or handling glass; wear absolutely everything—goggles, ventilation mask, rubber gloves, rubber boots and rubber apron—when acid etching, and work outside. Have nearby plenty of readily available water and some bicarbonate of soda in case of accidents. Put lids back on containers as soon as possible. Set the kitchen timer if you do not have an automatic cutout on your kiln; make sure nothing is placed on top of the kiln or can fall onto it; do not open the door at high temperatures unless absolutely necessary (for working with molten glass, perhaps) and you are suitably attired with goggles and gloves. Do not pick up the red-hot poker with which you have just stirred the glass. Personal hygiene should include thorough scrubbing of hands and fingernails when finished work, food, drink and tobacco should not be brought into the work area, and protective clothing should be worn: and stay in the work area. Children should not be allowed to enter into a workroom unless supervised by a responsible adult. *Commonsense and complete awareness of what you are doing is essential at all times.*

Safety timer A device to turn off the power to a kiln should the normal mechanism fail.

Sagger Fireclay case used to protect porcelain and other objects in a kiln from flames and fumes.

Sagging When glass is not supported it will sag, sink or bend when it is heated. The more common name for this is 'slumping'.

Salt glaze A glaze formed by the introduction of raw salt to the kiln at 1260° (2300°F). The vapour combines with the clay's silica to form the glaze, which is semi-gloss and has a slightly pitted appearance.

Sand Sand is composed of minute particles of eroded mainly siliceous rocks and thus is suitable to be fired in the kiln. Naturally coloured sands will adhere to the porcelain when applied with a mix of flux and medium. Fired quite high, this mix may be used to create scenes, designs, etc. Neutral sand may be painted once it is fired onto the glazed surface, or powdered paint may be mixed with the flux and sand and applied as a coloured texture. If the sand is not in direct contact with the glaze it will brush off after firing, as will any surplus sand. Naturally black, grey and other coloured sands lose their colour when fired.

Sand-blasting The removal of the surface glaze with sand or grit forced from an airblaster. Various grades of grit are used and the pressure is approximately 40 lbs (psi) of dry air. It should be used in a well ventilated area and a mask should be worn to prevent inhalation of the dust particles. Draw the design onto the glazed surface and colour in the part to be etched with a spirit-based felt pen. The sandblaster is held about 2.5 cm (1″) away from the surface and moved across the coloured-in area. Once all the colour is removed the piece is thoroughly cleaned, dried and painted with lustres or gold, etc. The airblaster may also be used to apply solutions, using less pressure.

Sang-de-boeuf This term of French origin describes a vivid red Chinese glaze derived from copper oxides. *Sang-de-boeuf:* ox blood.

Satsuma A soft crackled Japanese ware.

Scale Drawing or painting to scale is important. The relative size of objects such as fruit, e.g. pears and strawberries, violets and daisies, eyes in a face, all indicate correct proportions.

Schema A simple plan used as a guide for a more complicated design, e.g. geometrical shapes such as circles, triangles and rectangles used to illustrate the human form, squares and rectangles to illustrate a group of buildings.

Schira diluent Thinners used by Georges Miserez Schira for painting European style.

Schira medium Medium used for one-fire European style painting.

Schizzo Italian word for the preliminary sketches used to compose a design.

Scioto Manufacturer of hobby ceramic products.

Score To deface or abrade a surface lightly in order to blend a seam, repair a patch or to adhere another substance.

Screen printing medium Must be oil-based for use with waterslide paper. There are many from which to choose.

Scroller A fine long-haired brush which comes to a point.

Scroller

Scrolling Design made up of comma shapes in enamel or pastes or may also be penned in gold, silver, lustres or paint.

Scrolls Decoration consisting of comma shapes in either pen work or relief paste. Push a pen nib stylus or brush tip into a mound of mixed paste and lift in an upward motion. Poise the nib or brush above the surface so that the paste barely comes in contact with the porcelain. Draw the shape towards you and the paste will pull out in a tapering comma shape in the direction of the followthrough. Lift the brush or nib away from the surface to end the movement.

Scrubbing To apply a priming coat of an opaque underglaze.

S curve Pleasing line of design in the shape of an S. May be reversed.

Seam Build-up of clay where mould pieces join.

Secondary colours Made from equal amounts of two primary colours, i.e. equal parts of red and yellow will produce orange, equal parts of yellow and blue will produce green and equal parts of red and blue will produce purple.

Seed A very small gaseous inclusion in some glass. 'Seedy' glass has a visual texture caused by the presence of many bubbles. During fusing these bubbles may rise to the surface, causing blisters.

Seepage The gradual penetration of a solution through a porous body.

Selenium Metallic element (black in powder form) which is used in low-fired red, orange and amber colours. Frequently used in conjunction with cadmium, this is a FUGITIVE COLOUR and will change with heat. Selenium on its own creates a light rose colour in soda lime glass.

Self-hardening clay A combination of synthetic resin and inert pigments that will dry hard in a household oven and have the appearance of fired clay. Fimo is an example.

Seminar A short one, two or three day course in a certain subject. Attend as many as you are able. You will always learn something, even if only what not to do. Seminars are not always easy to arrange and much time is spent in preparation by the instructors, who disrupt their own schedule to give the workshop. Some thought should be given to this by people who thoughtlessly cancel late or do not turn up.

Semi-porcelain Ironstone like earthenware.

Sepal Leaf-like division of calyx of flower. See diagram on page 22.

Separator Another term used for shelf primer or kiln wash.

Sèvres Originally soft then hard paste porcelain from the town of Sèvres in France.

Sfumato The blending of outlines to give a soft atmospheric or smokey effect.

Sgraffito Design which has been scratched out of paint, slip, glaze or the top layer of a substance exposing the usually different colours of the layer or layers beneath.

Shade Colour to which black or some other colour has been added. Absence of bright light.

Shadow Area shielded or furthermost from light source. Looks good when painted with greyed colour of the subject, e.g. a red object will cast a shadow with a red reflection.

Shadow area Area not in path of light source.

Shadow leaves The cast shadow of leaves, flowers or other objects not necessarily in the design.

Shape One of the elements of design which is important to the final outcome of the painting. *See* ART FUNDAMENTALS.

Shaping up technique Outlining a form with brushstrokes to give it shape and body.

Shard Fragment of fired clay or glass.

Shears Tool used to trim a glass object in the process of its making.

Shelf primer (kiln wash) A mixture of hydrated alumina and china clay, binders and suspension agents which is used to protect and prevent glazes and glass adhering to kiln furniture and shelves. Follow the manufacturer's instructions but the usual practice is to paint the shelves with three or four coats which will last a number of firings, after which the primer should be sanded off and reapplied. To use in powder form, make a sprinkler from a glass jar covered with a double layer of nylon stocking.

Alternative uses: **1.** The powder may be mixed to a stiff paste and used to 'write' or create designs onto a primed shelf over which glass may be slumped. **2.** Alternatively, the powder may be sprinkled thickly onto a primed shelf or into a mould, which will give the slumped glass a roughened or textured appearance. **3.** Shapes may be pressed into the powder or placed on top of the powder and the slumped glass will take on these indentations or raised motifs. Imagination!

Shivering Glaze will crawl away from clay body as it shrinks if the two are not compatible.

Slumped glass used to add another dimension to a variety of porcelain shapes which are fused together to form quizzical, perhaps extra-terrestrial, shapes and figures (Fay Robinson)

A round sheet of glass which has been painted and then slumped over a cylindrical mould (Val Blake)

This interesting piece is made up of seven individual pieces of glass slumped together and coloured with oxides such as cobalt and copper (Val Blake)

Statement—Margaret Ramsey
*My work explores a fusion of
traditional and modern myths with
personal beliefs, symbolising the
invisible ties and restraints that
cultural and traditional beliefs,
practices and superstitions, can exert
on successive generations. The work
is what it is because of the lived
experience behind the image, rather
than of trying to be the image of the
experience and spring from everyday
life in suburbia. In this work, titled
'Dollar Bound Oracle', the multi-
functional properties unique to glass,
the appearance of being there and not
being there, where one can look at it,
through it and beyond, can appear at
one time as visible and invisible
barriers, just as traditional and
cultural beliefs can restrain or allow
freedom of thought and action. The
use of enamel with glass in varied
techniques produces design and
colour of vast opportunity. Screen
printing enamel fused between layers
of glass produces a repetitive motif
essential to the concept, with ease and
strong effect in this work.
My work originates in an emotional
response to the invisible presence
capable of unseen manipulation to
which we willingly comply. The glass
box—the grid formation of the walls
represent the invisible presence,
which in turn imprisons desire and
the free spirit within us all. The
repetitive pattern of the grid parallels
the ongoing desire of mankind to
provide and consume. The spaces of
the grid suggest possible escape.*

'Golden Traditions—Day Dreams VI' In this
1997 series, the glass is used as a canvas and a
more traditional technique of painting is employed.
The enamel is applied and manipulated to produce
the various effects desired, allowing the unique
properties of glass to enhance the overall
appearance. Gold fired onto the enamel-painted
glass carries with it its own history, traditions and
beliefs, which reflect in the reading of the piece.
The motifs are symbols of the hopes and dreams
generations of women have woven into their lives,
according to their beliefs and commonsense views
of myth, folklore, rites, ritual, religion and
tradition

Shrink calculator A table of values which allows for compensation for shrinkage and for accuracy in throwing or casting an object of a specific size.

Shrinkage Diminution of fired ware due to the moisture content being evaporated and the clay particles moving closer together during drying and firing. It is possible for a piece to diminish more than one-third in size. This shrinkage is usually described by percentage.

Siccative A medium to promote the drying of oils used on underglaze and overglaze colours.

Side load Load the brush with a circular motion into the paint, until the paint is spread across two-thirds the width of the brush.

Silica (silicon dioxide) Hard white or transparent mineral present in precious and semi-precious stones, quartz and sand. When heated it forms a glass-like material. It is usually combined with other agents such as a flux to lower a melting point which exceeds 1700°C (3090°F).

Silicon carbide (carborundum) Crystalline compound of carbon and silicon, second in hardness to diamond. **1.** Used as an abrasive in powder form or in blocks for polishing and rough grinding. **2.** Also used as a refractory lining for kilns and kiln shelves and furniture. **3.** An addition of 2% of fine silicon carbide will produce reduced copper glazes in an electric kiln and in the area immediately surrounding the silicon carbide particles in a leadless base glaze. Tin will aid colour development. Large quantities of silicon carbide may cause blistering or craters in the glaze.

Silk screening A technique to apply a stencil or design to a given surface. A frame of stretched silk is coated with an impermeable substance with the area of design resisted. The resist is removed once the coating is dry and colour is forced through the unprotected silk onto a paper, fabric or other surface. Alternatively, the surface of the paper or vessel may be resisted with a design or stencil and colour screened through a plain silk screen. Once dry, the stencil or resist is removed and you are left with the paint surrounding your negative space. Decals may be made by screen printing, with the design being photographed (in half-tone) and developed onto the coated silk with the aid of ultra-violet light. The design is then applied to waterslide paper and once dried a gelatinous coating is screened over the design. There are many variables to these techniques and it is not advisable to practice them commercially within the confines of the family home. Atmospheric conditions play an important role as the paper will stretch in humid conditions. Dust is also a problem.

Silk sponge Sponge covered in short hairs which has many uses.

Simili incrustation The decoration of edges with matt firing colours or gold base coats.

Simple syrup For penwork. Mix 1 part icing sugar, 1 part water and 2 parts powdered paint to an ink consistency. Use with mapping pen. An even simpler syrup is made by mixing your paints with a sugar-based soft drink such as cola or lemonade, etc. Do not use artificially sweetened liquid; they don't work because they don't contain sugar. Do not apply this syrup thickly as it will chip off. May also be used for monochrome painting.

Single strength glass Clear window glass, 4 or 5 mm thick.

Sinter To fire to the point where cohesion takes place.

Slab pottery Objects made from clay rolled into slabs.

Slaking The period of time allowed for plaster to mix with water.

Slip Clay with a high water content and creamy consistency used for making, cementing, decorating clay-bodied wares. Objects such as leaves, fabric or other shapes may be painted with slip, allowed to dry and fired. These shapes may then be painted as bisque or coated with enamel and fired, then painted with onglaze colours.

Slip casting Slip or liquid clay is poured into a plaster mould which leaches water from the clay so that it is then deposited onto the walls of the mould. Excess slip is poured off.

Slip thinner Used to acquire the desired consistency of porcelain slip.

Slip trailer Firm rubber or plastic bulb normally used for clay slip which may also be used to distribute thinned paint or lustres.

Slumping A verb, to slump. What one does in a chair after a hard day creating? Not in this case. When glass is heated beyond its melting point the molecules begin to shift; if heat is maintained the glass will take the shape of the surface or mould upon which it sits. There are tests which should be done to determine the proper annealing range of specific glasses if this information is not available. Slumping differs from sagging in that the cross-section of a slumped piece does not change noticeably.

Soaking Maintaining the temperature of a kiln for a period of time to allow the heat to fully penetrate the pieces being fired.

Soda glass Glass in which the alkali is sodium carbonate instead of potassium carbonate.

Sodium carbonate Sodium in glazes which creates brilliant colour reactions. More commonly used in preparation of frits because of its high solubility. Sometimes used as a casting slip deflocculent.

Sodium silicate (water glass) White powder or a liquid of varying viscosity used as a binder in making refractory moulds, as a low temperature flux and as a deflocculent.

Soft brick A porous refractory brick which can be carved with a file or knife or sanded into a shape. If coated with kiln wash it may be used as a mould. Used in insulating kilns.

Soft paste porcelain Simulated porcelain fired at a low temperature. Often glazed with tin.

Soft soap Potash soap supplied as a gel and used in the production of plaster moulds. Mix with equal quantity of warm water and store for use as a parting medium for plaster mould making. Paint onto the surface of a mould and wipe away excess with a damp sponge.

Soft ware Porcelain clay to which flux has been added.

Solvent Solution used to dissolve a substance. Turpentine, dipentene, pine oil, methylated spirits and acetone are common examples.

Smoking 1. Discolouration of glazes due to underfiring. **2.** Could be bad for your health if practised while painting and glazing.

Spalling The disintegration of ceramic ware when exposed to sudden temperature change.

Spanish colour (Spanish oil) Underglaze colour reminiscent of Lladro with traditional soft blues, greys and beige as well as soft greens, yellows, lilac, mauve and pink. The natural colour of the underglaze is not the same as the matured colour. The 'oils' are painted onto porcelain greenware and are absorbed by the clay body. Firing temperature is 1250°C (2280°F) and the piece may be left bisque or glazed with a crystal clear glaze. Spanish oils are best kept in the refrigerator and removed shortly before use. Use a non-absorbent plastic stirrer to agitate

rose, candy pink and violet oils. Apply three coats of these colours, drying between each. Wash your brush in warm water between colours. Once applied to the clay surface Spanish oils cannot be removed.

Spare Excess clay formed around the pour hole which must be trimmed away before opening the mould.

Spattering To apply small flecks of colour, usually with a (tooth) brush or by flicking a paint brush.

Specific gravity Found by dividing the weight of a volume of a material by the weight of an equal volume of water.

Spectrum glass Extensive range of coloured and textured glass.

Spike oil of lavender A volatile solvent used as a thinner for oil and ceramic paints. Has a similar use to turpentine but becomes more viscous and evaporates more slowly.

Spit out Air or gas bubbles occasionally blister or cause small ruptures or defects in a glaze.

Split-complementary Colour combination made up of a key colour and two colours adjacent to its complementary colour.

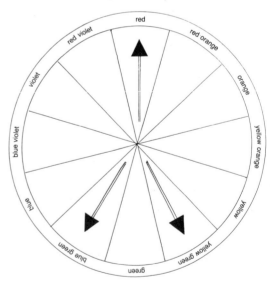

Split complementary colour wheel

Spodumene Active flux used in small quantities in glazes, particularly where low expansion glazes are required.

Sponge There are any number of uses for a sponge and many varieties available. Fine makeup sponges are ideal for very fine padding but take care not to lift off too much paint or lustre. Plastic sponge is available with a fine or coarse texture and may be used for making marks, sponging, padding, applying paint and lustres, etc. The coarser sponge is ideal for visual texture. Sea sponges have similar uses and it is possible to obtain a sponge on a long wooden handle for more difficult areas and the inner parts of your piece. Gilberton Gallery, Adelaide, has an extremely useful sponge brush and hardware or electrical stores have alligator clips which are great for gripping the sponge pieces while you work. (If you cover your sponge or sponge brush with cling plastic and then with fine athletic support bandage, you will protect the sponge and save wastage of the paint or lustre you are using).

Sponging To use a sponge instead of a brush to achieve the effects you require.

Sponge work Application of colour with the aid of a sponge. Sometimes referred to as 'wet grounding'. The mixed paint is thinned slightly with turpentine and applied by padding the colour onto the object to be painted with plastic sponge. The application should not be too heavy or it will chip off. It is better to apply several coats, firing between each for a rich, even colour. Suitable for borders, areas of solid colour, stencil motifs or for 'wiping out' a design from the applied colour. A solid colour may be fired onto an object and a second coat of another colour lightly applied with a sponge, leaving only the imprint of the sponge texture.

Sports bandage (athletic support bandage) Available from pharmacies and useful as an inexpensive alternative to silk for padding. I find it makes good animal fur when gently pulled through the freshly applied paint and good visual texture when used in 'print' mode.

Sprigg Clay relief cast in a mould, removed and applied to the surface of greenware.

Sprigg mould Moulds used for surface decorations.

Spun glass burnisher Burnishing brush which consists of fibres of spun glass; used for burnishing gold.

Square shader Brush which varies in width from 1 millimetre to 5 centimetres. The bristles also vary in length and are long and straight.

Squeegee oil Fluid composed of pine oil and solvent in varying viscosities, used for silk screening and frit application in fused glass work.

Stagger To separate successive applications of glazes by millimetres to prevent them flowing together.

Stain A prepared and fritted colouring agent for slips, glazes, overglazes, etc.

Stemmed glasses If firing stemmed glasses (wine, champagne) fire them upside down in order to distribute the weight more evenly and prevent the stems from bending or sagging.

Stamen Male fertilising organ of flowering plants, with anther containing pollen supported on a slender footstalk. *See* diagram under ANTHER.

Stamp A shape may be used as a stamp to print colour onto the painting surface by sponging a coat of colour onto a small area on your tile, pressing the shape into the paint, and stamping with it. Another method is to use a grounding oil or thick quick drying medium as a stamp pad, pressing the stamp into it and then onto the china; wait for several minutes until touch dry but still a little tacky and dust with the desired colour. Brush off excess dust and fire.

Stamping gold Bright gold used for stamping a design on china. Available as a paste or in liquid form which must evaporate a little prior to use. Liquid Bright Gold may be used if allowed to thicken for a few minutes by exposing to air. The paste is spread thinly on a glass slab, stamped with a rubber stamp and transferred to the porcelain. The liquid is used in the same way. The stamp is usually of embossed rubber.

Stencil motifs A simple shape is sketched onto card or thick paper and cut out. You will now have a positive shape and a negative shape (the card which has a hole in it the shape of the object you have drawn). Place the card with the cut out hole onto the porcelain and colour the exposed area by painting, pouncing with a sponge dipped in mixed paint or airbrushing. Alternatively, place the cut out shape on the porcelain and paint, sponge or airbrush colour around it. The motif may be repeated as often as desired to form the design. Combine the two for interesting effects. Frisk film, self-adhesive labels, mesh tape, in fact, any fabric or paper

Square shader

with an adherent on the back, may be used for most stencilling.

Still life Painting of a subject that once had life.

Stilts Kiln supports for glazed objects during firing.

Stilts

Stippling A 'broken' look achieved by tapping a wet painting with a flat deersfoot or similar brush (e.g. to simulate the appearance of distant leaves on trees and shrubbery or the fur of an animal) or by tapping a glass surface with a pointed tool to produce a pattern with small dots.

Stone With reference to glass, an imperfection which may be a piece of furnace brick or crystalline contaminations in the glass.

Stoneware Hard, dense, opaque pottery made from siliceous clay or a mixture of clay, flint and sand.

Stone Washed Glazes Trade name for glazes which have the appearance of stoneware. They are non-toxic and safe for eating utensils.

Strain The change in dimension or deformation of glass due to stress.

Strain point The temperature at which the internal stresses in the glass are reduced to low values in four hours. At this point the glass is substantially rigid. The data for determining the strain point are compiled using the same procedures used for determining the annealing point but for a slower rate of fibre elongation.

Strasbourg European design in the style created in the factories of the city of Strasbourg.

Strength of glass The ability of glass to resist damage from external causes. Glass may be exposed to heat or chemical treatment to increase strength.

Stress The result of placing too great a strain onto glaze or glass. Compressive stress is caused by contraction and tensile stress by stretching or expansion.

Stressometer A small polarimeter distributed by the US company The Fusing Ranch. It is composed of a light source with one diffusing lens and two polarised lenses which will give a visual indication of the amount of stress existing in two glasses which have been fused together.

Stria 1. A low intensity corded glass, commonly referring to antique glass. **2.** Linear markings. **3.** The raised ribs between grooves in fluted glass.

Striking Refers to reheating the glass after cooling to develop colour or opacity when the glass contains colloidal particles. Reheating above 595°C (1100°F) will increase the size of very small particles in the glass matrix or cause them to migrate together.

String Not in this case a piece of twine. It is a verb meaning to cause the enamel or paste to elongate or 'draw out'. The enamel or paste which is being carried on the stylus is touched to the porcelain surface and as the stylus is lifted the paste will stay in contact with the porcelain and be pulled along by the stylus in the desired direction. If it strings well the shapes will be long and well formed without lumps, without air bubbles and without breaking.

Stringer Very thin glass thread used for fine detail work and tests on glass. It is made by dipping a punty in molten glass and swinging it rapidly from side to side or by stretching flat glass with the aid of a torch and pliers. Stringers are finer than glass rods.

Stringer glass Hand-cast sheets of glass containing stringers to refract light and give a lineal appearance.

Strom clear Russian glass Transparent coloured glass with no texture.

Strontium carbonate Suitable for glazes for low temperature vitreous bodies; glazes containing viscous zirconium can be smoothed with the addition of strontia. Glaze fit, glaze hardness and scratch resistance are improved with the addition of strontia.

Study 1. Design used as a guide or pattern. **2.** What you should do with every subject you want to paint.

Style The techniques used in a particular method of painting or the characteristic painting traits of an individual.

Stylised flowers As in European style painting. Not photo realistic.

Stylus In our case a pointed tool used for tracing, paste work, drawing in unfired paint and placing pieces of glass or decoration in position.

Subject The feature of your painting. Study and know it well. Look at as many photographs, drawings and interpretations of the real thing as possible—and the object itself if convenient. Know its anatomy, habits, colours, varieties, anything at all of interest to give your own rendering realism and life. Even an abstract painting caricatures realism.

Substrate A technical term which refers to the base article or surface.

Sugar painting Mix 4 parts powder paint to 1 part icing sugar with a little water to ink consistency. It dries quickly so you will have to keep adding water. Work rapidly and apply your design either in a paint-in method or apply paint for a wipe-out design. With the paint-in method make every brushstroke exactly where you want it as you can't eliminate brushstrokes or blend as easily with this method as painting with oil. With the wipe-out method remove the colour from your brush with water and lift the paint from the areas of the design with the water-moistened brush. The piece may be fired or with care a second layer of paint may be applied for depth and details such as stamens on flowers, veins on leaves. (A second coat or detail may be applied with an oil-based medium prior to firing.) Take care not to apply the paint too thickly otherwise it will chip off. Wash brushes well but because they may retain grains of paint and sugar they should not be used for normal painting techniques.

Sulphide With reference to glass. Medallion or cameo of opaque glass encased in transparent glass as for a paperweight.

Super-realism Lifelike or photographic realism in a painting, including minute details.

Surrealism Movement in art purporting to express the subconscious activities of the mind and usually resulting in grotesque and imaginative symbolism.

Suspension Non-colloidal dispersion of solid particles in a liquid.

Suspension agent Chemical added to a solution to keep particles from separating.

Synthetic brushes Comparatively inexpensive brushes which are ideally suited to painting on roughened or textured surfaces and for uses to which you would not want to put your good sable brushes, such as applying resist.

Swischengoldglas Gold between glass.

T

Tacky Slightly sticky to touch—the surface required for applying dry powder paint for grounding, or even drier for dusting.

Talc French chalk (magnesium silicate). Used as flux in low-fired bodies and as a secondary flux in both high and low fired glazes. In large quantities it produces a typical opaque matt surface and interesting colour variations with cobalt and manganese.

Talent The ability or aptitude to execute (in our case) an art form easily. Very few people are natural artists and those who are credited with having talent usually work hard to develop it. We mere mortals need a great deal of assistance, practice and patience.

Tapes Adhesive design tapes used for detailing cars and other decorative surfaces are ideal for obtaining straight lines, masking out parallel spaces, borders and other areas which require definite division of colour. Available at hardware, car accessory and department stores.

Tar, oil of An oil used as a medium. It can also be added to raised paste to assist in its application.

Teacher A teacher has to know more than the student and to be able to execute it better. A *good* teacher is something else again. Teachers should have a knowledge of art, colour, materials used, and be versatile in their abilities, not only as painters but also in being able to impart and share the skills and knowledge they have acquired. They have also to be amateur psychologists. With regard to porcelain, most states in Australia have an association which is a stepping stone towards teaching. Aspiring artists are advised to join one of these groups to increase their own ability and to learn of some of the problems that go with teaching and how others have handled them. New South Wales has TIPA; in Victoria, aspiring teachers join APAT as Associate Teachers for one year and must then submit work for assessment. South Australia has a Teachers' Association to which artists apply and Western Australian TAFE Colleges include onglaze painting in their Diploma of Art and Design courses. There are prerequisites for joining all these associations or courses. There is also APAT (Australasian Porcelain Art Teachers), an association for teachers to meet and discuss methods, different techniques, hold workshops and once every two years, organise a major exhibition to which many international artists come to share their knowledge, demonstrate and give seminars. In the alternate year each state has its own prestigious exhibition. This Association is recognised internationally. To become a member, a porcelain artist must have taught continuously, with at least five pupils, for two years, be proposed by two existing members and, depending on the various state rules, pass an assessment. Other international organisations such as International Porcelain Art Teachers and World Porcelain Artists are available for teachers and each has its own merits. For pottery and ceramic artists there are an enormous number of associations such as the Ceramic Art Association which will provide you with the names of trained teachers. Duncan and Gare both have teacher training programmes. It is advisable for students to look for an accredited teacher if they have the opportunity and hopefully they will find one who is not only convenient but also a kindred soul. (Some teachers and students are truly star crossed!)

Teaching techniques There are as many way to teach as there are teachers. Some have a set project for the term, others, like Kit Ferry, of Ferry Ceramics, Sydney, prefer all students to have different projects so that each can develop at his or her own pace without the feeling of competition. Some demonstrate and encourage the students to do exactly as they do, others prefer students to develop their own traits and styles. (It is a good thing to remember that just as a signature is almost impossible to copy, so is an individual painting manner, so do not expect to be able to copy someone else's style without the same amount of practice you would need to forge a signature.)

Temperature conversion To convert to °F multiply by 1.8 and add 32; or multiply by 9, divide by 5 and add 32. To convert °F to °C multiply by 0.55 and subtract 32.

Template Pattern or guide which may be used to form an object or repeat a design.

Templates (the magic of) Innovative uses of stencils courtesy of Fay Robinson of Sydney. Simple suggestions: place a line of sticky tape across a tile or other surface, paint in your sea,

remove the tape and you have a straight horizon line, or use a round price tag to make a great moon. These handy tricks demonstrate the advantages of using a template or stencil and show the way to more complicated designs. Fay suggests placing a piece of glass over a detailed drawing, covering the glass with clear contact, and reproducing the design by tracing it with a fine waterproof pen. Remove the contact and position it on the glazed surface you wish to paint, making sure there are no bubbles. Cut along the design lines with an art or craft knife. Peel off and colour (paint, lustre, ground, texture, etc.) the darkest part of your design first and then selected other areas until the design is complete. This painting aid will keep you within the boundaries of your design. It may be used for straight lines, curves and swirls, numerals, borders, names, geometric shapes and repetitive designs. You can paint the positive or negative space, confidently paint bold colours, complete whole dinner sets or paint a tartan ribbon, and once you have practised a little all your work will have a professional finish.

Tempera Painting with pigments or colours which have been mixed with a natural emulsion such as egg yolk or an artificial emulsion such as oil or gum.

Temperature The measurement of heat intensity in Celsius or Fahrenheit degrees. *See* Cones—conversion chart; Conversion formulae for temperature.

Tempering glass To strengthen glass by cooling the still softened glass suddenly from red heat to cause the surface to harden and become rigid. The inner part of the glass will continue to shrink, compressing the outer surface. The toughened glass cannot be cut as it will shatter.

Tensile strength Caused by stretching or expansion.

Terracotta A reddish brown clay used in pottery which may be painted with onglaze colours, enamels or other ceramic paints as bisque. It may also be painted with a kiln wash and used as moulds.

Tertiary colour Colour created by mixing two or more secondary colours or equal parts of secondary colours and one primary colour.

Tessera Small pieces of glass, porcelain or other ceramic used in mosaic work.

Test tile It is always a good idea to know the materials you use; test tiles are designed to show you the colour of the paint pigments, how they blend with each other, how they fire at various temperatures, how and if they mix with other products. *See* illustrations on page 110.

To make a sample test tile: Paint a shaded stroke of all your blue paints right across a tile leaving the top centimetre or so bare. Write in their brand names to identify them and fire. Then paint another stroke of all your pinks, roses and rubies down the tile, starting in the unpainted area at the top and leaving an area of the original blues showing down the left side of the tile. Identify these colours as well and fire. You will now have a record of all your blues, pinks and a range of mauves and purples you did not know you owned. Make tiles of other useful colour combinations such as autumn tones, blues and greens, etc.

Prepare a test tile of all your *enamels*, without the addition of colour pigments and foreign substances such as sand and glass. Label well, allow to dry and fire. Note results in pen ink on the tile and fire again, this time to test the tolerance of the enamels to further firings. On a separate tile, fired at the same time, try the various additives such as sand, glass and colour and note these reactions as well. Experiment with size and height.

Prepare a test tile of your *texture pastes* as for enamels.

Lustres provide another opportunity to make a test tile; diagonal bands may be added to the lattice pattern previously described. Lustre tiles could have a stripe of lustre on a dried unfired stripe of another lustre, as well as firing between applications. Also prepare a sample of the same lustre applied upon itself several times, firing between each layer. Experiment and save the results for future reference.

Texture Texture is both visual and tactile. It may be obtained by a variety of methods. To obtain a visual effect try brushstrokes, stippling, mottled colours, etc. and for a tactile effect use one of the many commercial preparations available, such as Texture Coat, Ruff-It, Petit Point Paste, Base for Raised Gold, enamel, and of course there is the addition of sand, glass, stones and other solid matter which tolerate heat.

Texture coat White powder which may be mixed with most liquids—medium, milk, sugar solutions, glycerine. etc. It will react differently with each one and according to the various firing temperatures and the varying viscosity of the mixture. It may be applied by brush, sponge,

pen, print, etc. and may be coloured with the addition of about 1/6 or 1/8 of dry powder paint. It may also be painted after firing, and will fire a glossy, semi-transparent white without additives. Firing temperature is between 700–820°C (1290–1510°F). The higher the temperature, the flatter the result.

Texture pastes *Texture Coat, Texture Paste, Ruff-It, Base for Raised Gold, Hancock's Raised Paste, Petit Point Mixture, Dresden Raised Paste, Gold Underlay,* the various enamels, etc. There are many textured pastes on the market and each of them is different. Always follow the manufacturers' instructions initially for tried and proven results and to familiarise yourself with the characteristics of the paste—and then experiment! (Where I have been given them, the instructions will be listed under the name of the manufacturer.) The pastes can be smooth or rough, shiny or dull. Some are suited to hard glaze porcelain and others more suited to soft glaze surfaces. All require adequate drying time. Each paste will react according to the many variables including the human element. Application, the porcelain, the amount and type of solution with which it is mixed, the amount of time it has been allowed to dry, the additives, the weather, the heat of and position in the kiln and numerous other factors must be taken into account.

Some methods of application:
• Padding with assorted textured sponges and shapes.
• Thinned texture paste flowed onto an area.
• Thickened paste padded with wrinkled foil, plastic wrap, paper or cloth.
• 'Printing' with shaped objects such as leaves and grasses, stamps, cut outs, potato prints, coarse sponges, anything!
• Pressing with woven fabrics.
• Drawing a comb, fork, satay stick or similar object through the paste at various times while it dries.
• Flicking off a toothbrush or dropping from a pointer.
• Pressing with a palette knife or credit card.
• Syringing through various nozzles, cake icing cones.
• Pressing through a garlic press, strainer.
• Wrapping in plastic wrap and pulling into a pattern. Leave plastic wrap in situ and fire. The plastic will burn off in the kiln and your design will be intact, which will not be the case

if you try to remove it before firing; fabric can also be left in place.

Thermal shock The breakage which occurs when a piece of porcelain or glass is subjected to sudden changes in temperature. This may happen in the kiln or weeks or months later. It can be attributed to poor firing technique and insufficient annealing (in the case of glass). You can determine when the break occurred by looking at the edges of the break. If they are smooth and rounded, the fracture occurred as the temperature rose in the kiln; if the break is sharp-edged the fracture occurred as the temperature was falling.

Thermocouple Thermoelectric device used to measure temperature accurately.

Thinking What you should be doing all the time! However, take a moment to think laterally. Is the way you are going about whatever it is that you are doing the only way? The best way? What are the alternatives?

Thixotropy The thickening of slip when left to stand; when stirred, it becomes a pourable liquid again.

Tiefschnitt *See* Intaglio.

Tiles Glazed squares or rectangles of porcelain or other clay. Most tiles have a softer glaze than porcelain and will absorb paint and pastes more readily. They come in various sizes, in both ceramic and porcelain. To make your own first wedge or knead the clay to remove any bubbles, rolling it like pastry onto a cloth, sand or plastic wrap surface and cutting into the desired shape. Allow to dry until leatherhard and then fire. There will be some shrinkage as the moisture content is reduced. The clay may be imprinted, carved, antique etched, etc. After firing the tile may be glazed, partially glazed, or painted. Care should be taken when firing tiles to protect them from uneven heat; do not place them against the wall of the kiln close to the exposed elements.

Time/temperature curve The time take to attain a desired temperature during the firing process. The longer it takes to bring the kiln to the desired temperature the lower that temperature has to be to mature the products being fired. The more rapidly a kiln is fired the higher the temperature should be to mature the contents. The length of time that the clay body is subjected to heat determines the maturity of the paints used, not the actual temperature. For instance, if you load your kiln with only two or three pieces, switch it to 800°C (1400°F) and it takes 2 hours to attain that temperature, the paints will react in a certain manner. Then if you fully load your kiln, switch it to the same temperature and it takes 3 hours to reach thaat temperature, the paints will have been subjected to heat for a longer period and the reaction will differ from the previous example.

Tin colours Yellows.

Tin glaze Lead glaze to which tin oxide has been added.

Tin oxide **1.** A white powder used with raised paste to facilitate its application. Use 1/8th quantity of tin oxide to paste. **2.** Also used for polishing glass. **3.** Opacifier which produces a bluish white glaze at all temperatures.

Tint **1.** Addition of white to lighten a colour. **2.** To slightly darken pure white porcelain and opaque white glazes on other clays with a pastel colour, to give 'tooth' or a less slippery surface on which to paint.

Tipping Adding another colour to the tip of an already loaded brush to obtain an effect.

Titanium dioxide Used in crystalline glazes, it results in cream coloured matt finishes.

Tondo Circular painting.

Tools There are a great many commercial tools available and even more makeshift ones. You will find uses for pottery and ceramic tools, woodcarving tools, normal household tools, products such as Scotchbrite, tissues for painting as well as cleaning, credit cards for stamping—the list is endless. If you need something to do a job, look around you. Tools are everywhere.

Tooth A slightly roughened surface to facilitate the application of paint. Attained by a smooth coat of a pale pastel colour fired onto the glaze before the design is painted on.

Top loading Loading two or more colours on top of each other on the brush to create different colour combinations.

Tormented colour Overworked paint! The result is a dull, lifeless, muddied painting, lacking in freshness and spontaneity. Do not pussyfoot!

Touch dry Unfired paint is touch dry when it no longer feels tacky but there is a slight 'pull' when contact is made.

Trace To make a copy of a subject by placing a sheet of transparent paper over the painting or sketch and drawing the outline and detail which shows through. Tracing should only be used to give beginners confidence and to attain accuracy from your own sketches. You can learn a lot from copying and developing your own techniques and style but very little from continuing to trace. An effective tracing procedure is to place graphite paper transfer side down (test it first) onto the glazed surface and place your drawing over the top. Fix in position with adhesive tape. Using a stylus carefully go over the drawing, making sure all the lines are repeated. When you have finished remove both the papers and you will have your tracing. (At this stage you may like to lightly dust the transferred design with a pale colour powder paint and fire it. The fine line design will be permanently in situ and ready for further treatment.)

Tracing box *See* LIGHT BOX.

Trailing Trailing 'slip' over a clay surface or glass mould with the aid of a bulbous container and nozzle to form a decorative pattern, or laying threads of hot glass onto a glass object to form a decorative pattern.

Transfer paper Carbon paper, graphite paper and paper coated with a soft pencil or pastel. The paper is taped to the painting surface, face down; the design is placed on top and also taped in place. Pressure is applied to the design with a stylus or other ball point instrument and the pencil or graphite transfers to the painting surface.

Translucent Permitting diffused light to shine through.

Transparent effect 1. Transmitted light which clearly reveals the image behind. **2.** The effect obtained when applying colours over previously fired colours, e.g. an uneven wash of blue over a fired pale green will allow some of the green to show through.

Triadic colour scheme Made up of three colours equidistant on the colour wheel. See diagram in next column.

Triptych Painting in three panels.

Trivet Stand for tiles.

Trompe l'oeil Painting to deceive the eye. Illusionism.

Trunks of trees Tree trunks are easier to sketch or paint if the plate or tile is turned upside down and the trees drawn from the base to the top and 'pulled' towards you. The broader base of the trunk will taper to the division of the branches which can be pulled towards the tips in the same manner. Roughened bark can be

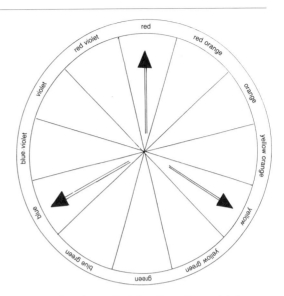

Triadic colour wheel showing primary triadic colour scheme

applied with textures or marks can be drawn into the wet paint with a stylus or some other tool such as a sponge or twisted hairy ball of twine. Look for all the unusual colours in bark, the reds, blues and greens, and apply them lightly.

Tungsten carbide Extremely hard, fine powder used in abrasives for grinding and in tools for etching.

Turnback That part of the petal or leaf which folds over. As a rule it should be lighter in colour than the main part, which is darker immediately under the fold because it is in shadow. Most importantly, it should be in proportion to the rest of the leaf or petal and have a straight or slightly concave edge.

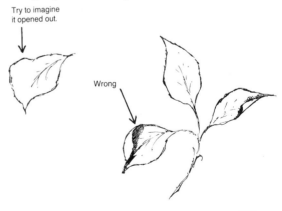

Turning   To turn (form) a pot on a wheel or to trim a leatherhard pot on the wheel.

Turpentine   Colourless or yellow volatile, flammable solvent used to remove unfired paint from painted surface, to clean brushes, to repel paint, as a very fast drying medium to apply paint, and as a thinner for mixed paints. It may also be used as a wash; for signature ink and outline painting. Art turpentine or *pure gum turpentine* is more expensive but is more pure and has a more agreeable odour than household or wood turpentine. It is produced by distilling the balsam of pine trees. *Alternatives:* Water-based mediums, lavender oil, spike oil of lavender and, in some instances, white spirit. It can cause allergic reactions and skin irritation, although it is not considered a health hazard.

Turps repel   Selected paints mixed with medium are applied to the porcelain surface and dabbed with a turpentine-soaked brush. The paint will run and dribble over the area as the object is tilted and turned. When dried and fired the shapes and patterns frequently lend themselves to manipulation by an active imagination. Faces, animals, landscapes can be seen and enhanced with extra lines and colour in a subsequent firing. Other methods include: **(a)** wetting the surface with turpentine and adding paint, either dry powder or mixed, and letting the colours run or turn; **(b)** loading a turpentine-filled brush with mixed paint and allowing it to flow over the area with movement of the plate or tile; **(c)** using lustres rather than paints with any of the previously mentioned methods. Paints mixed with different mediums give different results as do different brands of paint. There are several types of turpentine available and each of these will react differently. The results are entirely unpredictable but a lot of fun.

U

Underglaze   Design painted on or colour applied at the bisque stage prior to application of the glost glaze.

Underglaze colour sticks   Hobby Colorobbia underglaze sticks are used on bisque fired clay in the same manner as pastels are used on paper. The underglaze may be left as applied, blended with water, and coated with hairspray to prevent smudging while working. The painting is fired to approximately 1000°C (1830°F). It should be coated with a transparent glaze if surface is for food preparation.

Underglaze painting   Design painted onto a porcelain or ceramic bisque blank with oxides or paint pigments. The design is allowed to dry and the piece is dipped in glaze and fired.

Unfluxed gold   Paste gold which is purchased in the form of a circular pat of paste. For use over a painted surface where there is already flux present in the previously applied and fired coat of paint.

Uranium oxide   Compound formed from uranium and oxygen used in glazes. Must be stored in a metal container as it is slightly radioactive.

Uroboros glass   Glass with deep rich colours mainly used in Tiffany style lamps but with a small range of fusible glass. Wide range of colours, each one individual. Available from Australian Stained Glass, Pyrmont NSW.

Utility ware   Functional pieces used for eating and drinking. Must be lead-free.

V

Value   Confusing term given many different meanings. Dimension of colour denoting the relative darkness or lightness of a colour. Imagine the colours of a painting as if they were shades of grey in a black and white painting. Could you differentiate between two adjacent colours if they were grey and had no border or outline?

Value glass   Used in the manner of a magnifying glass. The colours are reduced to shades of grey and their values can be determined.

Vanadium colours   Greens and blues.

Vanadium pentoxide   Used in glazes it gives a variety of colours from yellow to brown.

Vehicle   **1.** Matter to utilise one substance with another, e.g. the liquid which is used for grinding the powdered paint or the liquid used to adhere paint to a surface. **2.** Liquid with particles held in suspension.

Vent 1. A hole in the kiln wall to allow moisture, air, smoke, fumes, etc. to escape during the firing process. The kiln is usually vented during the early stages of firing and then the bung is replaced. This prevents the marring of the brilliance of the lustres and metals. The vent also allows the escape of excess heat after reaching the fusing stage for glass. **2.** Small holes in greenware to allow trapped gases and air to escape, particularly when pieces have been attached to the main body.

Versatile Underglazes Trade name of Duncan Design Coats underglazes for use on bisque and greenware.

Vetro a fili Filigree decoration of continuous, uncrossed threaded lines in clear glass. (Italian term.)

Vetro a retorti Filigree decoration in which parallel lines of intricately twisted threads are embedded in clear glass. (Italian term.)

Viscosity The internal property of a liquid which influences its rate of flow. As viscosity increases the liquid becomes stiffer. With glass, the viscosity increases with decreasing temperature until the glass temperature falls below strain point, at which stage the glass is so stiff it becomes a solid.

Vitreous Pertaining to glass. A vitreous or glazed surface is said to be impervious or waterproof.

Vitreous enamelling Usually done on metal sheets, forming a base for onglaze artists to paint. A primer coat of a mix of feldspar, silica, quartz and special clays is sprayed onto a prepared metal sheet and fired. A coat of white enamel is baked onto the primer coat. This surface may then be painted on as any other glazed surface. It is fired normally.

Vitreous paints For painting on glass. Mixture of ground glass and pigment oxides to provide colour. The oxides may be one of, or a mix of, iron, copper, cobalt, chromium, manganese, nickel, titanium dioxide, etc. and the ground glass is usually composed of silica, alumina, borax and lead. The paints come in powdered form and are mixed with water and gum arabic or other mediums such as white vinegar or acetic acid, turpentine or one of the essential oils.

Vitrify To glaze and fire a piece and induce a hard impervious surface.

Volatile To evaporate rapidly, to become gaseous. When organic binders, oil mediums and wetting agents are heated they will volatilise. It is important that the oil you use remains stable until the kiln is sufficiently hot to soften the glaze to allow it to absorb the paints and oxides. If the oil evaporates too soon the paint will run. Mineral oils such as motor oil and other open mediums such as household oils, paraffin, baby oil, etc. are more volatile than the vegetable oils like copaiba. The volatile oils should be used sparingly and be as dry as possible when applying paint.

Volatile solvents Organic liquids used as thinners and cleaning agents which evaporate at a low temperatures. They are usually flammable and immiscible with water but must be readily mixed with the other components being used. The most common are turpentine, white spirit, acetone, ethyl alcohol, kerosene and spike oil.

W

Walker Ceramics Australian owned firm founded in 1885. It is still family owned and family run and the major manufacturer and supplier of ceramic products (the majority of which are Australian) to Australasia. Much of the information and advice in this book has been provided by the generosity of David Walker, of Walker Ceramics, 55 Lusher Rd, Croydon Victoria. Walker Ceramic products include onglazes, lead free stoneware glazes, lead-free middle fire glazes, earthenware glazes, lustres, one-stroke underglazes, underglaze crayons, underglaze pencils, glaze stains, body stains, underglaze stains, frits, raw materials, clays and slips. *See* Product Information, page 106.

Warm colours Yellows, reds and oranges give the appearance of being closer and exuding heat. To help subdue a dominant portion of a background painted in these colours give it a wash of a cool colour such as blue. It will then recede.

Warm glass A term given to kiln-fired glass.

Warp A twist or bend in a flat shape or form. Warped glass is usually caused by incompatible glasses or incomplete annealing.

Wash of colour The application of colour in broad flat areas to gently colour a black and white sketch, to push an intruding or displeasing flower or other area of design into the background or to highlight part of a design.

Waterglass Common name for sodium silicate.

Water smoking When moisture escapes from the clay during the initial stages of firing.

Weathering Deterioration of glass and glazed surfaces by exposure to adverse conditions, evidenced by crazing, frosting and colour change.

Wedging To remove air from a lump of clay by repeatedly slamming it down hard onto a bench top, cutting it in half and rejoining it many times.

Welding To blend and seal two edges or surfaces together, as in blending clay pieces.

Wet felt Pliable refractory fabric for making moulds.

Wet on wet Application of paint on freshly applied unfired paint. To be done with great care as the first stroke applies paint which dries rapidly. The second application will move the first coat of colour unless you are extremely cautious.

Wheel engraving The use of a rotating wheel to grind a pattern into the glass surface.

Whink (*Caution—Acid*) Product equivalent to Rustiban available in USA. Diluted hydrofluoric acid used to remove fired painted designs.

Whiskers Long fine hairs on the cheeks of animals. Very difficult to render realistically as they are so light and fine. Best done with a very fine scroller, mapping pen or rubber tip and thinned even further with the rubber tip. Light or white whiskers are wiped out in the first fire or painted in with fine enamel lines on the last fire after all painting in that area is finished. Dark brown or black whiskers are painted in the last fire with either paint or coloured enamel. Understated whiskers are better than an overabundance.

White granite Hard dense porcelain similar to ironstone.

White relief Thicker than normal white paint which is applied for relief decoration.

White spirit Another name for dry cleaning fluid. A solvent frequently used as a substitute for turpentine.

Whiting Calcium carbonate used in shelf primer or kiln wash.

Windows of light Areas of light in the design. Very important. Without these light patches the design would be dull, colourless and lifeless and the painting would have very little contrast.

Wipe out To move freshly applied wet paint and create a design. First outline the design, then partially remove paint from within the lines, leaving sufficient for shading and moulding.

Wipe-out tool Instrument equipped with a pointed rubber or synthetic tip at one end and a sharp rubber or synthetic blade at the other. There are many varieties of wipe-out tool and many other objects which can be used for the same purpose. Typist's erasers, rubber dental picks, and most useful of all, fingers—every one of them, and each has a sharp blade at the end in the form of a fingernail. Covered with a tissue, all ten are very effective.

Wissmach glass Extensive range of coloured glass made in USA.

Wood ash Glaze ingredient composed of well burnt trees, shrubs or plants which may be used in a rough state or well washed and sieved. In the rough state, particles of wood and carbon would be sieved with the glaze. If the ash is washed these particles float to the top and can be removed, the water dissolves the soluble salts of potassium and sodium and the fine ash settles. This procedure may have to be repeated several times, the residue sieved through an 80 gauge mesh and allowed to settle, then dried. The quality of the ash is affected by the age of the tree or plant, the dryness of the timber, the soil and the preparation.

Woodtone Glazes Trade name of satin glazes which have small flecks of dark colour which simulate a wood grain when brushed out.

Wool sponge Open textured sponge which is soft when wet.

Worcester Porcelain made in the factories in the town of Worcester, England.

Working range The range of temperatures in which it is possible to form glass. Slumping occurs at the lower end of the range; at the upper end of the range glass may be combed or raked.

Wrico Pen A pen which can be filled with gold or platinum and used for penwork and decoration.

Wreathing Wave marks forming on the surface of a cast clay object, caused by irregular pouring.

Wrythen Spiral effect given by vertical ribbing.

Y

Z

Yellow cake Uranium oxide in unprocessed form.

Zigzag saw A ceramic tool used to cut designs in thick unfired clay.

Zirconium oxide Refractory oxide opacifier.

Zirconium silicate Waterground zircon suitable for refractory washes, low expansion glazes, matt and crystalline glazes. May be used as an opacifier for semi-opaque glazes.

Product Information

ALEXANDER'S PRODUCTS

Designer Paint Range A range of onglaze paints for application to china. Due to advances in technology these paints are finely milled and do not exhibit grittiness in either appearance or physical nature. The high gloss and clear finish is chip resistant and the recommended firing temperature is 700–820°C (1290–1510°F). The success of these paints is due to three main factors: 1. bonding flux; 2. glazing compounds; 3. colouring agents.

Bonding flux An additive which permits the basic components of the porcelain glaze and the ceramic onglaze paint to fuse together at a lower temperature to form a homogeneous bond. If too much is added, chipping can be a problem where the paint is applied heavily and colour deterioration can result. The flux Alexander's use in Designer Paints is a perfect combination for creating optimum paint adhesion, with no detrimental effects of colour loss or chipping.

Glazing compounds These are predominantly lead-based compounds which readily dissolve other essential ingredients in glazes and in the paint pigments, to form a brilliant high gloss appearance. These lead compounds have a lower melting point with a wide softening range which is what enables the paints to exhibit their outstanding characteristics.

Colouring agents The colouring agents are formulations of many chemicals, including cadmium, chromium, cobalt, copper, iron, manganese, nickel, tin, titanium and selenium, to mention the most common elements. The chemistry of forming colours is extremely complex and is further complicated by the reaction between the glaze and the chemicals used. For instance, cadmium-based colours should not be mixed with other colours. The Designer Range has been extensively tested to ensure all colours will intermix, even pinks, reds and purples.

Lead content All ceramic onglaze colours, or china paints, require the addition of a large percentage of lead to enable them to work properly. This is the reason for the health warnings as required by the Australian Health Department on all the paint labels. It is important to follow general commonsense when using powder paint. All paint dust should he kept to a minimum, hands should be washed and care should be taken not to transfer powders from hand to mouth.

Manufacture Most of the paints used in Australia today are manufactured in Germany or England and there is a massive range available which seems endless when trying to select colours. Most colours are designed for commercial use (tiles, transfers, etc.) with a wide range of firing temperatures, fast firing, slow firing, underglazes, and onglazes. The Designer Paint Range has been developed from the paints considered most suitable for painting by hand. The recommended firing temperature is 700–820°C (1290–1510°F).

Ferrule There is a difference in the ferrules used in the production of brushes. Alexander's consider that nickel plated brass ferrules are the best and most suitable for the uses to which porcelain painters put their brushes. The various types of ferrules are listed in descending value:
1. Plated brass seamless
2. Nickel plated soldered
3. Clear anodised aluminium seamless
4. Aluminium seamless (not anodised)
5. Soldered tin
6. Unsoldered tin
A painter's hands would soon turn black using an aluminium seamless ferrule (not anodised).

The term 'silver' may imply that it is a cheaper ferrule and not a nickel plated brass ferrule. Therefore the description of a brush which reads 'sable hair, silver ferrule' would suggest a cheaper brush using inexpensive (so-called) 'sable' hair with a nickel plated soldered ferrule.

Flo-line brush Full bodied Kolinski sable brush with a built in liner.

Golds

Liquid Bright Gold AA grade
Degussa 11 % Liquid Bright Gold
Liquid Burnish Gold premium AA grade
Professional Liquid Burnish Gold 30%
Gold For Glass Low firing gold (520–630°C, 970–1165°F) especially for glass. Fires *bright gold* on top and underside of glass.

Golds and lustres Simple rules which must be followed are:

Firing Allow gold or lustre to dry properly before firing. For best results, fire between 680-820°C (1255–1510°F). As ventilation is most important do not load kiln too closely and leave bungs out until approximately 500°C (930°F) to allow gases and contaminants to escape. Always allow kiln to cool slowly with bungs in place.

Application Porcelain surface must be clean and dust-free. Use a separate brush for each colour and keep clean. Use gold and lustre thinners to clean brushes. Gold and lustres should be applied in an even tan coloured coat, not too heavily and with only one coat per firing. Applied over bisque or matt surfaces a dull finish will be the result. May be applied by brush, stippled or sponged to achieve different effects. To slow drying time for large areas, a little thinner may be applied.

Storage Will last longer if stored in tightly sealed containers in a cool dark place. If gold or lustres thicken, add a little gold or lustre thinner at time of application.

Problems

Cracked or blistered gold—Applied too heavily or overfired.
Gold has areas of purple, blue or brown—Applied too lightly or over thinned.
Poor gold adhesion—Insufficient kiln ventilation. Applied over dirty glaze. Insufficient firing temperature.
White spots or spots of glaze showing through—Gold or lustres applied on a moist or dirty surface.
Dull or cloudy gold or lustre—Poor kiln ventilation. Contamination in gold or lustre. Dirty

brush. Satin or matt surface.
Fingerprints—Clean glaze before application and keep fingers clean of gold or lustre.

Odourless Brush Cleaner Has a non-irritating aromatic fragrance and is bottled in 500 ml containers. Has a similar solvent power to spirit of gum turpentine.

Oils and mediums Copaiba Medium, Grinding Oil, Pen Oil, Rosemary Blend, Australian Open Medium, Grounding Oil, Sabatella, Fat Oil, Clove Oil, LavenderOil, Balsam of Copaiba.

Australian Stained Glass Supplies, Sydney

Wide range of glass of various types, glass tools such as band saws, glass cutters, pliers and shears, equipment for lead, soldering and copper foiling; etch pens and etching creme, putty and patinas, cutting rules, flux and putty brushes, safety equipment, light boxes, grinders and accessories and a comprehensive stock of books.

Carey's Products, Adelaide

Carey's Base for Raised Gold or Enamel Place a small quantity of powder on a glass mixing slab or tile and add a few drops of Carey's Enamel Medium. Grind until the mixture is crumbly. It is easier to have the mixture holding together well and then add a little more powder to bring it back to the crumbly texture required. Remember if it is too oily it will spread or crack when fired. Add perfectly clean turpentine until the mixture strings. If you add too much turpentine, keep mixing as the turpentine will evaporate. For easy application use the needle end of an NT cutter. Fire at 740°C (1365°F), although it will take up to 800°C (1470°F) without ill effect. [*Author's note:* I find this an excellent dry powder paste which can be mixed with almost anything and which will withstand several firings. It may be left glossy white or coloured with 1/8 powder paint or the same proportion of mixed paint. It may be applied as is enamel or base for gold. It may be used as a fine or rough textured surface over a large area or as high build-up, given sufficient drying time. It will tolerate additives such as pieces of glass, sand, stones, etc., being painted or lustred and gilded. I have even replaced a large 2 cm (3/4") chip from the rim of a plate with it by gradually building up the depression and edge in successive firings.]

Carey's Acid Etch Powder Draw or trace design and apply Carey's Cover Coat over design and any other part not to be etched, e.g. the rim of a plate or a raised design on the porcelain. Mix a small amount of Acid Etch Powder with Carey's Seminar Medium, just thin enough to paint, and brush it over the exposed area. Pad with silk over cotton wool but do not over-pad. Carefully remove Cover Coat. Fire to 760°C (1400°F). If you wish to accentuate your design, such as roses, violets, forget-me-nots, leaves, etc. apply Carey's Base for Raised Gold. Fire to 740°C (1365°F). Before applying the Liquid Bright Gold, wash and rinse the china in clear water to rid it of any impurities. This is essential to prevent discolouration of gold. Be sure the china is completely dry before applying the gold. Fire to 720°C (1330°F). A second application of gold should be given and again fired to 720°C (1330°F). Apply gold a third time if necessary. For a different effect, apply the mixed powder with a piece of foam sponge. Instead of using Base for Raised Gold, the lines of the flowers may be penned with the Acid Etch Powder mixed a little thinner.

Carey's Copaiba Medium Excellent quick drying medium.

Carey's Seminar Medium Semi-open, non-sweating medium which is lint-repellant and suitable for humid conditions. Open enough to allow for correction of work, while drying sufficiently to allow work to be fired. Do not use to mix and grind paints unless colour is to be used within a few days.

Carey's One Fire Medium Ideal for painting in Dresden style. Paints must be mixed and applied smoothly. Fire to 800°C (1470°F).

Carey's Grinding Oil For mixing powder paints, which will remain workable for seven or more years when kept in a covered container. Does not attract lint. Mixed colours are compatible with pen oils.

Carey's Pen Oil No. 2 A new and improved version of pen oil. May be added to mixed colours from palette and used and fired immediately.

Carey's Cover Coat Water-based masking agent which is not attacked by grounding oils.

Grounding Oil (Gwen's) Slow drying oil with good colour absorption suitable for large areas.

Metallics and lustres If you know you are going to apply metallics or lustres on a piece, apply one more coat of glaze to the piece than normal and fire as close to Cone 4 (1060°C, 1940°F) as possible. Clean piece with either Med-Mar Glaze Cleaner or acetone, remembering to wipe off the residue left by the acetone. Do not use rubbing alcohol to clean as it contains an oil.

Lustres may be applied by a variety of methods: a soft wide brush, an air brush or even your finger. Be sure your brush, or finger, is clean and dry before using it to apply lustre. If using Mother of Pearl or Rainbow Opal, stroke the brush in different directions to increase the multi-coloured effect. Fire at Cone 018 or 019, 715°C (1320°F); (standard cone, normal low fire). Allow the lustre to dry before firing, otherwise it will have a frosted appearance. If applied too heavily the lustre will chalk off after firing.

Gold, platinum and palladium Follow the same basic instructions as for metallics and lustres. Apply the gold, platinum or palladium in a thin even coat and *do not* go over the unfired gold. If you do, these areas turn brown before firing and will be dull after firing. If the gold, platinum, etc. rubs off after firing it is because it was not fired high enough. Moisture will cause white spots after firing. Black specks are caused by dust or contamination before firing. If, when applying Gold Bronze, Gun Metal or Red Copper it pools in deep recesses, it will fire off and leave bare areas showing. To rectify, clean with Glaze Cleaner and apply another coat all over. Do not touch up as this will show.

Hard spot If a large black spot appears which does not fire out, it was caused when the slip was being poured. The glaze will be thin where the 'hard spot' is and lustres will turn black on this thinly glazed area. If there are tiny bubbles in the glazed surface or pinpoints in the ware, a blemish will result, particularly with lustres.

Frosting If Mother of Pearl appears dull there could be a number of causes. Too hot a fire or too long a firing cycle, poor circulation of heat, too heavy an application or firing before the lustre was dry.

Antique Etch To give the appearance of erosion with age. Apply with an eye dropper or brush to cleaned greenware that will fire to Cone 06-05 (1000–1045°C, 1845–1915°F). Antique Etch is thin so the application must be controlled as

'Tawny Frogmouths'
1st and 2nd fire

1st fire—shapes of flowers identified in background and 'wiped out'

3rd fire
(photography A. Patten)

2nd fire

'Roses'
Background, applied at random leaving light and options

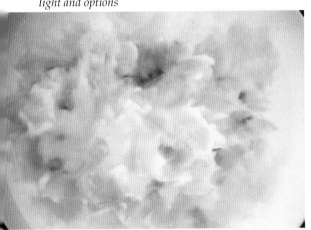

3rd fire

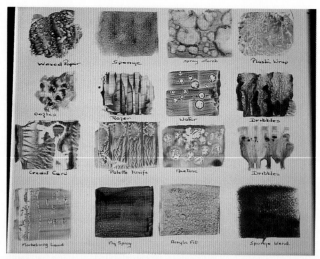

Fun with wet paint *The paint was either pressed, padded or dampened with various tools and solutions*

1st row: *Waxed paper, sponge, spray starch, plastic wrap*
2nd row: *'Ooples' with turpentine, razor, water, dribbles and runs*
3rd row: *Credit card, palette knife, acetone and more dribbles*
4th row: *Marbelising liquid (yes, for lustre), flyspray, acrylic fill and sponge*

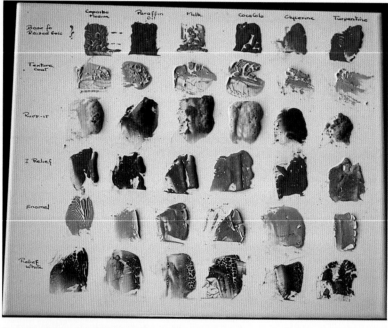

Test Tile of Pastes *All substances were mixed to a fairly stiff consistency, dried overnight on a ceramic tile, fired very slowly to 800°C (1470°F), in my kiln. None of the substances chipped off in the first fire and would not be expected to on a tile. All were shiny with the exception of Ruff-It.*

Remember: *It is impossible to predict accurately the results of texture because the amount of liquid added, colour added, china on which it is placed, thickness of application and time/ temperature curve all have an effect on the final result.*

Base for Raised Gold: *Copaiba medium flattened just a little, interesting separation; Paraffin— separation, slightly flat uninteresting blob; Milk— interesting separation; Coca-Cola—little separation; Glycerine—flatter, otherwise no change; Turpentine— very little separation.*
Texture Coat: *Very interesting separation with all mediums.*
Ruff-It: *The textured surfaces vary with the amounts of each liquid applied.*

I-Relief: *Smooth, slightly flattened surface with very little separation with all liquids.*
Enamel (Fay Good's Dresden): *Copaiba medium— very interesting striated separation; Paraffin, Milk, Coca-Cola—retained height with a small amount of separation; Glycerine—flat; Turpentine—interesting separation.*
Relief White: *Most interesting of all—good separation with various shapes with all mediums.*

it will immediately start to erode the greenware, causing interesting craters and raised areas. The amount applied governs the depth of erosion.

Antique Effect with Wild Dove Iridescent grey brown lustre. Apply lustre to relief or textured work, rubbing back from raised areas. Repeat another complete coat and fire to Cone 019 (680°C, 1260°F). On a plain surface first apply Antique Etch and when dry, fire and glaze. Coat with Wild Dove.

Blue Storm Iridescent dark blue lustre. Use as Wild Dove or first apply Liquid Bright Gold or Liquid Bright Palladium or Platinum and fire. Then apply Blue Storm for a most unusual effect.

Metallic Flo-Base Apply a heavy coat of the solution to a glazed and fired surface and immediately drop Liquid Bright Gold onto the wet areas so that it runs. Results in a lacy gold pattern.

Weeping Gold (Not to be confused with Mottling Gold.) Apply over a glazed surface with as wide a brush as the object will permit. On a vertical surface, place loaded brush at the top and pull all the way down. A full brush will usually carry 25 centimetres (10"). On a clear white glaze this will result in feathery runs of gold over a lavender pink background. Fire at Cone 019 (680°C, 1260°F).

Weeping Platinum As for Weeping Gold.

Painting on soap Using Carey's Soap Medium and Carey's Soap Sealer. Mix china painting colours with a minimum of Soap Medium so as to leave them slightly dry on the palette. Moisten brush with Soap Medium and paint in the usual way. Do not use water with medium as drying time will be increased. Wipe outs are done with a brush moistened in the Soap Medium. Keep mixed paints in a covered container to prevent them from absorbing moisture from the air and wash brushes in water. When design is completely dry, thoroughly fill a 10 or 12 mm (3/8" or 1/2") flat brush with soap sealer and flow it over the painted design without actually touching and scratching the design. Second and third coats may be applied when previous coats are completely dry, about 10 minutes. Full drying time is 24 hours. Wipe sealer from brushes and wash them in the special Sealer Brush Cleaner and dry. It is possible to use methylated spirits for cleaning provided it is done immediately. If the Soap Sealer is contaminated with turpentine it will become milky.

CELIA'S PRODUCTS

Celia's Petit Point Used as a background and looks like tapestry. *Method:* Celia's Petit Point Mixture, small piece of sponge, fine wedding veil netting, 2 pegs. Dry powder paints (not reds) can be added to the mixture for toning. Draw a pencil line around the area you wish to set off for the Petit Point base. Place a little of the mixture from the jar onto your palette and add turpentine to suit application. The mixture must be thin. It should run and spread on the palette. Dip the piece of sponge into the mixture and dab it onto the area to be treated. Take a large enough piece of net to pull round tightly underneath the article, twist and tighten then secure with the two pegs to hold the net tightly in place. Dip the sponge into the mix again and wipe evenly, but not too thickly, over the area. Set aside to dry, e.g. for one hour under a lamp or beside a warm kiln, or overnight if dried naturally. When dry, remove the net and tidy the edges with a small pen-knife. Fire at 790–815°C (1455–1500°F). Leftover mixture may be replaced in the jar. After firing, go over the Petit Point gently with a piece of wet and dry sandpaper to smooth. To paint, have your paints runnier and thinner than normal as the Petit Point base absorbs the paint like blotting paper. Reds will turn rusty brown.

Celia's Pre-mixed Acid Look Meant to be used for fine designs using a mapping pen. Place a small portion from the jar onto the palette and mix with pure turpentine to a thin milky texture which flows smoothly from the pen or brush. Fire at 800°C (1470°F) and then apply lustres, Liquid Bright Gold or Silver, Burnishing Gold or Platinum, and fire again at 800°C (1470°F). The acid look should be applied very thinly as when painted with gold. The gold will turn black if the mixture is too thick.

Celia's Pre-mixed Glaze Acid This mixture will remove the glaze where it is applied and the decoration can then be covered with lustres, gold or silver for a matt finish. Mix well in the jar before use as the oil on top is part of the formula. Use masking lacquer to protect surface areas not to be treated and either sponge, paint or pen the mix onto your design. For pen or brush the mixture should be a little thicker than milk and slightly thicker for larger sponged areas. Just apply and do not smooth. Fire at 790°C (1455°F). It is important to place the article in the kiln where the temperature is correct, i.e. 790°C (1455°F); when the powder is rubbed off after firing the glaze will be unchanged if underfired, or the powder will be difficult to remove if it has been overfired.

Celia's Pre-mixed Gold Base Frost To give a satin finish to gold painted china. Mix in the jar to the consistency of thick milk before use, as the oil on top is part of the formula. Use masking lacquer for areas not to be treated and cover two or three sponges with fine pure silk. Place some of the Gold Base mixture onto the palette and apply with a silk covered sponge. Use a second sponge to fine dab or buff so that you have a very fine application. Fire at 800°C (1470°F). Apply Liquid Bright Gold in one or two coats, depending on the quality.

Celia's Pre-mixed Raised Paste or Coloured Enamel *Yellow pre-mixed raised paste* is used for painting scrolls and trimmings which are to be covered with Liquid Burnishing Gold, Liquid Bright Gold or Platinum. For painting flowers, for example a blossom, use a No.1, 2 or 3 pointed shader from Celia's French brush range. Take the mixture from the jar onto your palette, add a little pure turpentine, and stir with a palette knife until you have a very smooth texture and until there are no lumps of powder.

Method Push paste to an edge around flower petal; then flatten the brush on the palette, no paste added, and pull down the strokes to the centre of the flower. This must be done quickly and neatly with no dry lumps to be seen—it does need a little practice. If any dry paste is left on the back of the brush, wipe away on a dry cloth. The mixture for painting flowers and leaves must be rather thin, just firm enough to hold the raised edge on the flower. Add pure turpentine frequently. For a pleasing embossed effect it does not have to be raised to extreme. Fire at 790–850°C (1455–1560°F). The raised paste and enamel can be used for scrolls, drops, large dots down to small dots as a pattern. For scrolls, drops and dots use a mapping pen. When applying on the china as a drop, dip the mapping pen into the mixture then use the press, lift movement. The pre-mixed enamel and raised paste can be placed straight in the kiln; no drying time is needed when used as a painting material. If the enamel is used as a high texture application, then set aside to dry one or two days before firing. When gold or platinum is applied over raised paste and pre-mixed

enamel, fire only at 600–650°C (1110–1200°F). *No more.*

White raised paste has a powder added to the mixture so that it can be used for scrolls, dots and lines on lustres, backgrounds and floral decorations, but where the pre-mixed enamel stands glossy and translucent, the raised paste will stand semi-matt. The white raised paste stands out extremely white on dark backgrounds, very dark lustres, gold and platinum. It is very suitable for snow scenes. Fire at 790–815°C (1455–1500°F). If gold or platinum is used over white raised paste fire at no more than 650°C (1200°F). The raised paste may be stippled over a hairline or small crack.

Pre-mixed coloured enamels may be intermixed, with the exception of red and yellow. Orange matures at 700°C (1290°F). Salmon, Scarlet, Red, Deep Red and Black mature at 740°C (1365°F). Rose Pink Yellow, Light Green, Green, Aqua Blue, Mauve, Brown and White for mixing mature at 790–815°C (1455–1500°F). For a lighter tone add the pre-mixed coloured enamel to some pre-mixed white enamel. Do not add dry powder paint as this will disturb the formula and cause failure.

CERAMIC SOLUTIONS

Safety Data Please take appropriate precautions when air brushing and do not eat food while working with ceramic materials. All Ceramic Solutions products which are deemed to constitute a chronic health hazard are labelled with a red sticker. All underglazes used on food utensils must be glazed with certified 'Food safe' clear glass glaze which has been fired according to instructions. Once fired, the glaze must not be prone to crazing or shivering to preserve the integrity of the ceramic ware. Ceramic ware which does not meet this requirement cannot be considered food safe and should not be used for this purpose.

Ceramic Solutions provides an encompassing service which puts the customer first. They are available to answer any questions on their products and techniques.

Ceramic Solutions Acrylic Stains and Sealers Formulated to be applied to bisque clay bodies not intended for firing. The sealer is applied on top of the acrylic stain to seal the surface. Some colours are best applied over an undercoat of white or grey to ensure colour does not appear opaque. Not for storage of food and beverages but for decorative purposes only. To apply—shake well for several minutes and apply three full even coats with a soft art brush or air brush (taking airbrushing precautions) and then a coat of sealer. May be thinned with water to assist application. Clean brushes with water and wash hands thoroughly with soap. Storage should be in a firmly closed container to avoid drying out of the contents. The stains and sealers are composed of acrylic co-polymers, organic pigments, metal oxides, rheology modifiers, preservatives and water.

Ceramic Solutions Hobby Leaded Clear Glaze
Mauve liquid glaze (the colour assists application by making glazed areas apparent) used to seal and protect ceramic ware from moisture and discolouration caused by contact with food and liquids. Ensure all previously applied Underglazes and One Strokes are perfectly dry and apply two or three coats in a cross-hatch manner using a soft glazing brush and allowing each coat to dry prior to application of the next coat. *The application of lead glazes by spraying is not recommended.* Clean brushes with water and wash hands thoroughly with soap. Storage should be in a firmly closed container to avoid drying out of the contents. The glaze which is fired between Cone 06–04 (1000–1060°C, 1845–1940°F) on bisque which has been previously fired to Cone 04–03 (1060–1095°C, 1940–2000°F) must not craze or shiver over the course of time and if this does ocur the ceramic ware should cease being used for food purposes. The glaze is composed of clay, a number of fritted compounds including lead bi-silicate, rheology modifier, organic colourant, preservative and water. If fired incorrectly or has crazed, the glaze should not be used for the storage of food and beverages as doing so may lead to lead poisoning. Refrain from eating, drinking or smoking when using the glaze and if pregnant or considering pregnancy, restrict use of the glaze to classroom/studio only. The Hobby Leaded Clear Glaze is not recommended for use in Health Care Facilities. It was tested by a NATA approved analytical laboratory for conformance to BS 6748 which tests for heavy metal release and the results of the test concluded that the Ceramics Solutions Hobby Leaded Clear Glaze was well within the acceptable limits and therefore is food safe when fired correctly.

Ceramic Solutions One Strokes Wide range of translucent colours popular for handpainting art works and functional wares either on greenware or bisque or opaque white glazes, for a finish similar to Majolica. They have a firing range of 1060–1300°C. May be applied by single strokes with a suitable brush or by sponging or airbrushing. When fired correctly, compounds such as water, carbon dioxide and traces of other organic and inorganic matter are released. Flaking, bleeding or running under the glaze indicates incorrect firing technique.

Ceramic Solutions Sovereign Coloured Glazes The glaze which is fired between Cone 06–04 (1000–1060°C, 1845–1940°F) on bisque which has been previously fired to Cone 04–03 (1060–1095°C, 1940–2000°F) is best applied and fired onto white clays. The glaze may by thinned with water to suit application technique which may be by cross-hatch strokes with a soft glazing brush or applied by spray with appropriate precautions for airbrushing, i.e. in a spray booth equipped with an exhaust fan and wearing a proper face mask. Cleaning and safety precautions as Ceramic Solutions Hobby Leaded Clear Glaze.

Ceramic Solutions Underglazes These underglazes are non-toxic when used with care following the directions supplied. They are intense glazes composed of a range of ingredients including clays, oxides, fritted compounds, rheology modifiers, preservative and water which can be used on greenware or bisque, hobby, commercial or stoneware clay and which have a firing range of 1060–1300°C. When fired correctly, compounds such as water, carbon dioxide and traces of other organic and inorganic matter are released. Flaking, bleeding or running under the glaze indicates incorrect firing technique. To apply, first clean the ceramic ware with a damp sponge, then apply glaze either with a sponge, brush or air brush. Glaze may be thinned with water to adjust for technique used. Clean brushes with water and wash hands thoroughly with soap.

DEGUSSA PRODUCTS

Apparently Bright Gold was first developed in Meissen in 1830. The formula was kept a closely guarded secret for many years, and eventually came to the Degussa factory. Initially, there were problems with adhesion; however, after much experimentation a practical method was developed to produce large quantities of a good preparation at reasonable prices and comparatively easily, and during the last century the Degussa production has become world wide with subsidiary companies in many countries. Degussa expanded into a product range which included other precious metal preparations, and other decorating colour for glass, porcelain, enamel and earthenware; also stains, frits, glazes and special raw materials. The gold preparations have been developed to meet the many demands of commercial and amateur artists. They have to be compatible with various solvent systems and suitable for different application techniques. They must fire perfectly under extreme firing conditions, demonstrate chemical and mechanical resistance, and, as well, be in accordance with environmental and work regulations.

Precious metal decorating products can be categorised according to their : 1. Viscosity: liquid/pasty or solid (powder); 2. Fired appearance: glossy or matt; 3. Precious metal content: gold, platinum, palladium or silver.

Liquid/pasty with a glossy finish: Bright Gold, Bright Citron Gold, Bright Platinum, Bright Palladium, lustre.

Liquid/pasty with a matt finish: Burnish Gold, Burnish Platinum, Burnish Palladium, Burnish Silver, Argalvan.

Solid preparations have a matt or satin finish: Painter's Gold, Powder Gold, Powder Platinum, Powder Palladium, and Powder Silver. The appearance of the bright preparations in their unfired condition is transparent, usually brown to black coloured liquids which look like varnish. They have a specific precious metal content.

Bright Gold is based on pure gold and fires with a red to yellow gold shade. The yellow Bright Golds contain a small percentage of silver. *Bright Platinum* and *Bright Palladium* are based on platinum and palladium and have a grey/white metallic appearance when fired.

Lustres can be composed of precious metals as well as base metals which give them their metallic iridescent appearance.

Burnish and *Matt* preparations contain precious metal in fine powder or tinsel form. They are matt when fired and obtain a gloss by being burnished by sand, a glass brush or an agate pencil.

Painter's Gold is a chemically precipitated precious metal powder, frequently containing flux, which is mixed with thick oil for handpainted gold decoration. Also used for the dusting of steel prints and for the production of decals. Often contains mercury compounds and appropriate safety measures must be observed.

Dusting or *powder products* contain pure precious metal, mainly in flake form.

Bright Gold and *Bright Citron Gold* can be mixed with Burnish Gold. For a higher gold content, *Powder* or *Painter's Gold* may be mixed with Burnish Gold; however, the flux content will vary and adhesion should be tested prior to application to piece.

Gold content: The gold content of Bright preparations ranges between 6% and 24% and it is suggested that a 12% preparation be used for painting. For *stamping* no less than a 12% preparation should be used and 15% is recommended. The gold content of Burnish Gold ranges between 12% and 40%; 16.5% is standard for liquid preparations, while paste has a content of 28%. A higher content is used for stamping, up to 30%. There are special preparations, e.g. High Temperature, Fast Firing Gold, which generally has a higher gold content of up to 60%. The thickness of a layer of Burnishing Gold is three to six times that of Bright preparations and it is therefore more durable (and more valuable).

Storage The maximum recommended storage time is approximately one year as the preparations are subject to changes during storage, becoming more viscous. This can be remedied by the addition of thinning oil. Bright Citron Golds may be stored from six months to one year after which they become so thick they are no longer workable. Black Burnish Golds also become so thick in six months that it is difficult to use them. Other preparations become fluid during storage and should also be used within six months. If preparations are not to be used immediately they may be stored in the refrigerator or cool cellar. Precious metals are formulated for the various surfaces to which they are to be applied, such as porcelain, earthenware, majolica, glass and enamel. The object to be painted must first be thoroughly clean and free from dust, fingerprints, water stains and any other impurity. It is usually sufficient to rub with a textile or leather cloth which has been dampened with water and ethyl alcohol. However, if detergent must be used, a thorough rinsing is necessary as the detergent will leave a thin film on the surface. Glass to be fired may be treated with a 'mudding mixture', which mainly consists of ochre with the addition of copper sulphate to improve the adherence of Bright Gold; this creates a spotless fired film on the exterior surface and a more beautiful appearance on the interior surface. Other preparations are for frosting the glaze or glass by etching, or by firing a flux or colour. *Simili incrustation* is the decoration of edges with matt firing colours or gold base coats. The fired base colour is then painted with Bright Gold and fired again at a slightly lower temperature. The various methods of application include painting, edging, printing, spraying or machine transfer. Bright Gold should not be shaken as this may have an unfavourable effect or damage the decoration. Burnish preparations should be shaken very well prior to use and from time to time during the application. *Screen printing* preparations such as Burnish Gold pastes are intentionally more viscous and it is necessary to add thinning oil to attain the correct consistency prior to application.

Thinning oil needs to be used as there is loss of solvents through evaporation; however, this should not exceed 20% to 25% of the precious metal content. For edging and spraying a thin volatile oil is used; painting a large flat surface requires a medium-flat oil and stamping a fat oil. There are a variety of oils available for the different requirements.

Environmentally-friendly Burnish Gold preparations do not contain *mercury* and are more voluminous and therefore have to be applied in a thicker layer to attain the same gold content. They also contain a larger quantity of resin and appear more viscous and definitely require the correct thinning oil. Higher temperatures require a fatter oil. The more recent formulae should be applied with a smooth constant flow with no overlap, as these areas may be obvious and may also craze and crack.

Screen printing Decals are produced by means of a silk screen or it is possible to apply the design directly to the surface with the aid of a screen. There are screens available with the correct mesh to suit Bright preparations and Burnish preparations.

Offset printing Generally uses high grade powder golds with a content of nearly 100% for the production of decals. The addition of a flux is necessary for adhesion.

Steel printing Painter's Gold is mixed with varnish or flux and printed onto tissue paper. However, it is also possible to use thickened Liquid Bright or Burnish Gold if the print on the tissue paper is transferred immediately to the piece for decoration. The addition of some varnish is most helpful. For indirect application, powdery precious metals are dusted onto the pre-printed gold surface and fired. As the basic surface already has a flux it is not necessary to use flux for this firing.

Stamping The application of gold by rubber stamp is generally thinner than when painted on and therefore requires a higher content gold preparation. This is poured onto a plate and treated with a rubber roll or spatula until the necessary consistency is obtained through the evaporation of the solvents, with consequent increase of the gold content. There are specially developed stamping oils available for this work and the addition of only a very small quantity is necessary.

Machine application The decoration of large quantities of ware with the same design. There are edging and stamping machines which apply the gold with both brushes and rollers.

Spraying Used to decorate large surfaces. After application the painted layers of the precious metal dry to a relatively hard surface and are relatively insensitive to dust. They may be handled with caution, taking care not to scratch or knock the object or deposit impurities on the surface.

Firing There are two separate phases in the firing of precious metals and lustres. First is the evaporation of fumes when the organic components are volatilised, carbonised and finally completely burned off with the oxygen in the air with increasing temperature. The precious metal layer starts to develop at the end of this phase when the temperature is approximately 420°C (790°F). It is essential that there be sufficient oxygen in the kiln during this phase and that the kiln be ventilated for this purpose and to allow the fumes to escape. In the firing of the preparation the flux additions and the metal oxides of the precious metal and lustre layers interact with the silicate components of the glaze, the glass or the enamel and cause mechanical adhesion through a temperature range of 520–830°C (970–1525°F). If the kiln heats too quickly the time/temperature curve could cause a Bright preparation to fire dull or matt or the development of the adhesive power could be reduced. The evaporating fumes could cause problems in the early firing stage and Bright Gold, particularly Bright Citron Gold, may fire dull. In extreme cases, insufficient ventilation could lead to the decomposition of a decoration, especially if the ware is closely stacked or loaded. Contours and shapes of borders may blur or even bleed during the firing process. If air vents cannot be left open, it is advisable to slightly open the door during the initial stages of firing, i.e. up to approximately 420°C (790°F). The layer of precious metal which is produced during the firing process is very sensitive to fumes or other reducing gases; a lack of oxygen prevents the precious metal from fusing with the glaze, allowing it to be easily wiped off after firing. Bright preparations will lose their brilliance and metallic appearance without sufficient ventilation.

Temperatures Temperatures used to fire the precious metal preparations allow for the time/temperature curve to be sufficient to cause the precious metal to fuse with the glaze, glass or enamel. The temperature recommended signifies the peak temperature in the muffle and the temperature of the hottest zone in a continuous kiln. In normal kilns heating is terminated when the required temperature is reached and additional soak is usually not necessary. When firing glass the temperature should be maintained within distinct limits to avoid deformation of the glass and it may prove necessary to maintain the highest permissible temperature for approximately 10–30 minutes to obtain sufficient adhesion. The firing temperature has to vary according to the ceramic base materials and is dependent on the softening point of the glaze or glass. A guide for the conventional firing of porcelain is approximately 800°C (1470°F), for glass approximately 500–580C (930–1075°F), and for enamel 700–800°C (1290–1470°F). Test fires should be performed on all surfaces to be painted as not all are suitable for decoration with precious metals. Too high a temperature will reduce the adherence of the precious metal layer and may cause an unattractive appearance or even the disappearance of the preparation. On soft glazes, colours or enamels the fired precious metal may crack (which may be desirable in some cases). On an ivory porcelain glaze, Bright Gold and Bright Platinum are very sensitive to excess heat and, with a temperature 30–40°C (85–105°F) in excess, will adhere badly or not at all. The same excess in temperature will not adversely affect a normal layer of gold on white porcelain. Bright Citron Gold will lose its characteristic green colour and, according to the degree of excess heat, will become yellowish or reddish. Silver containing Burnish Golds will turn from green to yellow to red at excessive temperatures. The longer the firing cycle, the lower the temperature to obtain the same effect.

Too low a temperature will reduce the adherence of the precious metal to the surface.

Bright preparations need little attention once removed from the kiln. In some cases of certain glazes or glass the bright preparation may have a matt film which may be easily removed with a wet cloth. To check adhesion of decorated glass after firing, the ware should be dipped into water or wiped with a wet cloth; humidity could influence the adherence at a later date if it is not satisfactory at this stage. The Bright decoration on glass may be overcoated with a ceramic flux and refired to refract the gloss of the gold and protect it against mechanical stress; this causes electrical isolation as well.

Burnish preparations have a dull, non-metallic appearance and have to be polished or burnished, either with moist fine sand or a glass brush. A spectacular finish will be obtained with the use of an agate, bloodstone or steel wool. This mechanical burnishing will affect the cohesion of the gold particles and improve the adherence. This procedure improves resistance to the chemical influence of detergents or acidic foods as well as enhancing durability, brilliance and attractiveness. The karat value of Bright Gold decoration can be designated at 22–24 karat and that of Bright Citron Gold approximately 17 karat. The karat value of Burnish Gold ranges between the two. The content of reddish golds is about 22–24 karat and of green Burnish Golds about 18 karat. Powder golds range in value from 19–24 karat. The thickness of the gold decoration also has to be taken into consideration.

FLORAL PRODUCTS

[Floral products are no longer readily available, however, I have left this section in the book as they are undoubtedly still in a large number of workrooms and studios.]

Acid Under Base A texture paste applied with a sponge, brush or pen to a glazed surface and fired at 780–815°C (1435–1500°F). Gold or lustre may be applied over the matt area to give an etched look without the use of acid.

Floral Enamel A raised and shiny enamel originally developed for scrollwork and dots and to be used in conjunction with Liquid Bright Gold. It should be mixed to a stiff consistency and penned on. If it is too sloppy or fired too high, it will flatten; however, it may be used in a 'sloppy' state and applied with sponge or a spatula. Colour may be added to the enamels but beware of reds as they will fire out. Lustre may be sponged over the fired enamel and this will effect a colour change. Enamel for stiff work should be fired at 780°C (1435°F) and up to 860°C (1580°F) for flat work.

Flux A powder product mixed with medium to a stiff consistency for the application of glass beads which are designed to stay on, or for a bed for glass sand to be sprinkled into and chipped off. Fire to 780–810°C (1435–1490°F) for glass to fuse. Glass can be chipped off with a spatula. Take care—chip down and away from eyes. Gold and lustre can now be painted on this unglazed area for a matt effect.

Grounding Oil Thick oil used for solid colour effect. Oil is spread evenly with a brush or sponge, adding turpentine if too thick and sticky. Pat off excess oil with a sponge covered with silk and apply dry powders evenly and not too thickly as they will chip off if too heavily applied. Do not open kiln door until cold.

Liquid Bright Gold Will mature at 600°C (1110°F). Paint over bare porcelain, other glazed surface or enamel for a shiny effect, or over Acid Under Base or paint for a matt appearance.

Lustre Applied with pen or brush, sponged on or dipped in water. Several light coats are more effective than one or two heavy coats. Various colour combinations may be used, however it is advisable to use lighter colours first.

Masking Lacquer Painted over an area to be protected from the application of grounding or lustre after which the masking lacquer is peeled off and the piece fired. Brushes are cleaned with methylated spirits or acetone. Cover Coat serves the same purposes as Masking Lacquer but is water-based.

Metallic paints Comprehensive range of colours available. May be grounded or multi-dusted with other compatible colours. May be used for normal painting or, thickly applied, they may be used to enhance ordinary paints. Fire 780–900°C (1455–1650°F).

Raised Paste Yellow paste used for scrollwork. Fire at 780–815C (1455–1500°F) and paint with Roman or Unfluxed Gold. May be used for stamens on flowers in dot form.

Texture Coat A powder which may be used with a variety of liquids to achieve a stiff crackled appearance. Mix with milk, lemonade, glycerine, oil-based mediums, etc. for different effects. Applied with pen, sponge or spatula. May also be mixed with tin and zinc oxides. Different kiln temperatures will give different effects (780–860°C, 1455–1580°F). Colour may be added to the mixture or the fired product painted with golds or lustres.

Floral Fun with Texture

Requirements

Floral Flux—Floral Water-based Medium

Floral glass beads—Floral Texture Coat

Floral Liquid Bright Gold—Floral Liquid Bright Platinum

Floral lustres—Floral metallics

Sketch a design onto the porcelain. Mix flux with water-based medium and paint design with mixture. Cover fluxed area with glass beads and fire to 815°C (1500°F). Chip off glass bead layer and decorate with gold, platinum, lustres, metallics or paint. If powdered paints and metallics are mixed with water-based medium they may be applied during the same firing.

Texture Coat may be used to add raised surfaces to your design. Mix with water-based medium, apply to design, fire and decorate with gold or platinum.

Glass beads Mix flux with water-based medium, add glass beads and apply the mixture with a palette knife to the porcelain. For an enamel like appearance fire to 1000–1100°C (1830–2010°F) before any colour is painted on. For a normal appearance, fire to 800°C (1470°F).

Copper enamel may be added to some designs; best results are obtained if it is mixed with water-based medium and applied on the last firing.

FAY GOOD'S PRODUCTS

American Marble Oil Marbling Oil is used for both mixing and painting. Mix your colour to a normal painting consistency with marbling oil and brush on using short strokes; try to obtain a mixture of light and dark values. Dip the article into a container of very hot water where the marbling will take place immediately. Take the piece out of the water and allow to dry before firing. Re-dipping is not recommended as too much colour may be removed. Experiment as results vary and can be very effective, unusual and very different—as well as frustrating at times. Too much colour and not enough oil will not give good results whereas for the most part you can achieve an effect which is rewarding and worthwhile. Further information on marbling can be obtained from the book *Gardens and Garlands* by Celée Evans, self published, USA 1990.

Australian Open Medium An open medium used for painting and mixing paints. If desired, paints may be mixed with this medium (and will keep indefinitely) and painting done with copaiba medium.

Citrus Solvent Turpentine substitute and a boon for those allergic to turpentine or its aroma.

Dresden Base for Raised Gold Can be mixed with any medium you wish. Can be put on top of wet paint. Liquid Bright Gold can be fired on top of the scrollwork done with this powder. Can be fired repeatedly. Fire to Cone 016–017 (780–820°C, 1435–1510°F).

Dresden Raised Enamel Mix with enamel medium and pure gummed spirits of turpentine. A very hard enamel used for jewelling work. Can be coloured with powder paint if desiring to make coloured enamel. Fire to Cone 016 or 017 (780–820°C, 1435–1510°F). Can be fired many times if necessary.

Dresden Raised Paste and Gold Underlay Grind powder on a glass slab with completely denatured alcohol. Allow to dry back to powder. Mix powder with Essence of Grasse or Dresden medium (for raised paste) until like pie dough, then add only pure gummed spirits of turpentine or Dresden raised paste thinners until creamy. Fire to Cone 017 (800°C, 1470°F). Do not take out of the kiln while hot. Allow the kiln to become completely cold before removing the article. This paste can be coated with *Liquid Bright Gold, Roman, Unfluxed* or *Liquid*

Burnishing Golds. Fire again to Cone 018 (760°C, 1400°F).

Note: The application of paste should not be too raised, only a light relief decoration.

Dresden Thinners Used to thin raised paste after mixing with *Dresden Raised Paste Medium*. Also good for those allergic to turpentine. Can be used for pen oil.

Enamel Medium Mix enamel powder with a few drops of this medium until crumbly consistency, thin with pure gummed spirits of turpentine until it strings.

Essence of Grasse (French fat oil) May be used to mix paints, to ground, etc., but cannot be used as painting medium.

Essence of Chamarre An open hyperallergenic medium used for mixing and painting. Paints will keep open indefinitely when mixed with this medium. If desired, copaiba medium may be used to paint.

French Acid Etch Paste Used as a substitute for acid etching. Mix powder with any medium you would like and apply only a thin wash of mixture in the design of your choice, e.g. scrolls, flowers. Fire to Cone 016 (800–820°C, 1470–1510°F). Second fire, coat with Liquid Bright Gold and fire to Cone 018 (760°C, 1400°F).

Gold Contrast Varnish A water-soluble product for applying gold or lustres over a dark surface. Brush the varnish where you want to apply gold or lustre and allow to dry. This will create a coloured film over the area so that the gold or lustre will be easy to see as it is applied. When fired the film will burn away without affecting the gold.

Grounding Oil Cover the area you wish to ground with this medium and then pad with very fine silk until only a thin, very even wash of oil is left. Cover with dry powder paint, remove excess and fire. This grounding oil will stay open longer than most and it is important to pad it well. You do not need to have a lot of oil on the china.

Ground Resist–Red Water-soluble plastic film painted on areas to protect from grounding, paint, golds, etc. If too thick, add a drop of water; clean brushes in water. It is advisable to keep separate brushes for this resist.

Grounding Resist–Green Acetone based film, stronger than red resist film. Peels off easily before firing. For use in conjunction with air brushing or water-based mediums. Clean brushes with acetone or nail polish remover.

CERAMIC SOLUTIONS

4/16 Corner Korong Rd & Orthla Avenue West Heidelberg 3081. Tel: (03) 9459 7284 Fax: 9530 4742

Underglazes

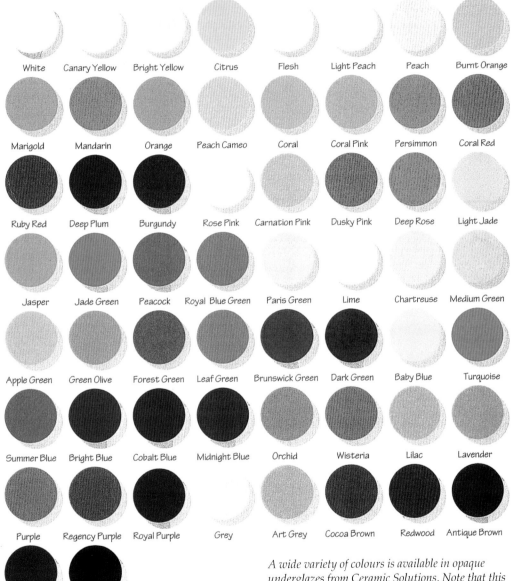

White · Canary Yellow · Bright Yellow · Citrus · Flesh · Light Peach · Peach · Burnt Orange

Marigold · Mandarin · Orange · Peach Cameo · Coral · Coral Pink · Persimmon · Coral Red

Ruby Red · Deep Plum · Burgundy · Rose Pink · Carnation Pink · Dusky Pink · Deep Rose · Light Jade

Jasper · Jade Green · Peacock · Royal Blue Green · Paris Green · Lime · Chartreuse · Medium Green

Apple Green · Green Olive · Forest Green · Leaf Green · Brunswick Green · Dark Green · Baby Blue · Turquoise

Summer Blue · Bright Blue · Cobalt Blue · Midnight Blue · Orchid · Wisteria · Lilac · Lavender

Purple · Regency Purple · Royal Purple · Grey · Art Grey · Cocoa Brown · Redwood · Antique Brown

Crimson · Cobalt Black

A wide variety of colours is available in opaque underglazes from Ceramic Solutions. Note that this reproduction may vary slightly in colour from the originals (Courtesy Ceramic Solutions)

Opaque Underglaze - Made In Australia

Colours are reproductions and may vary slightly from original.

Earthenware Glazes
Lead Free

ALL THESE GLAZES ARE FOOD AND DRINK SAFE

Colours available in lead-free earthenware glazes from Walker's (Courtesy Walker Ceramics)

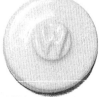

WEG101 Clear Gloss

WEG100 White Gloss

WEG110 White Satin

WEG111 White Matt

WEG200 Ivory Vellum

WEG119 Turquoise

WEG116 Golden Brown

WEG132 Egyptian Blue

WEG202 Turquoise

WEG211 Aventurine

WEG162 Rockingham

WEG131 Italian Blue

WEG201 Olive Green

WEG114 Primrose

WEG207 Jade Blue Break

WEG115 Dark Blue

WEG209 Sea Green Break

WEG161 Honey

WEG164 Victoria Green

WEG210 Oatmeal Break

WEG206 Peacock Break

WEG166 Black

WEG117 Tryolite

WEG163 Raspberry

WEG165 Grey Jade

WEG147 Black

I-Relief Mix with oil, water-based medium or milk, in other words any medium you choose, to a dryish mixture. Every oil or mixture used will produce a different result. Apply with a knife or toothpick. I-Relief shrinks in firing and has a semi gloss finish. Dry approximately two hours before firing to 800–850°C (1470–1560°F). If underfired it will have a matt rough surface. Correct this by firing to a higher temperature for semi-gloss. When fired it will be a creamy beige colour. I-Relief can be used as a glue to fire beads on. China can be repaired with I-Relief also, but please experiment. I-Relief on kiln furniture acts as a cement, so be careful not to allow unfired pieces to drop off porcelain when using furniture in the kiln.

Ivory, Pink, Crystal Clear Glazes These are definitely NOT to be used on food-bearing surfaces. The glazes are generally applied to the white porcelain by mixing them with any medium, painting them on, padding well so as not to leave brushstrokes and then firing to a temperature of about 860°C (1580°F). This gives a gloss over the whole surface. When applying colour over these glazes it is essential, especially when using reds, to lower the firing temperature considerably. Normal painting on top of the glazes should be around 720–760°C (1330–1400°F).

Lead in paints The reason for stating the firing temperature on the label of paint phials is that all paints contain a certain amount of lead, and the danger lies in paints not sufficiently matured in the firing being put to domestic use. Correct firing is essential so that the leachable lead content does not cause lead poisoning.

Medium for Raised Paste Add a few drops to the raised paste powder until it is a crumbly consistency and then add pure gummed spirits of turpentine until stringy.

Metallic Colours for Grounding Grind powder on a tile with completely denatured alcohol (or methylated spirits) and allow to dry completely back to powder. Apply grounding oil to area to be grounded and pad very well. Place dry metallic colour onto oil and lightly rub into oil with a cotton ball. It is not necessary to use a mop brush as this powder flies more than normal powder. Fire to Cone 016–017 (770–795°C, 1420–1460°F). All onglaze colours fire at 800–840°C (014–016). All reds will take a high firing.

Pearl Colours for Glass and Porcelain These are the metallic type finishes painted or ground onto your choice of ware. The colours have a very soft sheen when fired onto white porcelain or clear glass but will change dramatically when fired onto a dark surface, i.e. over black or dark blue.

Glass pearl colours fire to 560–600°C (1040–1110°F) and pearl colours for glass fire at 800–900°C (1470–1650°F).

Pen Oil Add a few drops to powder paint and mix to ink consistency. It may be mixed in larger quantities and stored in a glass jar.

Petit Point Mix Stir mixture well and place a small amount on a tile. Thin with turpentine or Citrus Solvent. Tie bridal tulle tightly over porcelain piece, sponge the mixture over the tulle and leave to dry for a few days. Remove tulle and fire to Cone 015–014 or 800–840°C (1470–1545°F). Paint with normal painting colours and fire to Cone 018 or 740°C (1365°F). Petit Point mix can be coloured with a small amount of ceramic powder if you want it tinted rather than white.

Powdered Gold 97% pure gold powder. It can be applied to white porcelain or over raised paste. It will adhere when stippled to a sticky surface such as padded grounding oil. It is fired to 800°C (1470°F) or at a temperature suitable to the type of ware used and needs no further burnishing when taken from the kiln. Expensive to purchase but very economical to use.

Pre-mixed Enamel Stir in jar well. Remove a small amount onto a mixing tile. Add only pure gummed spirits of turpentine if necessary. Can be refired repeatedly. Fire to Cone 016 or 017 (780–820°C, 1435–1510°F).

Pre-mixed Raised Paste Take a small amount from the jar and add only pure gummed spirits of turpentine until stringy and creamy. Fire to Cone 017. Do not take out of the kiln while hot. Allow the kiln to become completely cold before removing article. Coat with any of the golds.

Ruff-It Texture paste in form of white powder which may be mixed with most solutions, each of which gives a different result. Fired at a range of temperatures which will also have an effect on the appearance of the fired paste.

Texture Paste This can be used through a syringe and piped onto the porcelain giving a spaghetti-like effect. Burnishing sand mixed with it and sponged onto the porcelain will give it a rough texture. Fire to Cone 016–015 or 800–840°C (1470–1545°F). Gold can be applied to the fired paste. Available for porcelain and for glass.

Underbase Acid Look Pre-mixed paste, yellow in colour. Apply to porcelain very thinly and fire. Paint with *Liquid Bright Gold* and fire again. The gold will appear matt. A very useful imitation acid etch effect. Add burnishing sand for use in modern techniques.

White Raised Paste Available in either pre-mixed or powder form. Has better adherence to porcelain than *Dresden Raised Paste*. Can have either *Liquid Bright Gold, Platinum* or *Burnishing Gold* applied over the fired paste.

Weeping Opal Lustre This is an effect type lustre which will give a tear-like appearance. Brush the lustre in one direction and then in a cross direction. Stand the piece upright until dry. As it dries, the lustre will weep down. Fire when dry. Apply over fired *Liquid Bright Gold* or *Platinum* for an interesting effect.

White Transfer Paper Ideal for applying a traced pattern to a dark surface. Can be used for tole painting.

Kitty Drok Products
(Courtesy of Alexander's)

Covercoat Water-soluble red liquid which dries to form a plastic film to cover and mask previously painted areas when grounding or using lustres or gold, etc.

Copaiba Medium Open painting medium but not as open as the *Odourless Medium.*

Crystal Clear Glaze Gives a high gloss to painted areas. *Do not* apply over red. Fire at 780°C (1435°F).

Grounding Oil Thick quick-drying oil which does not attract dust. Powder paints may be applied straightaway. For large areas, add a drop or two of turpentine to keep it open.

Mixing Medium Stays open indefinitely but does not allow paint to spread. Does not attract dust and may be used as pen oil if mixed with paint from the palette and thinned with turpentine. To preserve brushes, wash in turpentine and wipe off excess. Dip into mixing medium to keep brush hairs supple and soft.

Odourless Medium A medium which does not have a strong smell and has more grip for painting on the porcelain surface. A very open medium which dries sufficiently to be non-slippery; for use for dry dusting.

Pre-mixed Enamels Ten colours are available; gold can be applied over these enamels.

Petit Point Paste Apply over a glazed surface to obtain a bisque finish. May be used to obtain a raised effect under gold work as well as in place of Acid Under Base. May also be used for repair work, repairing chips or flaws. Dries quickly to allow easy removal of netting. *Do not apply red over Petit Point paste.*

Josephine Robinson: Gilberton Gallery, Glass and Porcelain Products

Amethyst Gemstone Kit The most highly valued stone in the quartz group. This kit is for the rumbled variety as it shows more colour variations and vein markings, making it easier to duplicate. The particular colours include purple, a dark wine colour and a black. Paint a relatively smooth coat of the lighter purple and texture with crumpled cling wrap to obtain an irregular pattern. Fire. Mix 8 parts of the dark wine colour and 1 part black and apply over the first coat, texturing as before but leaving some solid patches of colour. Fire. Apply a third coat of the darker mix sparingly and fire again.

Designing tape For controlled narrow bands of colour and gold this easy-to-use tape may be applied in many ways. Will stretch for curved surfaces. Available in 4 metre lengths.

Dispersing Kit Textural effects with china paints comparable to watercolour techniques. Paint and fire the first coat. Thin regular paints with the dispersing oil and paint areas of the second coat then, standing 60–100 cm (2'–3') from the porcelain, lightly spray the wet painting with dispersing oil. Check results after a minute or so, adding more spray if needed. A third firing will allow detail and finishing touches. Firing temperatures are 800–825°C (1470–1520°F).

Etched Look White powder compound which, applied to glass and fired, gives the appearance of etched glass. There is also a Matt Etched Look.

Faux finishes Malachite, turquoise, sodalite, amethyst.

Glass Crystals Clear and coloured glass crystals suitable for decoration on glass—patterns, borders and texture on glass surfaces. To use, paint surface with glass glue and sprinkle the glass crystals liberally on the prepared area. Clean surrounding area and fire in the range of 540–580°C (1005–1075°F).

Glass Pearl range Pearlised colours developed for painting on glass. Interesting effects are created when colours are applied over dark backgrounds, especially blue or black. Fire at 560–600°C (1040–1110°F).

Glass Products Glass Relief for Gold Kit Powder to be mixed with gold relief medium to a slightly runny consistency. Apply with brush, pen or embossing tool. Clean surround with water and fire to 580°C (1075°F).

Gold Leaf Impressions Kit Comes complete with the mixing agent, texture paste and enhancer. Gather fresh leaves and keep pliable until use. For matt impressions, mix 4 parts of the texture paste and 1 part of the enhancer with the mixing agent to almost ink consistency (very thin). Select a pliable leaf and apply mixture to underside; press to clean or painted porcelain or glazed surface and remove by lifting from one corner, not the centre. Add additional detail with mixture and pointer brush if desired. Fire at 720°C (1330°F). Paint with Liquid Bright Gold and fire again at 670°C (1240°F). Subsequent firings should be 630°C (1165°F) to avoid the gold cracking off the impressions. Matt impressions against white china or wet paint produce an etched look. For gloss impressions, follow the same procedures but omit the enhancer.

Graining comb A wooden triangle with a variety of rubber teeth. Apply paint with open medium, pad with a sponge, then run the comb over the wet paint in C strokes, overlapping, zigzagging, simulating herringbone, making your own designs.

Intaglio Kit Engraved design. Establish the perimeter of the design to be engraved with a chinagraph pencil. Mix paste well and mix again! Apply as thin a coat of intaglio paste as possible with a palette knife and using a very fine sponge, distribute the product evenly over the designated area. If your hand slips and you wish to start the process again, responge the entire area. Fire to 735C (1355F). Apply a good coverage of *Pollyanna Liquid Bright Gold* and fire again at the same temperature.

Kits All kits come with instructions.

Malachite Kit Mix and paint the two lightest colours with large smooth cross-hatching strokes to give a good coverage. With soft paper towelling held loosely over the index finger, simulate the markings of the malachite stone. Using a 2/0 scroller and the darker colour, paint

on the dark lines that run through the stone. Fire at 800°C (1470°F).

Matt Underlay for Matt Burnishing Gold Kit Contains 1 vial powder and 1 underlay medium for easy gold and etching imitations. Mix underlay powder with underlay medium to a slightly runny consistency and apply with a brush, pen or embossing tool. Fire to 800°C (1470°F). Apply one coat of gold and allow to dry. Apply a second coat of gold and fire to 800–820°C (1470–1510°F).

Marbling Lotion and Marbling Gold For gold and lustres. Creates interesting freeform patterns with wonderful plays of colour which are unique to each piece.

Peelable Resist A resist for use on both glass and porcelain.

Petit Point Gloss Enamel A gloss Petit Point paste which dries in 30 minutes, is fired at 800°C (1470°F) and may be painted. Kind to brushes. Add only pure turpentine to suit application.

Pollyanna Enamelling Plus An enamel for porcelain which can be fired more than once at 800°C (1470°F). May be coloured with dry or pre-mixed paint and painted over wet paint for highlights. It is suitable for scrollwork and the application of gold, paint and lustre once it is fired. It may also be used as a flow enamel with the addition of turpentine. There is no drying time and it will not pop off.

Pollyanna One Fire Wet Grounding Mix dry paint with *Pollyanna Grounding Oil* until crumbly. Add lavender oil until the consistency of pen oil and apply with sponge brush by dipping brush into the mixture and pouncing on the china. Keep pouncing until you hear a smacking sound. Fire at 800°C (1470°F) (some pinks a little higher). Clean sponge brush in Preen or similar product and rinse in cool water. Dry on a paper towel.

Portrait paints Powder paints specifically developed in flesh tones for painting portraits.

Raised Paste for Liquid Bright Gold Kit Contains 1 vial of powder and 1 raised paste medium. The ivory coloured raised paste powder is mixed with the raised paste medium to a creamy consistency and applied with either a brush, pen or embossing tool. Clean well with water and fire to 800°C (1470°F). Apply Liquid Bright Gold over the raised paste and fire to 750°C (1380°F).

Silk Look A white powder product for glass decoration. May be painted on or grounded with *Pollyanna Grounding Oil*. Fire at 520–580°C (970–1075°F). The higher the temperature, the greater the transparency.

Silky Matt Gold Beautiful lemon matt gold which burnishes itself in the kiln and is dishwasher resistant. It has a slight matt film after firing and looks like pure burnished gold but usually needs no after treatment. The firing range is 650–900°C (1200–1650°F). Must be stirred well before use.

Sodalite Gemstone Kit Sodalite comes in all shades of blue, interspersed with white calcite and many fractures which show several shades of brown tones ranging from beige to deep amber. Found mainly in Brazil and the USA and occasionally confused with lapis lazuli. Mix 8 parts of the darker blue and 1 part black and paint a smooth coat on the porcelain surface. Texture the paint with a crumbled 25 cm (10″) square of plastic cling wrap. Draw in the large white veins with the chisel end of a wipe-out tool. For stone variation, paint a smooth coat of the lighter blue and texture as above. Fire. Carefully paint light orange/brown into the wiped-out vein lines. This requires a separate fire as the blue and orange paint will make the wrong colour if painted together. For the third fire paint and texture again a smooth coat of the lighter blue and wipe off any marks on the orange veins. A variation would be to paint and texture this third coat with the darker colour and use Liquid Bright Gold on the veins.

Sponge brush Soft fine sponge with wooden handle. An invaluable tool with many uses. May be washed after use.

Turquoise Gemstone Turquoise is a gemstone that tones and strengthens the entire body. It aids circulation, lungs and the respiratory system. The colour is pale green/blue with black diagonal lines. Paint glazed surface with turquoise green/blue and turquoise blue, varying the tone of the two colours. Pad irregularly with a sponge, making some areas much lighter. Slightly moisten a 2/0 scroller with medium and take out the veins, keeping a diagonal pattern across the area. Add some dark veins with the 2/0 scroller and black, flattening the scroller to give thick and thin lines. Fire at 800°C (1470°F).

Spritz It Designing liquid for making texture and bubbles.

White Gloss Enamel Does not require a drying time. Add only pure turpentine to suit application.

Northcote Pottery

Northcote Pottery is a historic pottery founded in 1897 in Thornbury, Victoria. Only one kiln remains and has been restored as a gallery for Australian potters. Clay delivered to the pottery is crushed in a hammer mill and sieved across a fine screen. Water is added and the wet clay fed into an extruder to remove all air. The clay is cut into lengths, coated with a lubricant and pressed into basic plant pot shapes and, if required, hand finished. The pots are dried and fired in a tunnel kiln to 1000°C (1830°F) for 20 hours.

Cookson Matthey 93 Series Onglaze Powder Colours Range of 25 low metal release, intermixable, durable onglaze colours for direct painting and printing and indirect printing applications; suitable for conventional and faster firing cycles.

Firing For firing cycles of 4 or more hours the following temperatures are recommended.
Bone china: 720–800°C (1330–1470°F)
Porcelain: 760–830°C (1400–1525°F)
Vitreous china: 720–800°C (1330–1470°F)
Earthenware: 680–780°C (1255–1435°F)
All Series 93 colours (except iron red and the cadmium colours) are intermixable in all proportions. There is a mixing white and a mixing flux to extend the palette. Cadmium colours are intermixable with each other. The gold colours are fully intermixable with each other and other basic colours with some limitations. Tests are always recommended.

Dishwasher durability test Immersion in a 0.5% Calgonite solution at 78°C, in accordance with Johnson Matthey Test Specifications shows no appreciable deterioration of either colour or gloss after 32 hours exposure which is an accelerated alternative to 500 consecutive dishwasher cycles.

Metal release test Immersion in 4% acetic acid at ± 2°C for 24 hours in accordance with DIN51031, 1986, resulted in typically less than 0.3mg Pb/dm² and 0.03mg Cd/dm². Dishwasher durability and metal release generally improve as firing temperatures are increased within the ranges indicated.

Screen Printing recommendations Mesh sizes of 71–120T (180–305) for all applications and powder to medium ratios are dependent on application—Decals 10:7 to 10:5 and direct printing 10:6 to 10:4

Storage of colours Store in sealed containers and avoid extreme climatic conditions.

THERMAL CERAMICS

The following information is courtesy of Thermal Ceramics, Sydney:

Ceramic fibre has low thermal conductivity, extremely small heat storage per unit volume and is lightweight and flexible. (It is not as strong as fire brick and has a low resistance to corrosion.) It will withstand temperatures ranging from 1100–1400°C [2000–2550°F]. The following products and their uses pertain to kiln and glaze artistry.

[*Author's note:* I have used a number of the following products when slumping and find their versatility great for making moulds of specific, individual and unique shapes. I have fired each of these home-made moulds a number of times and find they last reasonably well, the actual number of firing times depending on care and the use to which they are put. It is advisable to use the Hardener on the moulds prior to firing.]

Kaowool bulk fibre: General purpose insulating bulk fibre which comes in a standard form and also with zirconia; used as furnace back up insulation, fillers, asbestos replacement. Fires to 1260°C and 1400°C respectively and is available in 10 kg bags.

Kaowool blanket standard Mat composed of needled interlocking fibres which are strong, flexible and lightweight with low heat storage and thermal conductivity. Used as kiln lining, making moulds and forming shapes over which to slump glass. The standard form fires to 1260°C and is available in thicknesses of (a) 13, 19, 25, 38, 50 mm; (b) 9, 13, 19, 25, 38, 50 mm; (c) 9, 13, 19, 25, 38, 50 mm; and (d) 9, 13, 19, 25 mm. The width is 610 mm and the length varies with the 9 mm being 10 metres, the 13, 19 and 25 mm is 7.6 metres and the 38 and 50 mm is 3.8 metres.

Kaowool blanket with zirconia: Has similar properties as the standard blanket however is used for high temperature applications. Fires to 1400C° and comes in thicknesses of 19 and 25 mm, width of 610 mm and length of 7.6 metres.

Lt Batt: A flexible low temperature grade alumino-silicate material. Fires to 900°C. Available in 25, 50 mm thickness and 600 mm width and 915 mm length.

Wet Felt: Made from the standard blanket, saturated with hardener. It is strong and pliable and easy to cut or mould. It will set rigid on air drying, producing a strong, lightweight material. Available in 6, 13, 19, 25 mm thickness and in width and length of 610 mm by 915 mm. Will fire to 1260°C.

Triple T: Wet felt which expands 2 to 3 times original thickness on heating. Available in three temperature grades, 1200°, 1400° and 1600°C. Available in thicknesses of 6, 12.5, 25 mm and width and length of 600 mm and 900 mm respectively.

Kaowool board There are several types of board available:

1200 Vacuum formed board from fibre and binders which comes in thicknesses of 5, 10, 12, 20, 25, 30 and 50 mm and the two sizes available are 500 x 1000 mm and 610 x 1000 mm. The firing temperature is 1260°C. May be cut, shaped and sanded to form moulds and other free form shapes.

1400 As 1200 but fires to 1400°C. Comes in 20, 25 and 50 mm widths and 500 x 1000 mm and 610 x 1000 mm slabs.

1600 Another vacuum formed board from fibres and binders which fires to 1600°C. Thickness is 25 mm and the size is 500 x 1000 mm.

S Vacuum formed board from fibre, fillers and binders for improved hardness. Thicknesses are 10 and 25 mm and the available size is 500 x 1000 mm.

HS45 Durable high strength board formed using fibre, unique fillers and a multi-component binder system. Comes in 10 and 12 mm width boards, 500 x 1000 mm and fires to 1300°C.

Millboard Durable high strength board utilizing fibre, fillers and binders which is available in 3 and 6 mm widths, 100 x 100 mm, and fires to 1150°C.

Rigidised Durable high strength board composed of fillers and a multi-component binder system and available in 1260, 1400 and S material. Sizes and firing temperatures as per board used.

Kaowool paper Manufactured on conventional paper making machines from ceramic fibre and using a binder to maximise tensile strength without impairing flexibility. Available in thicknesses of 0.5, 1.0, 2.0 and 3.0 mm measured under compression. The widths are 500 and 610 mm and the lengths vary from 80 m down to 15 m. The firing temperatures are 1260° and 1400°C.

The available textiles are:

Rope which comes in a variety of diameters from 6mm to 50mm and varies in length from 400 m for the thinnest rope to 20 m for the thicker rope. It fires at 1260°C.

Cloth and tape which also comes in various widths and lengths.

Mastic Mouldable form of Kaowool fibre for hand moulding. Available in a 5 kg pail, and fires to 1260°C.

Coatings:

J Cote Chrome alumina coating for resistance to chemical attack, high velocity and abrasion which comes in 5 kg pails and fires to 1600°C.

Hardener Inorganic hardening agent for high velocity and abrasion resistance is available in 5 litre pails and 200 litre drums. Fires to 1600°C.

Cements: 1. Kaowool adhesive for fibre to fibre or fibre to refractory products and for refractory surface coating. Available in a 5 litre pail and fires to 1600°C.

2. Kaogrip adhesive for fibre to low porosity surfaces. Also available in a 5 litre pail and fires to 1000°C.

3. Veneering refractory mortar for modules. Available in a 20 kg drum and fires to 1550°C.

WALKER CERAMICS

Body stains, glaze stains, underglaze stains Colouring oxides or agents with stabilisers and modifiers which may be added to clear, coloured or opaque glazes, mixed with clay bodyand clear glaze to make engobes, added to clay body or slip to produce a coloured body or applied to bisque as an underglaze. *See* manufacturer's directions for individual products.

Casting Clays Filter pressed and powder, earthenware and stoneware bodies are available to make casting slips. To prepare, add water in amounts as directed. Slips may be coloured by adding body stains. Recipes provided on request. Slips are available in earthenware, stoneware and terracotta. All slips are easy to pour and use, with with good green and fired strength. Firing temperatures are normally 1000°C (1830°F) for biscuit, 1060–1250°C (1940–2280°F) for earthenware glazes and to 1300°C (2370°F) for stoneware.

Cerama pens Pens which contain metallic bright gold or silver which are easy to use for linework.

Clays Stoneware, special stoneware, fine white stoneware (PB 103), white earthenware, pink earthenware, white porcelain, hand building terracotta, school terracotta, throwing terracotta, fine throwing terracotta, terracotta earthenware, are among the 60 different bodies available.

Decorative colours, onglazes and lustres Colours which are applied over previously fired and glazed ware and fired at a lower temperature, usually between 700–800°C (1290–1470°F). Clean greenware and fire to bisque Cone 4. Apply lustres thinly and evenly. Brushes should be kept scrupulously clean or, if possible, a separate one used for each lustre. Best results with opal and mother of pearl lustres are caused by stippling and swirling with the brush when applying the lustres. Lustres painted on satin or matt glazes will be satin or matt; overfiring will result in fading, distortion and burn-out while underfiring will result in poor adhesion. Recommended procedure is to fire low for one hour with all bungs out, medium for one hour until smoking and odour has disappeared and then fire on high until desired temperature is reached with the top bung in and others out. The lustre will thicken if exposed to air and may be thinned carefully with gold or lustre essence, one drop at a time. Do not thin halo or metallic lustres. Thickened lustres may be used where precise brush control is required or for edges and decorative sponge work.

Egyptian Paste Self-glazing lead-free clay suitable for jewellery. Add water to powder to make paste and form shapes by rolling or hand modelling. Hang beads and buttons, etc. on nichrome wire and allow to dry for complete glazing. Colours are obtained by the addition of oxides to the basic white clay powder.

Engobes Available in white earthenware, white stoneware and terracotta. White engobes may be coloured with body stains. Firing temperatures for earthenware 1060–1250°C (1940–

2280°F), stoneware 1260–1300°C (2300–2370°F), terracotta 1000–1100°C (1830–2010°F).

Glazes Available in powder and liquid form, with best results obtained when used on clays recommended by the Manufacturer. Liquid glazes should be shaken vigorously and stirred and if still too thick a little water may be added. Powdered glazes may be mixed with Walker painting medium, following the manufacturer's instructions for correct consistency for brushing and dipping. Water may be added if necessary.

Cadmium selenium glazes: Bright vivid sensitive glazes which are totally unsuitable for food utensils. Apply in a similar thickness to opaque glazes to bisque ware which has been fired to complete maturity and dry completely before firing. If too much water has been added to the glaze, add more dry glaze. Do not let it settle and then pour off surplus. Fire alone, preferably in an uncrowded electric kiln, as these glazes are intolerant of steam and kiln gases caused by greenware and other glazes. If using a gas kiln it should be fully muffled or the ware set in saggers. Firing temperatures vary so follow manufacturer's advice. Remove plugs when firing is complete to allow naturally rapid cool.

Earthenware lead free glazes: Suitable for food and beverage utensils and fired at earthenware temperatures. Exciting colour range including Peacock, Jade Blue, Sea Green. Varieties include *base, coloured gloss, coloured matt* and *gloss break*. Base glazes are either transparent or opaque white to enable the artist to achieve individual colours. Techniques: **1.** Apply underglaze design to greenware and fire to bisque temperature, then coat with a transparent glaze. **2.** Alternatively, apply an underglaze design over an unfired opaque gloss, satin, or matt glaze. The design will remain sharp over a matt glaze but spread over an unfired gloss glaze. **3.** Apply one glaze over another either by dipping, brushing or spraying. An oxidising atmosphere will give different results to a reduction atmosphere.

Fritted lead glazes: A number of these glazes are not suitable for food and beverage utensils and these are clearly identified. All other glazes in this range are non-toxic when fired correctly. Red and white lead are not used at all as they are considered dangerous materials.

Middle fire glazes: All these glazes are lead-free, stable, suitable for food and beverage utensils, available in powder and liquid form and suit a wide variety of clays. Firing temperature 1250°C

(2280°F). Varieties include satin and glass base glazes, gloss glazes in flats and breaks, matt glaze and satin glaze.

One stroke underglazes: Translucent range of intermixable colours suitable for one-stroke application on greenware, bisque or unfired glaze. To apply, remove small amount of colour from the jar and bring to desired consistency for brushing, sponging, spraying or airbrushing with the addition of a little water. Fire between 1000–1220°C (1830–2230°F).

Stoneware glazes: Wide variety of colours in this lead-free range, suitable for food and beverage containers and available in liquid or powder form. These glazes are intermixable, allowing double dipping, mottling, pouring on or painting over and under each other, providing a great range of unique and individual results; as well, they are stable in oxidising and reduction atmospheres.

Liquid underglazes Suitable for all stages of expertise (and lack of it), these pre-mixed, ready-to-use Australian opaque, lead-free, intermixable underglazes are suitable for both stoneware and earthenware temperatures and may be applied to greenware and bisque. *Brushing:* Thoroughly clean surface and using a fully loaded good quality sable or ox hair brush, apply two or three coats of underglaze, drying in between, in alternate directions to avoid streaking. *Sponging:* Pour a small amount onto a palette and with a slightly damp sponge, apply three coats, drying in between. *Airbrushing:* Thin with water to correct consistency and apply, making sure the apparatus is cleaned thoroughly between colours. *Banding:* Apply with brush or sponge to rotating greenware. Do not let brush rest on greenware when it is not rotating. *Majolica:* Apply a heavy coat of glaze, allow to dry and smooth back with a dry sponge prior to applying a coat of underglaze over the unfired first coat. *Polishing:* Buff applied underglaze when it is almost dry with soft tissues in a circular motion. Keep surface moist with spray. *Antiquing:* Apply thinned underglaze to bisque surface and texture with a damp sponge. Glaze with transparent or semi-transparent glaze. *Raised design work:* Thicken underglaze by exposing a small amount to air and apply in lines of various depths to create pattern. *Sgraffito:* Scratch a design into the applied, slightly damp glaze. *Slip trailing*: Dampen greenware and apply slip which has been thickened with underglaze. *Spattering and stippling:* Apply two or three coats, using several colours, with a stipple brush.

Mask It   Resist which is applied thickly to greenware, decoration or glaze, is brushed or sprayed on. The latex mask can be peeled off or it will fire off in the kiln.

Underglaze pencils   Range of vivid colours in pencil form for applying to bisque ware. Most are suitable for a wide range of firing temperatures.

Wax resist   Mask to protect portions of the clay body from stains, underglaze or glaze. Will fire off in the kiln. Apply resist, allow to set, then simply paint on decoration. The colour or glaze will not adhere to the wax which may be wiped clean or left with a little of the residue.

Plyrite binder   May be used to thicken any colours except cadmium/selenium glazes. Mix colour and binder to thick mud consistency and apply. Will shrink during firing to approximately half its unfired height.

Hints

Students

1. Arrive on time. However, if you do arrive late, try not to disrupt the class. They have paid for their lesson. Do not stay later to make up time as your teacher will have planned the day.
2. Paint the class projects. There is time at home for you to do anything which is not included in your teacher's curriculum. Also, if you do not want to do what the class is doing this week, it will not be long before you do want to and your teacher is going to be exasperated at having to say it all again!
3. Take care of borrowed aids and designs.
4. Have all your own equipment labelled. All unlabelled 'found' equipment usually finds another home.

Things to do before painting a piece

1. Remove labels, tags, etc.
2. Clean with methylated spirits.
3. Check which way is up by looking for hanging holes. Mark top with graphite or grease pencil.
4. If flawed, plan your design to disguise flaw.
5. Plan the line of your design and, if you must, draw a pencil line to keep you on it. Draw another shorter design line across it so that you know where to branch your groupings.
6. Sketch some of the blossoms you intend to paint on paper, cut out and position them on the plate until you are pleased with the composition. Do not pick up the brush, paint a flower, turn the plate around three times and paint another at random at half or twice the size of the first one and hope to join the two together. It only works for the experienced—sometimes.
7. Think in threes. Three of everything: light, shade, values, colour (that is, three colours on the one petal, leaf, roof line, tree, etc., not the whole design). Large, medium, small areas; original colour, shaded colour and reflected colour. Foreground, middle distance and background. Threes!
8. Leave plenty of light. Even dark areas have light—especially the pupils in eyes.
9. Paint a different colour over a fired colour for a translucent effect—one of the advantages of painting on porcelain or glazed white ceramics.
10. Keep your palette clean and dust-free but do not be discouraged by a messy palette—it simply means that you are mixing the loads on your brush and blending your colours, for which you are to be congratulated. Just clean up after each painting session.
11. When painting a flower always start with the centre, even if you will not be able to see it in the finished painting. The centre is the part which holds the flower together and, therefore, the most important part. It has to be there. If you paint the petals to the centre, the sepals to the centre and the stem to the centre, your flower will be in proportion.

Things to do after painting a piece

1. Check for design faults.
2. Clean edges.
3. Clean base or underside.
4. Sign it.
5. Turn upside down or cover with plastic wrap.
6. If it does not look right before it is fired, it will not look right afterwards.

Practical Pointers

- Too much oil can cause paint to run in the kiln. Some open mediums should be used *very sparingly*. If your painting *looks* wet then it is probably too wet.
- Hold your plate in the palm of your hand. *Thumbs leave prints!*
- Put cotton wool pad soaked in turpentine or oil of cloves in your palette if your paints are not mixed with an open medium or grinding oil. Hopefully, it will keep them fresh a little longer. The oil of cloves will certainly have a more pleasant odour.
- Mix *grainy powder paints* with methylated spirits or turpentine before mixing with normal grinding oil.
- *Do not* put nylon net in your turpentine jar. It will shred your brushes.
- Add flux to a last-minute touch of colour (but not the reds, they fire low anyway) if you want to fire it at a lower temperature than normal because of pastes or enamels in the kiln.
- When painting *medallions* and smaller pieces of porcelain, sit them on a piece of plasticine or Blu-tack onto a slightly larger shard or tile to facilitate holding them. They may be transported to the kiln and fired, still in the same manner.
- Place your *vial of gold* on a piece of plasticine or putty and then in a slightly larger jar to stabilise it. If it spills, you will be faced with an expensive accident.
- When painting *animals* or *portraits,* trace the subject onto clear *plastic* or *acetate,* outlining all the features and colour changes in detail. Use this tracing to check your work for shape and form by holding the pattern above your work.
- *For those who cannot paint roses.* Lightly sketch a rose design in *very fine* line penwork, using violet of iron for your outlines. Have three roses, supporting leaves and stems and a few faintly outlined shadow leaves and shapes. If you have used pen oil, fire; if you have used simple syrup, Coca-Cola or something similar, once it is dry, you may immediately rouge in a creamy yellow rose, using the pad of your finger dipped in oil and then, in yellow paints, adding deeper

colour at the base of the bowl of the rose with an old gold and a little Golden Brown. Use the Golden Brown to give a rich colour and depth to the centre. Stay within your outlines and mould the contours of your leaves and petals with slightly deeper colour towards the outer edges. Keep only a light application in the centres. While you have the yellow tones on your finger, paint a few highlights on the leaf areas. Now paint in a pale pink rose using Blood Red very lightly for the outer petals and a little more heavily for the shading. There is such a wide range of values in Blood Red you may not have to use another colour for variation. Add a little reflected colour to your leaves with the pink. Paint in the third rose with a slightly darker tone of red or orange and paint in your leaves in the same manner using greens and blues. You may have to use a cotton bud for the fine stems. Clean the colour off the white porcelain outside the lines and fire. A simple *one fire finger painted plate or vase* that the rawest newcomer could produce as a morale booster.
- When choosing your porcelain or ceramic blank take into consideration the basic principles of composition, the natural surroundings of your subject and your treatment of it.
- Know your subject. Use fresh flowers when possible and try to draw outlines, various aspects, the leaves, buds, etc. Learn to 'look' at objects. Which geometric shapes best suit what you are trying to draw? Where is the vanishing point for straight converging lines? Where are the shadows?
- Apply a line of dots along a marked ruler for even spacing and accuracy. Use the curved edge of a plate or saucer, marked with a plate divider, for a circle or arc.
- Try to salvage *hardened lustre* with lavender oil. You will probably not have a true colour; however, the gloss is usually there.
- *Clouds* are not all white! Not all clouds are white!
- Before firing *gold* applied to *raised paste* (fired of course), clean up the edges with a craft knife once the gold has dried.

- Paint with *yellow, pink or rose very lightly* in the first fire. They can be disastrous if applied with a heavy hand.
- Paint a *difficult subject* a very, very pale grey to form and mould the shape and follow with washes of colour in subsequent firings.
- A mixed load of lustre and painted objects in the kiln will improve the gloss of the glaze.
- *Pinks* and *rubies* will appear yellow or brown if underfired and blue toned if overfired.
- The *sharpest detail* is found in the *middle values,* not in the highlighted areas or the darker shadow areas.
- *Matt paints* will be glossy if fired high.
- For shadow-filled backgrounds, wash colour over background and wipe out shapes. Fire, wash again with colour. Fire again. Do not overdo it.
- Make *highlights* larger than required for the first painting. They seem to get smaller whether you plan it or not.
- *Rocks,* when painted, should look well settled into the ground and not about to topple.
- Shadows of buildings and other structures should be all in the same direction, either in front of, beyond or to the left or right of the object obstructing the light source, not in every direction at once.
- *Texture* is both *visual* and *tactile.*
- *Do* clean your palette, preferably after each painting session and certainly before every lesson and seminar.
- Do mix your paints before the lesson, not during it.
- *Do* listen to the instructor. You have paid the instructor, not the student talking about the latest grandchild or favourite recipe.
- *Do* ask questions and *listen* to the answers.
- Do show the *baby photos* before or after the lesson, not during it.
- Do remember that a seminar is where you go to be *shown* a new technique. Then, go home and perfect it. Do not expect miracles at the seminar and remember, everything requires practice.
- *Do* take a notebook and *use it.*
- *Do cover a study* with clear plastic, especially if it is not yours!
- When painting wildlife pay particular attention to eyes, claws and facial features, etc.
- Very fine broken outlines of enamel in one or two areas of your design will help with strength and contrast.
- Link your traditional design with scrolls, lattices and grounding if it looks lost.
- An edge of gold may be all your plate needs to really 'finish' it. A band of gold frequently enhances an otherwise plain vase.
- Insect eaten leaves make a more realistic and interesting painting.
- If you do not like your finished product, lightly ground or dust it, outline the design which shows through in black, gold or enamel and paint in a background.
- Use a photocopier to enlarge or diminish designs, or have your colour photos reproduced in larger sizes for studies or seminars.
- Try not to fire a piece immediately after it has been painted. Look at it closely the next day to check for *faults.* It is said that these may be seen more readily in a *mirror.* View from all angles. Something which leaps out at you trying to attract your attention may be trying to tell you something!
- All surfaces should be thoroughly cleaned before applying *gold.*
- Do not apply *gold* to painted but as yet unfired porcelain.
- Allow used *turpentine* to settle and the sediment to fall to the bottom and pour off the clean turpentine into another jar.
- *Flat tiles* or *jewellery pieces* are easily raised with a palette knife so that fingers may be slid underneath to lift and carry, rather than on top where they leave prints.
- Raised *paste* for gold is yellow.
- Raised *base* for gold is white.
- Obtain an *antique look* by painting green lustre over fired gold.
- Always paint a design inside a box for interest. Preferably on the inside of the lid, as well as the base, which would be covered by the contents.
- *Skies* should be darker near the horizon.
- *Horizons* should never cut the tile or blank in half.
- Aim to use natural lines for your *line of design.* Contour lines in a landscape, fracture lines in stone or the character lines on the palms of your hands and, dare I say it, face?
- A well designed handpainted tile, plate or other fired object with your *name, address and telephone number* is good to have nearby when demonstrating. Viewers can take down particulars without interrupting to ask for a card.
- *A highlight* left as you paint is always interesting. One wiped out later may not be.
- When painting *trees* and *bushes,* stipple the tops with a *deerfoot stippler* for a muted, diffused

effect.

• Place your *eraser pencil* in the refrigerator and it will be easier to sharpen.

• *To transport a kiln* line it with cardboard and pack the interior with pillows. Secure the lid or door and pyrometer and tie in place.

• *To replace elements* which have popped out of their groove, heat the kiln for a few seconds, until the element wire is pliable, turn off the kiln and gently lengthen the wire by pulling open the coils slightly and replace them in their grooves.

• When firing *glass lamps,* allow plenty of space between the walls (and elements) of the kiln and the lamp to prevent sagging.

• Designs and monograms on cups are traditionally placed to the left of the handle.

• Add a drop of fat oil (evaporate some turpentine in a shallow dish until thickened and keep a small amount in a jar) to *blues* and *carmines* when painting a wash or tint.

• Too much fat oil will cause the paint to blister, but a little will help both the colour and adhesion.

• *Mother of pearl* may be used over fired paint.

• *Rose leaves* are not spread out like a handful of playing cards. The one at the tip is the largest, the centre vein being a continuation of the stem. The next pair on the stem are slightly smaller and have little or no stem of their own, and the last pair is about half the size of the second pair.

• *Leaves* should match the flower you are painting. Rose leaves do not really suit a daisy and vice versa.

• For *deep, rich colours,* try lightly grounding and then painting over the top of the fired grounding.

• If the darkest value in your design is next to the lightest value, the viewer's eye will go directly to that area.

• Try silk-screen printing a repetitive design on tiles. Simple designs can be made from contact paper.

• When setting up an exhibition remember *quality* is more important than *quantity.*

• *A concertina folder* is ideal for carrying a number of plates to class and to kiln.

• Do not fiddle with *happy accidents.* Leave them alone!

• *Contemporary fruit:* Squared and angled outlines make an interesting painting. Outline in black and dust or ground bright coloured interiors. *See* illustration on page 35.

• *Hide defects and flaws* on the glazed surface with the darkest part of the design, a line, glass incising, texture, etc.

• Did you know that Renoir (yes, the real one!) painted on porcelain before he painted in oils? So did a number of other very famous artists.

• Use *methylated spirits* to clean your work after *grounding* and *dusting.* It will not run into the applied powder paint as turpentine does.

• Plates and bowls or other concave objects not yet fired and covered with plastic wrap may be carried face to face without slipping.

• Forgotten a box for your freshly painted plate? Tape it face down to your palette or to a hard plastic covered book. You do cover your expensive reference books with plastic, don't you?

• Look at your painting in sections through a frame. You may be surprised.

• Use a very small frame or hole, about pea size, in a card to see just how dark a portion of the study or photo you are using is.

• Wrap plastic wrap around a piece of foam and then cover it with fine athletic support bandage before padding with *lustre.* It is most economical.

• Thin *lustre resist* with water.

• When painting a group of flowers have each of them facing in slightly different directions.

• *Do not dry raised paste* artificially.

• *Do not use Liquid Bright Gold over raised paste* as it will turn black.

• *Do not use glazes* such as *Crystal Clear* over iron colours (reds, red browns and some of the less expensive pinks) as they will disappear.

• *Underfired* pieces may be refired.

• Most onglaze colours will take a wide range of temperatures.

• Paints, golds, lustres and glass to be slumped may be fired in the same kiln load.

• Dust and moisture will leave white spots on gold and lustres.

• *Homemade lustre resist:* Crush a light coloured piece of blackboard chalk to a fine powder and add some clear glue to make a thin paste. Add sufficient water to attain poster paint consistency. Apply. Dry thoroughly and fire with vented kiln. Brushes can be washed in water.

• For a *bronze effect,* paint Roman Gold thinly over Russian Green.

• A drop of Liquid Bright Gold into opal or mother of pearl lustres will enhance the colours. Too much Liquid Bright Gold will turn the lustres grey.

• Paint designs on real eggshells which have

been blown. Gently and carefully pierce the top and bottom of a raw egg with a sharp needle. Blow through one hole (use your vacuum cleaner!) and the contents will come out the other. Once the shell is empty (feed the contents to your dog) and dry, paint it with your normal onglaze paints. Allow to dry. Spray with artist's finishing varnish. *Do not fire*. Alternatively, decorate with Ceramic à Froid, acrylics. etc.

• *Do not* wash porcelain or ceramic blanks immediately before painting them as the porcelain may retain some of the moisture. This may affect your paints and the firing process.

• *Grounding:* Mix a little dry powder in your grounding oil before application to enable you to see where you have covered the surface. If you are masking an area of design prior to grounding first trace the design so that you will be able to find the masking lacquer easily after the powder has been applied.

• Use masking tape or design tape for a straight line, particularly when dry dusting.

• For a full rich colour when dusting or grounding, apply the powder as soon as the oil is sufficiently dry; for a lighter coating, wait until the oil is much drier so that it will not absorb so much of the powder.

• Do not *ground* where there is a freshly painted, unfired object nearby. The powder flies about and may adhere to the wet paint (and it may not be your piece).

• *Firing:* Do not place large flat tiles on the floor of the kiln or against the walls and elements as the heat distribution is uneven and may cause fractures.

• *Do not* place wet pieces in the kiln as moisture may cause dullness.

• *Do not* allow glazed surfaces to touch. They may fuse with one another.

• *Do not* overcrowd the kiln; however, a full kiln will give better results than one with just one or two pieces in it.

• *Do* allow space between walls and pieces for expansion.

• *Do* heat to dry out an infrequently used kiln before firing.

• *Do* leave the air vents open until oils burn off and fumes escape.

• *Do* place a saucer of vinegar on top of the kiln if you are concerned by the fumes during firing.

• *Do* fire and cool slowly to avoid breakages.

• *Do* place small medallions, etc. on Blu-tack to fire so they can be easily placed in the kiln.

• If your *raised paste* will not string or lengthen easily, add a drop of enamel medium to it.

• There will *always* be some *additional expenses.*

• To choose a *design* for your porcelain blank, sketch the shape and *doodle* whenever you have a minute, are on the telephone, or waiting for someone. Doodling is often the answer to a difficult problem and may provide stimulus and ideas for future work.

• Try *doodling* to music and then searching for a design in your results with a frame of two L-shaped pieces of card that can be adjusted for size.

• A window or frame cut to the shape of your blank is helpful.

• *Matt silver* will tarnish. It will need to be polished.

• Paint porcelain *bisque* with paints mixed with *glycerine* if you do not have any lavender oil.

• To protect *fine slender brushes* keep them in a drinking straw.

• Protect *pen nibs by keeping them* in a drinking straw.

• Store your *grounding brush blender* or *mop brush* with a tiny plastic bag over the hairs to keep out the dust. Inflate the bag and secure with an elastic band to prevent weight on the bristles.

• Blend your *signature* with your painting. It should be obvious (who knows, it may be worth something), but not obtrusive, penned in a suitable colour and legible.

• Do not *eat* while working or you may: **1.** Drop crumbs, salt or sugar on your work. These will all leave white spots in the fired paint, the reason being that the majority of foodstuffs are water-based and fall onto the oil. The two do not mix! **2.** Ingest some harmful substance.

• Do not *put anything in your mouth* (including either end of your brush) while painting—you may *poison* yourself.

• If you must drink liquids while painting, put your cup or glass where you will not dip your brush into it in error.

• *Dull red*, painted very very lightly, will produce a beautiful *pink.*

• *Use disposable surgical gloves* if you are at all allergic (readily available from pharmacies) for finger wipe-outs, cleaning your palette, applying lustre with foam, etc.

• *Vacuum out your kiln* periodically to remove kiln dust. You will find your work much smoother and it will not require so much sanding.

• Add *yellow (just a little) to rose pink* to prevent it turning blue with firing.

Suppliers

It is not possible to list all suppliers of ceramic, glass and porcelain products as they are too numerous and frequently change. Therefore I have listed the wholesalers and several retailers who were kind enough to offer their expertise for the readers' benefit and some other well known retailers in each State or Territory. I am sure that they would be only too happy to supply names of retailers in any area.

Australian Capital Territory
Artisan Art & Craft Pty Ltd
89 Tennant Street
Fyshwick ACT 2609
Ph & Fx: 02 62806673

K B Craft & Leather
62 Oatley Court
Belconnen ACT 2617
Ph: 02 62516918 Fx: 02 6242 8693

A Peace of Porcelain
Gallery 11
Ginninderra Country Crafts
O'Hanlon Place
Gold Creek ACT 2618
Ph: 02 62302695 Fx: 02 6258 2115

Walker Ceramics
298 Canberra Avenue
Fyshwick ACT 2609
Ph: 02 62805700 Fx: 02 62805705

New South Wales
Australian Stained Glass Supplies Pty Ltd
39 Pyrmont Street
Pyrmont NSW 2009
Ph: 02 9660 7444 Fx: 02 9660 8888

Ceramic & Craft Centre
11 Green Street
Revesby NSW 2212
Ph: 02 9771 6166 Fx: 02 9771 6011

Cesco–Ceramic Supply Company Pty Ltd
P O Box 717
Guildford NSW 2161
Ph: 02 9892 1566 Fx: 02 9892 2478

Clay & Fire
145 Oak Rd
Kirrawee 2232
Ph: 02 9542 4738

Deirdre Fewell Studio Gallery
6 Kurramatta Place
Cronulla NSW 2230
Ph/Fx: 02 9544 1887
Mobile 015 104 143

Ellen Massey
1 Marigold Place
Milperra NSW 2214
Ph: 02 97733 9900 Fx: 02 9792 7373

Hilldav Industries Pty Ltd
108 Oakes Road
Old Toongabbie NSW 2146
Ph: 02 9688 1777 Fx: 02 9636 3961

Jaybee's China Supplies
'Aquila'
Grenfell NSW 2810
Ph: 063 43 1616

The Junction Gallery
17 Kenrick Street
The Junction, Newcastle NSW 2290
Ph: 049 69 5040

Kit Ferry Ceramics Pty Ltd
55 Macquarie Drive
Cherrybrook NSW 2126
Ph: 02 9875 1518 Fx: 02 9484 8421

La Maison de Ceramics
1 Revesby Place
Revesby NSW 2212
Ph: 02 9773 1171 Fx: 02 9791 0805

NSW Pottery Supplies
90 Victoria Road
Parramatta NSW 2124
Ph: 02 9963 0133

Porcelain Palette
23 Beaufort Street
Northmead NSW 2152
Ph: 02 9630 8025

The Potters Warehouse
108 Oakes Road
Old Toongabbie, NSW 2146
Ph: 02 9688 1777 Fx: 02 9636 3961

The Pottery Place
104 Keira Street
Wollongong NSW 2500
Ph/Fx: 042 27 1031

Thermal Ceramics Australia Pty Ltd
Endeavour House, Level 5
3-5 Stapleton Avenue
Sutherland NSW 2232
Ph: 02 9914 7627 Fx: 02 9914 7649

Walker Ceramics
98 Starkey Street
Killarney Heights NSW 2087
(PO Box 500 Forestville NSW 2087)
Ph: 02 9451 5855
Fx: 02 9451 7876/1800 655 775

Victoria
Ceramic Glazes of Australia
Factory 3/8 Eastgate Court
Wantirna South Vic 3152
Ph: 03 98871702
Fx: 03 9801 4650

The Ceramic Centre
Unit 19 Abruzzo Crt
391–401 Settlement Rd
Thomastown Vic 3074
Ph: 03 9464 3600
Fx: 03 9464 3511

Ceramic Hobbies
12 Hanrahan Street
Thomastown Vic 3074
Ph: 03 9466 2522
Fx: 03 9464 0547/1800 679 248

Ceramic Solutions
2/43 Mologa Road
West Heidelberg Vic 3081
Ph: 03 9459 7284 Fx: 03 9530 4742

The Glass Workshop
283 Lower Heidelberg Road
East Ivanhoe Vic 3079
Ph: 03 9499 4816 Fx: 03 9499 2499

The Ceramic Centre
Unit 19/391–401 Settlement Road
ThomasTown Vic 3074
Ph: 03 9464 3600 Fx: 03 9464 3511

Melton Ceramic Supplies
11 Production Road (PO Box 92)
Melton Vic 3337
Ph: 03 9743 9711 Fx: 03 9747 9148

Northcote Pottery–Matthey
Cookson
85A Clyde Street
Thornbury Vic 3071
Ph: 03 9484 4580 Fx: 03 9480 3075

Walker Ceramics
55 Lusher Road
Croydon Vic 3136
Ph: 03 9725 7255 Fx: 03 9725 2289

South Australia
Alexander's Fine Porcelain
6 Surrey Hills
Keswick SA 5035
Ph: 08 8297 5933 Fx: 08 8297 0543

Ceramic Fanfare
11/59 Barndioota Rd
Salisbury Plains SA
Ph/Fx: 08 8281 9033

Fay & Elliot Good
43 Devonshire Street
Walkerville SA 5081
Ph: 08 8344 4306 Fx: 08 8344 4477

Gilberton Gallery–Josephine
  Robertson
101 Walkerville Terrace (PO Box 156)
Adelaide SA 5081
Ph:08 8344 1688 Fx: 08 8344 8438

Melton Ceramic Supplies
74 Chapel Street
Thebarton SA 5031
Ph: 08 8351 9891 Fx: 08 8351 9890

Queensland
Alexander's Fine Porcelain
Ph: 07 5476 9885

Ceramic & Craft Centre
52 Wecker Road
Mansfield Qld 4122
Ph: 07 3343 7377 Fx: 07 3349 5052

Gold Coast China Painting
Supplies
109 Witt Avenue
Carrera Qld 4211
Ph: 07 5594 4269 Fx: 07 5579 8269

Lawnton Ceramic Arts
18 Paisley Drive
Lawnton Qld 4501
Ph: 07 3205 1462 Fx: 07 3881 0798

Pottery Supplies
51 Castlemaine Street
Milton Qld 4064
Ph: 07 3368 2877 Fx: 07 3368 3947

Western Australia
Jackson's Ceramic Craft
94 Jersey Street
Jolimont WA 6014
Ph: 08 9387 8488 Fx: 08 9383 7612

Ceramicraft of Western Australia
33 Denninup Way
Malaga WA 6090
Ph: 08 9249 9266 Fx: 08 9249 9690

Park Ceramics Pty Ltd
Unit 3 Welshpool Trade Centre
Cnr Leach Hwy & Welshpool Rd
Welshpool WA 6106
Ph/Fx: 08 9351 8900

NEW ZEALAND
New Zealand Hobby, Clay & Craft
Co. Ltd
Unit 1/180 James Fletcher Drive
Mangere, Auckland
Ph/Fx: 011 649 270 0140

Shand China Company
30 Waldegrave Street
Palmerston North
Ph/Fx: 06 355 0509

Western Potters Supplies
4/43A Linwood Avenue
Mt Albert Auckland
Ph: 09 815 1513

USA
Bell Inc.
Fx: 352 394 1270

Ceramichrome
PO Box 327
Stanford KY 40484
Ph: 606 365 3193

Duncan Enterprises
5673E Shields Avenue
Fresno CA 93727
Fx: 209 291 4476
Email: consumer@duncan-enterprises.com

Gare
165 Rosemount Street
Haverhill MA 01830

Holly Colorobbia
Italian Tile Decor Corp.
410 Market Street
Elmwood Park NJ 07407
Ph: 201 796 0722

Kathy Petersen's "the good stuff"
4919E 38th Avenue
Denver CO 80207
Ph: 303 377 0762 Fx: 303 377 0954

Kemper Manufacturing Inc.
PO Box 696
Chino CA 91710
Ph: 909 627 6191

Maryland China
54 Main Street
Reistertown MD 21136
Ph: 1800 638 3880

Mayco Inc.
20800 Dearborn Street
Chatsworth CA 91311
Fx: 614 876 9904

Mr & Mrs Dallas Inc.
1301 Avenue K
Plano TX 75074
Ph: 972 881 1699
Fx: 972 878 7528/1 800 878 7528

Willoughby's
PO Box 574
Shingle Springs CA 95682
Ph/Fx: 916 677 1071

CANADA
Alberta Ceramic Supplies, Ltd
8640 Coronet Road (62 Ave)
Edmonton Alberta T6E 4P3
Ph: 403 462 2582 Fx: 403 466 2529

Canadian Ceramic Wholesalers
12138 6th Avenue
Surrey British Columbia V3W 3H7
Ph: 604 596 9451
800 695 7423 (Canada only)
Fx: 604 596 5336

Ceramic Arts Ltd
3103 Mainway
Burlington Ontario L7M 1A1
Ph: 905 335 1515 Fx: 905 332 4403

The Ceramic Greenhouse
31 Trottier Bay
Winnipeg Manitoba R3T 3R3
Ph/Fx: 204 475 1456

Cobequid Ceramics, Ltd
PO Box 1031
Truro Nova Scotia B2N 5G9
Ph: 902 895 5313/902 895 5314
Fx: 902 893 7126

Creative Ceramic & Gifts Ltd
PO Box 1010
Saskatoon Sask. S7K 3M4
Ph: 306 931 7700 Fx: 306 668 1855

Sial
2860 blvd Le Corbusier
Laval Quebec H7L 3S1
Ph: 514 687 4046 Fx: 514 687 4105

UNITED KINGDOM
Cromartie Hobby Craft Ltd
Park Hall Road, Longton
Stoke-On-Trent
Staffordshire ST3 5AY
Ph: 011 44 1782 319 435
Fx: 011 44 1782 599 723

Howe & Ware
42 Gladys Avenue
Portsmouth
Hampshire PO2 9GB
Ph: 0705 661 987 Fx: 0705 665 839

Lalco Ltd
Units 4-8 Spedding Road
Fenton Industrial Estate
Stoke-on-Trent
Staffordshire SP4 2SP

Westfield House
North Avenue
Wakefield
West Yorkshire WF1 3RX